THE AUTHOR

Valerie Grove was born in South Shields in 1946. From Kingsbury County School in London she went to Girton College, Cambridge, to read English, and on graduating in 1968 immediately began work as a journalist on the Londoner's Diary of the London *Evening Standard*. She remained on the *Standard*, where she had her own weekly column and was the Literary Editor for many years, until 1985, when she moved to the *Sunday Times* as a regular columnist. Her previous book, *Where I Was Young: Memories of London Childhoods*, was published in 1976. She has been married for thirteen years to journalist Trevor Grove and they have four children.

THE COMPLEAT WOMAN

Marriage, Motherhood, Career:
Can She Have it All?

Valerie Grove

THE HOGARTH PRESS
LONDON

Published in 1988 by
The Hogarth Press
30 Bedford Square, London WC1B 3SG

First published in 1987 by Chatto & Windus Ltd

A CIP catalogue record for this book is available from the British Library.

ISBN 0 7012 0826 0

Printed in Great Britain by
Cox & Wyman Ltd
Reading, Berkshire

to T.

Contents

༄

CONTENTS

Introduction

'They do say,' Fay Weldon once told me, 'that if you are talking on a platform, and you are a woman, people find it impossible to concentrate unless they know your marital status and how many children you have. The audience cannot settle until they know. It colours their expectation: is she a cosy homebody? or does she partake of the male role? Nor do I resent their curiosity; for I too feel I need to know this.'

So do I. Women are by nature enormously inquisitive about other women's lives. How many children had Lady Macbeth? always seemed to me a pertinent question.

The twenty women interviewed in this book have had ninety children altogether. They are 'compleat' in the sense that each has had a lasting marriage, become a mother at least three times, and managed to achieve some distinction outside the home as well. 'Don't make it look easy, whatever you do,' I was told.

Freud asked what do women want and today we think we know: everything, of course. The fulfilling work, the man, the children. Not to renounce one at the expense of the other. 'Impossible' was the word most often used when I described, to anyone interested, the women I was writing about. Married twenty-five years or more to the same man? *And* her husband's equal in achievement? *And* with a larger than average family? Impossible! For a while the working title became *Impossible Women*.

'I've yet to be on a university campus,' Gloria Steinem, the American feminist says, 'where most women weren't worrying about combining marriage, children and a career. I've yet to find one where many young men were worrying about the same thing.' It is a female dilemma: as career prospects for women improve, early marriage and children recede. Is a three-dimensional life so impossible? The books on my shelves, from Hannah Gavron's *The Captive Wife* to Betty Friedan's *The Second Stage*, from Simone de Beauvoir's *The Second Sex* to Germaine

I

Greer's *Sex and Destiny*, tell mostly the bad news about marriage and motherhood. Nobody ever painted a bleaker, truer or more terrible picture of the imprisoned mother than Germaine Greer in *The Female Eunuch* (1970); but her solution – to propose that children could be raised on a communal hill farm in Tuscany – was never going to catch on. 'Motherhood,' Shulamith Firestone declared that same year in *The Dialectic of Sex*, another feminist tract, 'is a condition of terminal psychological and social decay.'

This is not an entirely mistaken view. Mothers who are also achievers in the eyes of the world are still rare after decades of progress. Reading through *Who's Who*, looking only for the women's entries, does not take long. Pages of Henrys, Georges and Williams with only an occasional Mary or Elizabeth. So many married men have done well: but why should they not? On them were bestowed education, votes, university places, professional jobs, and domestic slaves called wives who picked up their socks.

All my life I have been struck by the scant reference, in biographies and obituaries of men, to their wives and families. 'Dickens's children arrived in the world almost as regularly as his books,' noted Phyllis Rose in *Parallel Lives*. 'He enjoyed himself as a family man, the centre of a growing circle of devoted people.' Phyllis Rose's book was, at last, a recognition of the domestic life of famous men; Edna Healey's *Wives of Fame* (Mrs Marx, Mrs Darwin and Mrs Livingstone) was another. But even today this curious separation of men's public lives from their domestic commitments, and women's inseparability from theirs, persists. Only the devoutly incurious could fail to find the family factor interesting. Sir Peter Medawar made this comment in his own memoirs.

'The ultimate sentence of an obituary notice in *The Times* often takes the following form: "In 1839 he married Emma, youngest daughter of Josiah Wedgwood of Meare Hall, by whom he had ten children." And that's it: so much for what might have been half a lifetime's companionship, and for the shared joys or sorrows that are the landmarks of married life. If I were a woman and not yet a feminist, this graceless and perfunctory form of words would assuredly have made me so.'

What of those women who do achieve a singular mention in their own right? From *Who's Who*, which remains the measure of public recognition, a general picture of them emerges.

The women who predominate in this volume today, as in the annual

Honours Lists, are the backbone of the nation: they are headmistresses and hospital matrons, principals of colleges and governors of HM prisons, district midwives and Under-Secretaries at the Home Office. They have served their country as VADs, they organise the Women's Royal Voluntary Service, they run Citizens' Advice Bureaux. They become magistrates and members of the Church Commission. After attending good girls' schools and women's colleges, they do not marry. They keep cats, garden and travel a lot, and they live for ever.

This pattern persists. Women who achieve a *Who's Who* entry early in life often promise to be the splendid old ladies of tomorrow. Slowly, perceptible changes are taking place. More of the newer entries in *Who's Who* are mothers of families: Ann Mallalieu the barrister, Maureen Lipman the actress and Josceline Dimbleby the cookery writer, all of whom are probably more in tune with the aspirations of contemporary women.

But the overall likelihood at the end of the twentieth century is that any man in *Who's Who*, no matter how busy or successful, will be a married man with a family, while any woman picked at random will probably have sacrificed a family life. It is absolutely predictable that this vast and heavy volume opens with a male professor, and ends with a bishop, and that each is a father of five. Mothers of five within the pages could be counted on the fingers of one hand. Women of real achievement – like Ann Burdus, first woman chairman of McCann Erickson the advertising agency, Mary Goldring the economist and Livia Gollancz the publisher – have no family.

There remains, of course, an army of unsung and uncelebrated women who will never get into the male-dominated *Who's Who* nor even into any of the Dictionaries of Women's Biography which have now been assembled to redress the balance. These women are nursing geriatric patients, tying shoelaces in primary schools, looking after demented and incontinent elderly parents at home. We do not care to remember these women too often. But they represent another unequal male/female ratio. For every 100 of them, there is another spoonfed male earning a New Year's honour and a space to himself in the next edition of the book that should be retitled *Who's He*.

Among the few married women with children who have achieved an entry in *Who's Who* I discerned an old girl network: women from matriarchal families, and from the older women's university colleges, which breed the type of women certain to succeed. Perhaps women like

Mary Warnock and Elizabeth Longford (who both went to Lady Margaret Hall, Oxford) were bound by birth and inheritance to do well in life. But the same could not be said about Anne Blythe Munro, who left school in Glasgow at sixteen in the Depression, or Margaret Forster from the Carlisle council estate, or Mavis Nicholson from the South Wales mining town. They aren't typical women, any more than Mary Warnock is. This is not a book about typical women. These women are all extraordinary: in their durable marriages, in having more children than most people, in the professional success that makes them at least their husband's equal.

Would I call them feminists? The discussion of feminism has featured prominently in my life – you could not be a journalist and a woman in the 1970s and avoid the subject. But it was not nearly so central to other women's lives, I found. Some of the women whom I interviewed were feminists and said so; some were inadvertently so; and some would perversely deny that they were feminists at all. Possibly the last group have swallowed the tabloid press's view of feminism: man-hating, dungaree-wearing, etc. This is a blinkered view, but I have left their statements (eg 'You don't have to call yourself a feminist unless you feel downtrodden') without comment. 'Are you a feminist?' I would ask; and 'What do you mean by feminism?' they would respond. I would suggest that it began with equality between the sexes, which none could deny. Yet some women believe that their kind of equality and achievement has always been possible. Not every woman consciously recognises what we owe those pioneering women (for it was always women, however much they were aided by men) who challenged the status quo and turned women, so very recently, into working, voting, educated citizens instead of helpless bondslaves. Indeed, the view that feminism must be a negative force is widespread. Alice Thomas Ellis said she wrote her first novel because she was sick of the whingeing and whining of feminists. Well, whether declared feminists or not, there are no whingers here. 'You've just got to get on with it,' was their common brisk refrain.

Exactly how they got on with it varies. That is what I, as someone currently in the throes of trying to combine everything, wanted to ask them. How do you cope? people ask. I know what my own answer is: I couldn't, if I didn't have an unusually supportive husband and a hard-working and dedicated nanny. There is nothing unilateral about this kind of life, and I could not do a full-time job and have four young

4

children without this kind of support. How did others manage? I asked in a genuine spirit of inquiry.

I looked for clues and reassuring conclusions. What made them take on so many commitments? Perhaps they might all be the thrusting eldest daughters of encouraging fathers (like mine), for instance, or the fortunate wives of helpful husbands (like mine, without whom . . .) Neither was applicable. Often the reverse was true. The strong mother, the dead or absent father, the singularly undomesticated husband were more usually the norm in these women's lives. And would it be huge energy which they shared? or organisational skill? Some of this, a touch of that, but no pattern emerged. As for the crucial question of who irons the shirts and keeps the domestic chaos at bay while the mother earns the bread and rules the world – Her Majesty Queen Elizabeth II being the most publicly visible example of the Compleat Woman – these women had found various solutions to the question of help. Nannies and grannies, au pairs and treasures, in one case a mental hospital in-patient, and in one or two heroic examples, nobody at all.

Because they all have at least twenty-five years of marriage to look back on, these twenty women are all of a certain age: between forty-five and eighty. They belong to the generations of women who grew up after the first great wave of the women's movement (and therefore had votes, education and access to the professions) and before the second wave (and consequently also expected to have husbands and children). The Victorian wife had children but no career; the woman of the 1980s can have a career but finds children a pressing dilemma, always supposing she meets the good man who is hard to find. Betty Friedan, whose *The Feminine Mystique* was one of those influential books of the 1960s, had second thoughts in the 1980s with *The Second Stage*: asking how the career-minded young woman was to have a family before it was too late. No wonder the present generation is not reproducing itself. The three-or-more-child family (down to fewer than 10 per cent of households in 1981) becomes rarer every day. That's why I picked on three as a minimum number of children for my subjects. Most people realise that two is the sensible, manageable family unit. When the children start to outnumber the parents, things are different. I see all too clearly how possible it is to be submerged by motherhood.

For it is motherhood which divides women: what alters their lives is not marriage, or work, but children. As my own family grew, I sometimes found it frankly galling to be instructed on self-fulfilment by those who had never been in the coils of life with small children underfoot. 'The written attitudes of feminists about mothering are far from reality,' wrote Ann Dally (psychiatrist, mother of six, now divorced) in her book *Inventing Motherhood* in 1982, 'and far from what most people felt they needed.' The women's movement would always be peripheral, she said, if it was supported chiefly by those who ignored or disliked motherhood and children. What about the woman (I count myself one) committed to feminism in principle but equally committed to husband and family? Feminism and family life may be hard to reconcile, but reconciled they have to be.

There is no history of distinguished mothers, only the generalisation that the distinguished women of the past tended to be childless. A century ago, if I had interviewed twenty women they might have been the mothers of 180 children instead of 90, but the women would have had nothing to say about practising law or medicine, or teaching, or standing for Parliament. Even some of the writers among them might have published pseudonymously or privately.

In the sepia-tinted Victorian family photographs, the father always stood behind, the mother sat stony-faced in a lace collar with the brood of children around her and the latest infant in her lap. The father was something in the world; the mother was not. The women in this book are more like Mary Browne, in the cover portrait by Francis Wheatley, with her fishing rod and her rather excessive hat. These women are mothers because they have chosen to be; they have all the benefits of education, the vote, and the right to keep the money they earn. They are their own women and their husbands' match.

But lives that seem to have it all – perfectly fulfilled and apparently organised – are never quite that. All these women with their now grown children have been at times run ragged. They have managed or muddled through babies and adolescence, sleepless nights and schooldays, menopauses male and female; some have suffered the deaths of children and the problems of ageing parents; all have known matrimony in sickness and in health. I was struck by the emotional energy each of these women had needed. None of it had been without effort, or without sacrifice. Crowded lives are full of pitfalls and every child is a hostage to fortune. The Compleat Woman can never be a complacent woman. There was often the impression of a lonely struggle, and often still the nagging sense of things left undone.

As I write this, it is always Sunday and usually raining. I am trying to conjure up, and to be, the Compleat Woman. My husband has once again taken the four children out so that I can write in peace, and any minute they will be back with all the commotion which that entails ('I fell in the mud!' 'Is this mushroom edible?' 'Oliver lost a shoe!' 'Can Daisy stay the night?') but life and work without such interruptions is unimaginable to me. The pleasure of talking to these twenty women was the feeling that they understood. They had known the daily guilts and gratifications. I enjoyed talking to them as one enjoys talking to anyone with a kindred experience. Nuggets of their insight and wisdom would linger, often contradictory but usually right for the moment: 'Ambition dies overnight when you have children . . .' 'A mother's place is in the wrong.' 'Someone's got to spend time with your children, and if it isn't you, who will it be?' 'You're a fool if you take on work you can't cope with, nobody makes you do it.' 'Children are not the enemy.' 'I used to think it would be so lovely when they were all grown up, but now I think, Oh for a sticking-plaster . . .' and most comforting of all: 'There is no perfect solution. It was rather a relief to find out that there really is none.'

To Mary, Anne, Margaret, Alison, Evelyn, Beulah, Mavis, Drusilla, Anna, Fay, Barbara, Wendy, Sheila, Pramila, Shirley, Jill, Trixie and the three Elizabeths, thank you for knowing, and telling, what it is like.

Marriage & Motherhood

፝

MARRIAGE

Happy the marriage which has no history. 'I do wish you'd write about marriage when it has lasted. That's the difficulty – and the beauty of the difficulty! Anyone can *part*.' Thus Lynn Fontanne, half of the famous acting partnership the long-married Lunts, to her writer friend Enid Bagnold. If Bagnold had been alive I would have been hotfoot to Rottingdean as she would have been an ideal interviewee with her four children and her long marriage to Sir Roderick Jones. Yet hers was one of those complaisant marriages in which each partner allows the other an occasional fling.

'One has no idea what goes on between married settled people,' Enid wrote. 'Once a pair has weathered twenty years they have closed the front door. That doesn't stop what goes on behind the curtains. The entrancing gossip of bedroom life, the crackles of annoyance, the candlelit battleground, the truces, the fun, the love, the rage. In marriage there are no manners to keep up, and beneath the wildest accusations no real criticism.'

But all marriages, even the strictly conventional, are unfathomable. The very idea of marriage for life is barely defensible except in personal, subjective terms, but all usually agree that when it works, it works well, and all the marriages here have been reinforced by family life. No other manner of life could be imagined by any of these women. But within its broad confines, practically any agreed mode of shared existence is permissible. There are some very odd marriages. There are some extremely odd marriages in this book. The degree of togetherness, for instance, varies from the Smithsons' twenty-four-hours-a-day for thirty-six years, to the Kitzingers' agreement to 'fly wing to wing, like birds, but to inhabit different continents whenever possible'.

'When so much is changing outside marriage,' wrote Katharine Whitehorn recently in the *Observer*, 'it's odd we respect so few variations within it. People are peculiar: no two marriages are the same. A

9

marriage shouldn't be assumed to be useless, just because the couple aren't always in each other's arms. It may be all they want . . .'

I mentioned to one interviewee that I was shortly going to see another couple, X and Y. 'But X,' she protested, 'has not kissed Y for twenty years!' And although she may have been right, I am also certain that X and Y have a perfectly agreeable marriage on their terms. They undoubtedly have what Cyril Connolly in *The Unquiet Grave* called the duologue, marriage's particular charm: 'the permanent conversation of two people who talk over everything and everyone till death breaks the record.'

Drusilla Beyfus, at the end of her book *The English Marriage*, came to the negative conclusion that marriage cannot be tidied away into definitive pigeonholes. All that could be said was that certain elements in a good marriage seemed unlikely to change: 'Mutual affection, tenderness, a tolerance of the other person's idiosyncrasies, a pleasurable sex life, and a sense of sharing.' But not every contented marriage has even all of these.

From the suffragette era onwards there was an assumption that a woman must dwindle into a wife. 'A pithy saying arose among the suffragettes,' noted Elizabeth Longford. 'Husband and wife are one, and that one is the husband.'

The Compleat Woman does not dwindle: the fact of being married is but one dimension in a full life. But there can be no assumption that her particular choice is the good man that is hard to find. She may acknowledge the part played in her life by her amenable husband, encouraging and tolerant, but these husbands are not invariably more considerate or feminist than the rest of the male world. It is the women who are forces to be reckoned with. And the wives who pondered this subject would say with hindsight that they knew their husband was the marrying type, the uxorious type. The men themselves seemed embarrassed to be challenged about the marriageability factor. There is a kind of man who marries for ever, and cannot or will not express or analyse the reasons. 'We both need to be married. We're very uxorious types. Neither of us likes being alone and not having a stable companion,' say the Longfords. 'To analyse why our marriage has lasted would be like asking why one breathed.'

Evidence of happy marriages is scant in the writings of contemporary feminist authors. Eva Figes' view in *Woman on Woman* that 'a woman almost always gives up personal ambition as well as economic independence' in marriage was very much the received wisdom until the women's movement began to change things by its influence. One of the best feminist books on marriage, Lee Comer's *Wedlocked Women* (1974) acknowledged that a lasting happy marriage *was* conceivable: 'The lifelong union of a man and woman may well result in a happiness which touches all those with whom they have contact. But it is rare,' she adds, 'and it is always a statement to their resilience.'

Perhaps resilience *is* an essential requirement in marriage; it is a good thing on the whole in life. There is very little that a strong marriage cannot absorb or overcome. The marriages in this book have coped with various challenges – including the worst, the death of a child, as well as lack of money, loss of job, alcoholism, glaring political differences, domestic upheavals, anxieties over children, and problems with aged parents. Though infidelity was never mentioned, I suspect that some may have dealt with that too. Marriage can be very good, at its best, at dealing with adversity.

We all become biased, one way or another. To be married to one man and to make that marriage a fundamental, impassioned commitment undertaken willingly and wholeheartedly is our free choice. We may all stand accused, as married women, of personal bias, if we say we believe in marriage because it works for us; we may in turn accuse an unmarried writer of bias who declares, 'Commitment is a great, mysterious achievement involving faith and surrender. After the first delirium, marriage becomes a battle between two egos. It shares with other institutions the power to institutionalise its inmates.' (Thus the sensible and clear-sighted Irma Kurtz in her book, *Malespeak*.)

There are few poems to lasting married love; to happy couples the state of matrimony is too natural to be explained. I think many of the marriages in this book are like loyal friendships. Writing of her great fortune in finding a second happy marriage after an unhappy first one, Celia Haddon in *The Power of Love* wrote: 'I think of it as a close friendship rather than some permanent romance. It is a kind of shelter against the unhappiness of the outside world, a comfort and a consolation. I would not change it for all the romantic excitement in the world.'

'It is not lack of love,' wrote Nietzsche, 'but lack of friendship that makes unhappy marriages.'

At the time of writing, (in a year when governments, church leaders and medical researchers are exercised by the threat of AIDS) monogamy is back in style. There is a manifest reaction against one-night stands, serial affairs, and open marriage: *How To Make Love to the Same Person for the Rest of Your Life—And Still Love It* was an American How-to manual of 1986. But the marriageability factor observes no trends and requires no apologia. One of my favourite passages on marriage was written by the journalist Mary Stott in her memoir, *Forgetting's No Excuse*, which she wrote after she was widowed at the age of sixty:

'In marriage I was liberated. I know that saying this divides me from some of my young Women's Liberation friends, but it is the exact truth. I was liberated from the fear of inadequacy. What made me able to cope with disasters at work, what made me grow in courage, fortitude, even in independence, was that K. Stott loved me, admired me, was strong for me – and also depended on me. He thought I was the head of the house. I thought he was. I do not like to think what might have become of me if we had not met and married.

'Women who declare as an article of faith that women can never be "free" within the institution of marriage seldom know, literally, what they are talking about. None of them, as far as I can discover, has had the opportunity to find out how after ten, twenty, thirty years the marriage bond can become not a constricting ligature, but the rope on which climbers depend for each other's safety. With this rope you can securely climb.'

The husband of one of my interviewees, a psychiatrist, said when pondering the question of marriage: 'There was a survey, once, of extremely bright children in California, following up the pattern of their lives. It found that they had a lower divorce rate than most, and more successful careers. But then, they were more fortunate, better endowed at birth, had stronger teeth – and they all married someone who followed the same pattern. We are all creatures of habit; we're like ants when you get down to it. So you might as well flag down a passing ant and get on with it.'

'THE MEN THAT WOMEN MARRY'

The men that women marry
And why they marry them, will always be
A marvel and a mystery to the world
H. W. Longfellow

We know a good man is hard to find. But do they come in an identifiable package? What is the Compleat Woman's husband like?

I met some of them briefly and interviewed some at length. Others I was acquainted with already. One of them made my dining table. Not only do they not conform to a type, they are as different from one another as are their wives.

There are certain characteristics, however, that most of them share. Contentment with the married state, for one. And pride – often intense – in their wives. And a stated respect for a woman's right to do what she wishes with her life. There were no Andy Capps among the husbands. They were the sort of men who would say, 'I'd run a mile from a woman who expected to stay at home and do the flowers,' and, 'I certainly wouldn't have married her if she wasn't prepared to work like a maniac.' Essentially they were gratified never to have been bored by the busy women they had married. Over and over, I heard them say that they had never even discussed the question of whether their wives should continue working; the debate never arose. For most of them, if the home life could be managed – and it was up to the wife to make the domestic arrangements – it suited them very well to have a professional partner, a second income, a woman whose mind and opinion they valued.

Only one or two of the men had ever run the home and children single-handed while the wife got on with earning her living. One claimed to have got blisters on his hands from wringing out the nappies, but (partly because of the generation to which these men belong) it was generally assumed that they would be domestically less than competent. If they were not Andy Capps, they were not New Men either.

Men are never asked, 'How on earth do you manage to be a company chairman/an MP/ such a prolific writer and have four/five/seven children?' The assumption is invariably that there is a wife at home doing the spadework. But what if the wife is herself a company chairman/MP/prolific writer? It is true to say that even hard-working professional women still prefer to protect husbands from the real

THE PARLIAMENTARY FEMALE.

Father of the Family. "COME, DEAR; WE SO SELDOM GO OUT TOGETHER NOW—CAN'T YOU TAKE US ALL TO THE PLAY TO-NIGHT?"
Mistress of the House, and M.P. "HOW YOU TALK, CHARLES! DON'T YOU SEE THAT I AM TOO BUSY. I HAVE A COMMITTEE TO-MORROW MORNING, AND I HAVE MY SPEECH ON THE GREAT CROCHET QUESTION TO PREPARE FOR THE EVENING."

rigours of domestic life and all its tiresome and trivial distractions. Most of the women in this book patted their husbands on the back for doing anything with the children – adventurous, fun things like sailing, mushrooming, football, fossiling expeditions, games of chess. They would say: 'He enjoyed the children's company, but of course he didn't see them that often,' or, 'He got better with the children as they became more interesting.' As I sceptically say when someone is described as 'good with children', anyone can be good with children for an hour or a day at a time. But who reads *Topsy and Tim* and baths them night after night?

When a male colleague tells me that women have things all their own way nowadays, I advise him to look around the pub at 7 pm. It is full of men. If all the men there were women, spending fistfuls of fivers and loudly laughing, and you knew that most of them had children at home, even now being tucked in and told stories by their dutiful fathers who would wait for the womenfolk to drift home after the bar closed, what would you think? Answer: it would be impossible. It is unthinkable. Women are still not like that.

Men in essence have not radically altered their sphere of responsibility, not even the New Men who cook and shop more than Old Men

them was the son and brother of suffragettes: his mother and her friends had once had an audience with Asquith, he told me, and Asquith had greeted them with the words: 'What can I do for you, my pretty dears?'

They tended to admire and marvel at their wives' capacity for work, the deadlines they met, the way they found time to beaver away at the current project, labouring late into the night and never daunted by the prospect of additional piles of work. They liked their wives' financial independence, even if they confessed they would never have cared to be kept men. They said they had enjoyed having au pairs and nannies around ('discussing Westminster Abbey over the burnt toast,' one said) and they relished the idea of having larger-than-usual families even if it meant a period of domestic chaos. Several of them seemed to be – and confirmed that they were – extremely tidy creatures, who liked the knives and forks all facing the same way in the drawer. The question of professional rivalry – particularly when the two were in the same field – never arose. 'Jealous of her success? Good lord, no,' said Colin Haycraft, adding with a certain amount of truth, 'One only ever competes with one's own sex.' And John Vulliamy said: 'The funny thing is, when I'm talking to people and I say I'm Shirley Hughes's husband, their attitude changes – because they all know and like her work.' There spoke a Compleat Woman's man.

THE PRAM IN THE HALL

'You do not know what it is fully to be a woman until you have had at least three children,' declared Enid Bagnold. But she was not the reason why I picked on women with at least three children, to interview. I did so because having two children is sound commonsense. Two is probably the optimum number (thousands of busy women, and many who write on the subject of children, have two). Two is the popular choice.

The two-child family is balanced, fits neatly into any car, and even at their most unmanageable age two infants can be manhandled by a brace of strong adults. Two children are welcome in a spare room, so their parents are still invited to stay; two are company for each other. Most important, two children can be seen from birth into full-time school within a mere five-year-gap in a mother's career.

It is the three-child family that begins to be a crowd. Cars and friendly hosts are taxed and stretched, as are finances and tempers. In my view, most of the commotion in family life comes from internecine squabbling, two children versus a third. Larger families may look more picturesque for family album purposes, but the commitment to family life is that much greater. And I wanted to talk to women whose work achievement was all the more surprising and impressive, given the family involvement they had also chosen.

Those I talked to varied in their childbearing span from seven years to twenty-two years. A decade of nappies was the norm. The only mother-of-nine I met, Angela King, a schoolteacher in the west country, told me that, in her experience, four is saturation point. 'After four,' she said, 'you might as well have nine. The extent of taking over your life is the same.'

I know very few people with four children. In my own age group among my friends, I know more people without children than with any at all. The most popular household size in the country today is the single person unit, or the couple (more than half the households in the land). The four-person household amounts to only 18 per cent; the five-person family is down to 6 per cent. Households of six people or more, like my own, make up only 3 per cent at the 1984 census, and the number is falling. It seems highly unlikely at present that there will be any swing back to Victorian-sized families. So the kind of mothers I write about here may well prove to be the last of their kind. Since they are also the first generations to benefit from the opening up of the professions to women, they could turn out to be an historical aberration, uniquely of their time. I calculated that these 20 women's 90 children have produced as yet only 50 grandchildren – and 25 of those are Elizabeth Longford's.

'There is no more sombre enemy of good art,' wrote Cyril Connolly in *Enemies of Promise*, 'than the pram in the hall.' Every working mother has this great truth etched on her psyche as she tries to cut out domestic intrusions and apply her mind. It always seems to me that the childless *ought* to produce work of vast scope and genius, given all that solitude and those great swathes of self-centred time. While the fact that anyone who has small children gets any work done at all is invariably a small triumph over adversity. The crying child, for instance, encroaches even upon the best regulated households. Joseph Conrad used to complain that while he was trying to write he could hear the *breathing* of his sick child through the bedroom wall.

Consider the prevailing image of motherhood, in the successive guises it has assumed in living memory. In the middle of the twentieth century, when many of the suffragettes, having done their great work, began to recede into spinster aunthood, a new tide of ideology arrived: that of the Good Mother, its spokesman John Bowlby. 'A psychiatrist named Bowlby, in the mid-fifties, wrote about the trauma of mother–child

separation so forcibly that he terrified a whole generation of middle-class women into clutching their children's hands every minute of their dependency,' as Fay Weldon described it.

Bowlby's evidence did foster an immense burden of guilt. His declar-ation, 'The prolonged separation of a child from his mother during the first five years of life stands foremost among the causes of delinquent behaviour' (*Maternal Care and Mental Health*, 1952) became folklore, an unrefuted fact of 1950s' culture in the age of Never-had-it-so-good Toryism. Mothers must stay at home. Mothers and even brides gave up work. Fathers, who had had little enough to do with their children before, were now absolved completely. Delinquency is today still often attributed by public opinion to working mothers; working fathers are never blamed.

Mothers went along with this, giving up jobs to spend the required years at home; while domestic help became scarce anyway. The mystique of motherhood remained blissfully intact because until books like Hannah Gavron's *The Captive Wife* began appearing in the 1960s, wives who felt captive did not say so. Any misery and neurosis was kept a well guarded secret. But when it did all come out, the 'unfortunate wife-mother' became the prevailing image of womanhood against which the second wave of feminists launched their invective.

'The home is her province,' as Germaine Greer wrote in 1970 in *The Female Eunuch*. 'She wants her family to spend time with her for her only significance is in relation to that almost fictitious group. She struggles to hold her children to her, imposing restrictions, waiting up for them, prying into their affairs. They withdraw more and more into non-communication and thinly veiled contempt . . . Work of all kinds becomes hypnotic. She cleans, she knits, she embroiders. And so forth.'

But motherhood is intrinsically neither as noble and self-sacrificing nor as infinitely rewarding as it had been painted. One firm conclusion I can draw about motherhood after talking to all these mothers is that their memories are wonderfully selective. Just as the pain of childbirth is supposed to be forgotten, so is the chronic wear and tear caused by the sleepless baby, or the need for six pairs of hands, or the total invasion of privacy. When I was researching this book it was a long time before I met a mother who recalled being in a public lavatory when the little clinging hands of her two children came reaching out at her under the door and she admitted, 'I felt like stamping on them.'

Even Sheila Kitzinger, whose general picture of motherhood is thought to be roseate, can conjure up the ghastly plight of a mother at home with infants under five, in her book *Women As Mothers*:

'. . . The constructive play turns into a litter of cardboard boxes all over the kitchen, tacky flour-and-water paste in the coconut matting, and finger-paints on the curtains. The carefully prepared food is rejected with noises of disgust from the older child and is expelled from the baby's mouth in a great gob of goo.

'She pushes the protesting children in a pram to the supermarket, where the younger one sweeps tins from the shelves. In the end she slaps the baby's hand and gets a long, cool look from an older woman who thinks she is a baby batterer. She hates what she has become and scuttles back home, with both children whining . . .

'It is possible,' Sheila Kitzinger writes, 'that women have always been this unhappy . . .'

The careworn mother in a hostile society has become a repetitive theme, though it is not at all new. The Kitzinger account could be compared with the observations in her book *The Disinherited Family* of Eleanor Rathbone, the Socialist MP who fought for family allowances in Edwardian Liverpool. Hers is the same picture of ashen-faced weariness. 'The harassed mother is a very real phenomenon,' wrote Lee Comer in *Wedlocked Women*. 'There is no large-scale male experience like the depths of desperation every mother sinks to, having dragged, pushed and carried a boisterous or recalcitrant small child up and down escalators, on and off buses, in and out of shops and whose only recognition is the odd benign smile from an old person amid a sea of disapproving, condemnatory and hostile glances.' But it was the same long before escalators and supermarkets. A hundred years ago Elizabeth Cady Stanton, the American campaigner for women's suffrage who had six children, was referring to 'the isolated household' and 'the wearied, anxious look of the majority of women'.

Yet women will not give up maternity. For every account of harassed motherhood there is another on the bliss of childbirth. Stories of birth are of endless interest to those who are about to be mothers, or have just given birth themselves. Every birth is a story, each quite different, each ending with curiosity satisfied. The *idea* of motherhood, white-robed infant in its mother's loving arms, keeps the cycle in motion – not the picture of the scowling adolescent with green hair. Babycare books deal exhaustively with maternity rights and toddler tantrums but draw a veil over the worse that is to come. Occasionally an honest novelist breaks down this barrier.

'Standing by the toaster, Erica contemplates her children, whom she once thought the most beautiful beings on earth. Jeffrey's streaked blond hair hangs tangled and unwashed over his eyes . . . he hunches awkward-ly above the table, cramming fried egg into his mouth and chewing noisily. Matilda, who is wearing a peevish expression and an orange tie-dyed jersey which looks as if it had been spat on, is stripping the crusts off her toast with her fingers. Chomp, crunch, scratch . . .

'In her whole life she cannot remember disliking anyone as much as she now sometimes dislikes Jeffrey and Matilda.

'They were a happy family once, she thinks. Jeffrey and Matilda were beautiful, healthy babies; charming toddlers; intelligent, lively, affectionate children. There are photograph albums and folders of drawings and stories and report cards to prove it. Then last year, when Jeffrey turned fourteen and Matilda twelve, they had begun to change; to grow rude, coarse, selfish, nasty, brutish and tall.

'. . . The worst part of it all is that the children are her fault. All the authorities and writers say so.'

Contemplating such a refreshing account of mid-life parental anguish in Alison Lurie's *The War Between The Tates* I would suddenly regard the women I had interviewed as heroic survivors.

Our attitudes to children, childbirth and parenthood remain deeply significant. Are children welcomed? Is fecundity encouraged? Does the birth rate rise or fall? At the moment, it falls. We make a pretence of welcoming babies but we do as little as possible to make motherhood a comfortable state. We regard children as public nuisances and look on adolescents with undisguised suspicion. A nation carries on controlling its population until it does not replace itself: as in Sparta, Athens and Rome, so in Britain now. On the other hand, in Nazi Germany an Honour Card was awarded to mothers of three or more children ('the most beautiful name the world over is Mother') and people were reminded that it took a family of six children to compensate for every childless couple if the declining birth rate was to be reversed. It is always politically significant if a government deters parenthood (India, China, Russia today) or regards population as an asset as in Victorian England, or among the Founding Fathers in the New World. At the same time, it is worth noting what women's real feelings about children are, and how those compare with the feelings they think they ought to have.

'Well educated emancipated women should have no need of abortion,' wrote the economist Mary Stocks in 1971. I wish those who fulminate against abortion today, often childless young men, could appreciate that having an abortion is not a wanton decision taken lightly, or a sign of the decline of civilisation. Some of the women I interviewed were morally fixed against abortion. But others confided that they had at some point terminated a pregnancy. (I wish they could state their names, as did the brave French women who signed the 1968

Le Monde advertisement campaigning for the legalisation of abortion in France.)

Those in my sample who had had an abortion were the conscientious mothers of large families. Perhaps they had become accidentally pregnant within months of having a previous baby. Whether they regretted the termination or not, it had been an important and considered decision. Which is better, a regretted abortion or a regretted baby? Those who know nothing of pregnancy, or childbirth, or about bringing a new baby into an already crowded family, might ponder this. Abortion may feature in the life of an intelligent and happily married woman who loves her husband and is bringing up a stable family, but is responsible enough to determine precisely how large a family she and her husband can cope with.

And what are the children like, of these Compleat Women? I was often asked this. People long to know whether women self-indulgent enough to have large families while pursuing a successful working life produce delinquent monsters as Dr John Bowlby threatened.

I could have interviewed all of the ninety scattered children. But a child's view of his or her parents is no more reliable than a parent's view of the child. Few views are more biased than those of one family member on another family member. Families are hotbeds of secret resentments, even the very happiest families. Two children can view the same parent quite differently. Just as two parents can be worlds apart on the subject of the same child.

So I made no special effort to see children; but some happened to come along while I was visiting their mothers, and some I know anyway. Those children are, I have to report, no *more* peculiar or mystifying than others of their generations. Some have emigrated. Some are immensely successful; some have done even better than their parents. Some had been through difficult and recalcitrant periods in adolescence. Sometimes these very same ones had gone on to gain Firsts at university, to become professors, academics, musicians and serious writers.

In no respect, therefore, were they much different from any other sample of middle-class offspring. As the sons and daughters of working mothers they are no more blighted than most of us are by our mothers, working or non-working. We like to blame mothers, and as mothers ourselves we fully expect to be blamed in our turn. Or, conversely, we see the credit reflected on ourselves if the children do well. It is all misplaced egotism: so much anxiety is expended on the progress of children, from the cradle well into their adulthood – and nobody can say for certain that anything they do is because of parental influence.

Several interviewees mentioned how little influence they felt they had, in the long run, over grown children. Increasingly they go their own way – somehow reverting (in Fay Weldon's view) to precisely the character they had in the first few days after birth; and probably ending up, in middle age, very like their own parents.

What I have to report is that mothers do seem to have their favourites, and they do pick out the angels and the troublemakers very early in life. The impulse to favouritism can strike at birth; there is usually one child even among the largest brood who is 'simply the most beautiful baby you ever saw'. The beautiful one, the bright one, the funny one, the angel and the demon: all marked out, and often written down, within hours of life.

I would also conclude that the relationship between a mother and her eldest daughter is the single most complex described to me. One mother thought her eldest daughter a saint; another described hers as the most competitive person she had ever met; a third said she would always feel guilty about the pressure she had put on her eldest daughter. Eldest daughters were sources of huge admiration, wonderment, anxiety, pleasure and exasperation. They were 'spiky', 'strong-willed', 'astonishing'. I kept recalling that many of these women were themselves the daughters of strong mothers: I had a vision of a matriarchal line of women, each exasperating and becoming a source of wonder to her own mother, then going on to create another amazing young woman.

Phrases used by the mothers, too deeply personal to quote in the interviews, have stayed in my mind. One mother said she would wish to die in the arms of her youngest daughter. Another said that to see the loneliness of her daughter broke her heart. Even daughters who had been tearaways had come home to bring tears to the eyes. A father said, of one of his daughters: 'If I met her, I would marry her.' Interestingly, daughters were a far greater source of interest and conversation than sons.

In the course of producing four children of each sex, Elizabeth Longford told me she had come to the conclusion that a woman's excitement over giving birth to a boy is (unless she has only sons already and longs for a daughter) greater than the excitement of producing a girl. There is something inexplicably atavistic about this, but it is so – even if the mother is eventually much closer to her daughters than to her sons.

One of the most harrowing aspects of parenthood in middle age, I gathered, is to see the children moving in and out of more or less congenial emotional attachments. I heard once or twice about daughters' brutal and violent lovers. Mothers and fathers suffer dreadfully and helplessly over this. At such times I would feel I never wanted to see another mother-and-baby manual: there is so much sentimental claptrap about babyhood and teething problems, but any witless fool can cope with all that. It is coping with the brute who blacks your twenty-two-year-old daughter's eyes that ultimately tests a parent.

When they contemplate their daughters' future, these mothers point out that recently times have changed so vastly and rapidly that none of the old rules apply. Women now aged sixty grew up with quite different expectations from those of women now aged forty. For women of twenty, it is all going to be different again. Prolonged education, high unemployment, the cost of housing and of domestic help all conspire against youthful motherhood for the daughters of these women, and as for marriage, if they marry at all they will probably do so in their thirties rather than at twenty-two as their mothers did. The Family, as Betty Friedan now says, is the new Feminist Frontier: the 'biological clock' confronts the successful career woman who finds herself at thirty-eight suddenly desperate to have a child.

'The mothers of my mother's generation,' said one daughter who is now in her thirties, and divorced, 'knew so little about child psychology. The whole business of bringing up children – they didn't give it a thought.' It is true to say that an intelligent woman today would appear inordinately confident and courageous if she deliberately embarked on a family of five or six. Parenthood, for most mothers I interviewed, *was* more carefree. The dangers of road traffic and lurking child-molesters, which have now altered the parameters of childhood beyond all imagining, were then barely thought of. Childhood could once be, as Philip Larkin described it, 'a forgotten boredom': whole days of aimless wandering in solitude. My own mother never learned to drive; we children wandered, we cycled, we drifted for hours along the beach or cliffs. Mothers did not then spend their time chauffeuring. Children's lives are infinitely circumscribed now by home, school and organised activity.

Finally, though we live in the era of choice, and uphold a woman's right to choose, there is no choice for the infertile. Infertility is not a diminishing problem. And although those who yearn to have children can now be helped as never before – I write feelingly as one who must thank the wonders of modern science for my second pregnancy – it is still an unwelcome and bitter fact of many women's lives, which afflicts one in ten couples. The more control over gynaecological matters we appear to have, the less we seem to wield. Women of my generation are walking histories of gynaecological disorder – as bound, in a different way, to the vagaries of their bodies as were their Victorian forebears.

From time to time a survey is published to the effect that childless marriages tend to be happier. This comes as no surprise to those who are currently finding children consuming the majority of their time, energy and money, and causing so much disruption that they yearn for the pre-child honeymoon days.

On the other hand, children do concentrate the mind most powerfully on essentials. A parent may not be childish; parents have to grow up, and accept responsibilities, which is on the whole a good thing. Once children arrive they become the focus around which the rest of life has to be arranged. Without them we would all be better read, perhaps, and more widely travelled and possibly much richer – but altogether worse off. To me, the ultimate pleasure and motivation in having children is that they satisfy one's innate curiosity about what one's children would be like. The various answers they collectively provide are a source of unending interest. They are also the best excuse for vicarious fun in adult life – on high days and holidays and festive celebrations. It would be harder to justify a toboggan, a firework or a Christmas cracker without a child to hand.

Șɝ

Since this book was published, one marriage has foundered after twenty-eight years. Rather than excise that interview in this edition, I have retained it, with the subject's permission, as she represents a growing category of women who must soldier on when families grow up and even durable marriages fade.

Work & Help

❧

Even the diehard feminist has sometimes to be reminded of how recently the opportunities arrived for women to do any kind of worthwhile work, if they also chose to marry. Until well into this century it was not possible to combine marriage with schoolteaching, or with the Civil Service; the 'marriage bar' operated. No wonder 'Miss Buss and Miss Beale/Cupid's darts did not feel.' Had Cupid struck, neither would have run their famous schools. As late as 1950, Mary Warnock was the first married woman Fellow of St Hugh's College, Oxford.

Even though the medical profession was technically open to women since the heroic battle of Elizabeth Blackwell in 1870, a whole century later the medical schools were still secretly and disgracefully operating a quota, which kept the number of women medical students below 20 per cent.

Top female civil servants are still rare: there were only four women Deputy Secretaries in 1984 and only one of those had children. Christabel Pankhurst could have been the first English woman barrister, but, though she gained her LLB, she was refused entrance at Lincoln's Inn. The first woman accepted by the Inns of Court was Helena Normanton, called to the Bar in 1922 and later one of the first women King's Counsels. Sixty years later, in the 1986 list of new Queen's Counsels, the total of 50 included 45 men but only 5 women.

When Barbara Wootton began lecturing in Economics at Cambridge in the 1920s the university authorities had a problem: how could her name appear on the lecture list, if women were not allowed to be full members of the university (though they had technically been allowed to take degrees for some decades)? They solved the problem by listing her subject under the name of a male colleague. Everyone knew the lectures were Barbara's, but they could not say so.

Sixty-five years after winning the vote, and with a woman Prime Minister in 10 Downing Street, the representation of women at

Westminster remains preposterous – 27 out of 650 seats, at less than 4 per cent one of the lowest figures in Europe. Pressure groups like the 300 Group are doing sterling persuasive work, but it is an uphill struggle. In fact there is no shortage of women offering themselves as candidates for Parliamentary seats. But most fail at the final hurdle, the selection committee. 'You were the best candidate,' an aspiring woman may be frankly informed, 'but we selected the best man.' Many more women would come forward if it were not for the mad working hours – 2.30 pm to 10 pm – of the House of Commons.

The work-achievement catalogue is dismally familiar. Women make up only 10 per cent of university and polytechnic lecturers, 11 per cent of solicitors, 20 per cent of doctors, 5 per cent of accountants. As things gradually change towards the close of the twentieth century, girls' schools are desperately aware of the need for young women to rethink their whole approach to their future life, replacing 'little–job–marriage–babies' with 'career established – possibly marriage and children combined with continuing work – think what will I be doing at 40, 50, 60?'

Yet the idea that ambition is an unfeminine quality is still widespread. In the men's club atmosphere of the working world, women are labelled 'bossy' where a man would be admired for his drive. Young girls, perceiving this, might reasonably decide not to make the attempt.

That is why the power of the role model should not be underestimated. When young women see other women in influential positions a chain is established from generation to generation. I kept coming across examples of this. In one memorable chain, a woman doctor had modelled herself on a pioneering woman gynaecologist, who had herself been inspired by Marie Curie, for whom she had once worked. A young woman barrister told me she hoped to organise her life like that of Barbara Mills, the Queen's Counsel in this book.

It has been our misfortune that there were so few Compleat Woman role models among the pioneering women of the past. The usual prototype of the Victorian heroine is Florence Nightingale, who chafed at being enclosed in the genteel drawing-room life of a middle-class spinster daughter, and broke out of it to change the world – but never married or had children. If you search harder, however, it is possible to find examples of pioneering women who were mothers and also had other lives – isolated examples perhaps, but nevertheless there to show that a woman who bore children might also make her mark in the world.

Catherine Booth, co-founder of the Salvation Army, was a mother of eight. Mary Elizabeth Braddon, the novelist and playwright, had six children of her own and five step-children. Alice Meynell, the suffragist and journalist, was proposed as Poet Laureate after the death of Tennyson, and was a mother of eight. Julia Margaret Cameron took up portrait photography at the age of forty-eight, after having six children. Hester Thrale, Dr Johnson's friend, virtually ran her husband's brewery and household, and kept detailed notebooks about her five surviving children. Harriet Beecher Stowe, author of *Uncle Tom's Cabin*, had seven children. Lady Mary Bailey, when she was thirty-eight and had five children, made her 1938 epic solo flight from Croydon to Capetown. Elizabeth Cady Stanton, the American suffragist, was a mother of six; and Josephine Butler, campaigner for prostitutes, whose husband George was the prototype good man that is hard to find, had four children. Most fecund of all, Queen Victoria ruled the Empire and a family of nine.

While preparing this book I went to speak at a careers evening at a girls' school. It was a good opportunity to emphasise the importance of acquiring qualifications as soon as one can: no matter what happens later in a woman's life she has that base, one which was common to most of those I had interviewed. The headmistress of the school pointed out to me how perfect a teaching career must be for anyone intending to combine motherhood with work: the same school hours, long holidays, the chance to take a few years off and get back in.

I did talk to two headmistresses while doing my research and both had done just that – taken ten and twelve years out respectively to bring up four children apiece. One headmistress was married to a vicar. Her husband had suffered two coronary thromboses at the age of forty-eight, just at the point when she was starting back on the school career ladder. He made a complete recovery, but it led her to reflect that she might very well have found herself in her forties as sole breadwinner to a family of four. It is more important than ever to ensure that women, through education and training, are able to support themselves and if necessary their families. It falls to far more women than to men to be left in sole charge of a family at some time.

In Girton College Library the following letter of rebuff is on display, from novelist Charlotte M. Yonge on black-edged paper to the Foundress of Girton, Miss Emily Davies: 'I am obliged to you for your letter respecting the proposed college for ladies, but as I have decided objections to bringing large numbers of girls together . . . I am afraid I cannot assist you.

'I feel with regret that female education is deficient in tone and manner, if in nothing else. *Superior women will always teach themselves and inferior women will never learn enough for more than home life.*'

That is precisely the attitude – found as often among women themselves as among men – against which the women's movements had to wage their worthwhile war for so long.

❧

A ROOM OF ONE'S OWN

Writing fiction is the one profession everyone assumes a woman has always been able to combine with domestic life as easily as a man. Yet novels by married women with families remained scarce until this century, and later became an object of (male) critical jocularity in the 1960s and 1970s as the *kitchen table novel*, written between stirring the stew and bathing the baby, generally in Hampstead.

Let us take a sample of three dozen female writers whose work most women will have read: Jane Austen, the Brontë sisters, Virginia Woolf, Nancy Mitford, George Eliot, Iris Murdoch, Ivy Compton-Burnett, Barbara Pym, Katherine Mansfield, Dorothy L. Sayers, Beatrix Potter, Beatrice Webb, Louisa May Alcott, Emily Dickinson, Stevie Smith, Christina Stead, Edith Somerville, Rebecca West, Dorothy Parker, Elizabeth Bowen, Elizabeth Taylor, Freya Stark, Eudora Welty, Carson McCullers, Noel Streatfeild, Jean Rhys, Muriel Spark, Willa Cather, Joyce Carol Oates, Angela Carter, Margaret Atwood, Anita Brookner, Alison Lurie, Elizabeth Jane Howard.

The majority had no children. A handful of them have had one child apiece – West, Sayers, Howard, Carter. The woman who writes and also has a family is still exceptional; and even an enduring marriage is known to only a minority of those above. Cosy domesticity is plainly not conducive to the creative writing struggle. ('A woman who writes feels too much: those trances and portents!' wrote the poet Anne Sexton in *The Black Art.*) Until recently a woman writer was not a kitchen table person at all, but one with a desk in a room of her own.

The novelist Margaret Drabble, addressing an Authors' Day organised by *Cosmopolitan* magazine, described herself as 'very much a woman who has written while producing a family'.

'I wrote my first book while expecting my first child, my second book while expecting my second child, and my third while expecting my third child. Then I felt that was enough babies; I would keep on with the books.

'For a while I had a little superstition that they only went together, and my fourth novel, *Jerusalem the Golden*, was pretty sticky going. But that could have had something to do with having three small children under the age of five.'

Mrs Gaskell, Margaret Drabble reminded us, had been the first appreciable writer who was familiar enough with maternity to introduce it as an important subject. It had been a long wait for her arrival. In Jane Austen's description of children, said Ms Drabble, one could sense a kind of permissible *recoil*.

Now, she said, a large number of women writers have had children and have written about the experience of incorporating children into their lives. 'We are now free to describe what it's like to give birth, and the fury of dealing with one's darling beloved children.' She read aloud from Doris Lessing's account of Martha Quest trying to spoonfeed an angry child while maintaining an intelligent conversation with a male friend, hopelessly striving to appear the perfect mother. Martha ends up ramming the spoon down the child's throat and feeling she has failed on every count. 'This,' Margaret Drabble said, 'for many people would be a true confrontation.'

Now that her own children were grown up, said Margaret Drabble, she no longer felt she had to use in writing the experience of mother-hood; she would now, like every other sensible person, leave a railway carriage if she saw a baby in it. 'But when one is going through it,' she reflected, 'motherhood is a kind of sisterhood. Everyone is involved in sleeping problems, washing machines. It was a very important spring in my life.'

It is a tiny comfort to know that children need not necessarily be what Henry James called an incentive to damnation, artistically speaking. It is possible to argue that a writer's work might benefit from the experience of parenthood. Fay Weldon writes, in *Letters to Alice*:

'If you want to be a writer, don't. If you want to write, which is a different matter, nothing will stop you, not lack of time, nor the existence of husband, home or children; these things will merely sharpen your determination, not deter you. I do believe it is the battle the writer wages with the real world which provides the energy for invention.'

'HELP! I NEED SOMEBODY . . .'

Women who work need other women to help them. Put another way: women who work usually need women to work for them. There are exceptions to this rule, but on the whole if a woman works outside the home she has to find some kind of substitute for herself. And that often applies if she works at home as well.

Always, as Virginia Woolf observed, the doorbell rings and the baker calls. And she didn't even have any children underfoot.

The kind of help used by the women in this book varies from Charlie in the mental hospital (the Bewleys) to the Mills's nanny who ran a day-nursery for neighbourhood children in their basement. The Warnocks had a live-in mother as back-up to the series of nannies. Alice Thomas Ellis's last nanny, Janet, proved so indispensable that she has stayed on (the youngest child is fourteen) to look after Alice herself, organising her life.

The only common factor in all cases of employing helpers (nannies, mother's helps, au pairs) is the admitting of another person from outside the family into your home: those who have never done this cannot imagine it. It does tax a family's togetherness and tolerance to be always in the presence of an outsider; but it can also reinforce it. If the outsider becomes part of the family it is generally a testimony to character on both sides. On the other hand, as Drusilla Beyfus says, *you* the mother want to work, so yours is the need, and it is incumbent upon you to keep your help happy.

Mary Warnock says she saw her home as an institution that had to be staffed by capable, efficient people. But in the main the women here belong to the au pair generation: post-starched nanny era but pre-modern nanny, somewhere between the old nursery and below stairs habits, and the contemporary friendliness in which mother and nanny have lunch together.

In between come vaguely recalled short-term helps: 'We always had a Scottish girl . . .' 'someone from the village . . .' 'You could get some sad Swiss for three quid a week.' The real Mary Poppinses, who came and stayed and loomed large in the children's lives, are vivid exceptions, recalled with genuine gratitude. When I was embarking on parenthood, Joan Bakewell the television journalist and mother of two once told me, 'I've had them all, the anorexics and the compulsive eaters, the ones on drugs and the ones who drank, the ones with lovers and the ones with mothers, the one who stole my jewellery and the one who used the car and the one who phoned Australia . . .' a familiar litany of complaints. But if you eavesdropped on any nanny-mafia gathering you would hear similar terrible tales of employers. Yet there is never any shortage of questing mothers, nor of would-be nannies: there are ten pages of nanny ads in *The Lady* magazine every week.

To read these advertisements you would suppose that every couple is a thrusting dual-career family: 'BBC mum, doctor father', 'novelist and literary agent couple', 'mother finishing research degree, father practising international film law'. Their children are 'lovely, delightful, sweet,' etc., until the age of about two and a half when expensive adjectives drop out of the ads. Home is invariably 'hectic but happy', 'cheerful friendly house', 'chaotic lively fascinating household'. To match these frolicsome families, the nanny must herself be cheerful (most-used word) non-smoking, caring, loving, adaptable, reliable, affectionate, capable, kind, enthusiastic, a car-driver, a swimmer, a lover of pets *and* with a sense of humour . . .

By comparison with such a paragon any mother might end up feeling decidedly inferior.

No woman who lets another woman look after her children while she herself is busy working can ever be entirely free from the nagging expectation of a later reproach from the children. Two women I interviewed mentioned grown-up daughters who had later accused them of never being there, or of 'handing them over' to nannies; it is not a fact many want to face. Besides, as several said, whatever course you take, your children will reproach you, even for always being there. Several said how pleased they felt their adolescent children had been *not* to have over-attentive mothers fussing round them. But no mother would wish a child, later in life, to write as Dr Helena Wright the renowned gynaecologist wrote to her mother recollecting her childhood: 'To me you were merely a shadow, a shadow with three characteristics; you were always "busy" and you were always either ill or worried . . . I don't remember that you once spent time actually playing with us in the nursery. Nurse Minter was our chief companion . . . Why didn't you get to know your children a little?' (Poor Alice, Helena's mother, had devoted her energies like so many women of her class and generation, to social life and public-spirited charity affairs.)

My impression from these interviews was that when the time for help at home had passed, it was almost as if it had never been. Names and dates of helpers were blurred, conveniently forgotten. Mothers of a certain era can be astonishingly blinkered about the whole business, I reflected. 'I never had a *nanny*,' they say, even if a series of au pairs have slaved like Trojans. On the other hand nobody is allowed to mention the word 'exploitation' either. An interviewer once did so in the presence of Fay Weldon, who riposted: 'Either they live on social security or they work for me, which isn't very hard work, so that I can earn enough money for all of us.'

Nobody goes 'into domestic service' any more, yet there is somehow still a pool of available female employment as the Domestic situations columns testify. After the nannying years come the stop-gap years — 'Retired schoolteacher or other responsible adult wanted to supervise two nine/ten year old boys' homework Tuesdays to Fridays 4–6.30 pm.' This is the post-nanny age when the working mother realises that far from 'off her hands' when at school, her children need more supervision than ever. At exactly the same period, though, if a mother is working outside the home in business and career worlds, she is expected to work late at the office, or be available to see people. The working world does not recognise children's teatime, or bathtime, or homework or piano practice. *And somebody has to be there.* A career woman mother has to delegate part of her role and live with the results. 'At work,' as Jill Parker succinctly put it, 'one was only ever as reliable as one's hopeless Spanish au pair.'

The brisk, honest parenthood manuals of today address themselves more robustly to the help question than did those of a generation ago because the help trade is on the increase. Katharine Whitehorn's advice in *How to Survive Children* is to remember you have hired a mother's help to be *unlike* yourself. 'If you've hired a mother's help for qualities of cow-like tranquillity you absolutely don't have yourself, it's unfair to be furious if they take an hour and a half, reflectively stirring the water with one hoof, to do the washing up.'

Penny Vincenzi, mother of four, recommends mother's helps in her *There's One Born Every Minute*: au pairs work out most expensive because of the calls home to Italy, while grand nannies have to be lived

34

up to with posh prams, a cleaning lady, a third car. Libby Purves in *How Not To Be A Perfect Mother* gives an extraordinarily vivid portrait of life with a fully-trained treasure nanny. This treasure creates a gleaming, clinical kitchen and puts the baby in three pairs of freshly-ironed dungarees every day. But the atmosphere curdles as the husband starts saying he wishes to God the nanny would go off duty sometimes . . .

It is impossible for me to come to any conclusion about the help question. You only know what you have done yourself, and you may not even know whether that was the right course for years or decades ahead. I have only ever had one kind of help, our sterling nanny; and only one nanny. This was not planned. I had fancifully booked a place in a crèche, before having the first baby, and only after she was born did I realise what a daft solution that would have been. And so our Monday-to-Friday nanny arrived, the Angel of our House, ruling our roost. Even after eleven years I could not advise anyone else about following such a course because it is so particularly a matter of our lives and the way things have worked out. It is the most intimate and delicate of re-lationships and it is a testimony to our nanny's character that she has stayed so long and worked so hard. There is total dedication and trust. For that reason alone I could not imagine an ever-changing series of au pairs, as described by many women to me. Nor could I imagine not having a long Friday-afternoon-to-Monday-morning weekend in which to sample the really testing side of family life without our nanny, even though (as I was warned beforehand) having a Monday-to-Friday live-in help means that one is working seven days a week oneself. Could it have been better, organised differently? I can't imagine it, but I shall never know. I am grateful that it has all worked so well for so long.

Of all the elements in a busy life embracing family and job, the easiest part to delegate is the domestic drudgery. Innumerable famous women, widely assumed to be superwomen, admit to never having hoovered, dusted or laundered from one year's end to the next. There *is* a short-term satisfaction in gazing upon a gleaming surface that you have achieved yourself – few women would deny that. A few might even go along with Margaret Forster and insist on doing it all themselves. But on the whole it is quite an easy satisfaction to give up. After all, even ladies of leisure in the past had domestics and dailies, so why should a woman putting in an honest day's work herself have any qualms about it?

Mary Warnock

Baroness Warnock, *Mistress of Girton College, Cambridge*

b. 1924

m. 1949

GEOFFREY WARNOCK

*Sir Geoffrey Warnock, Principal of
Hertford College, Oxford*

3 daughters, 2 sons

KITTY FELIX JAMES STEPHANA (FANNY)

GRIZEL (BOZ)

Mary Warnock

To have had five children, to become headmistress of a girls' day school while bringing up the family, and then to run Girton College, Cambridge, while continuing to write on philosophy and education, seems altogether too crowded a life. Mistresses of Girton were always spinsters in the first century of that pioneering women's college (founded 1869). Mary Warnock was not the first to be a mother, but the first to be a mother of five. A considerable inspiration, I suspect, to the young women in her charge.

When we met, she had just chaired the Committee of Inquiry into human fertilisation and embryology and produced the 1984 Warnock Report, which created a whole new field for moral philosophers, embracing the great questions of life and death. In the midst of the controversy she was appointed Mistress of Girton, and that month I went (as an Old Girtonian) to hear her speak at the college's annual reunion. She talked of her committee work; it had been her first encounter with the lumbering Civil Service way of doing things. Documents required in London had to be posted to Scunthorpe to be typed; delay was a besetting problem. In Cardiff one night she had sat up typing till 3 am so that her committee could all have copies of a report the next day. This is typical of her industriousness. 'Mary is never cast down,' says her husband, 'by the prospect of huge quantities of work.'

She has written six books of philosophy (her latest being on *Memory*) and four on educational subjects; she is a newspaper columnist (recently for the *Daily Telegraph*) and a frequent reviewer of books for Sunday papers and weekly journals.

Baroness Warnock is quick, animated, frequently running her fingers through short, wiry grey hair which then stands up wildly. It is an alert face dominated by spectacles. We met for the main interview in her apartment at Girton. The college is the archetypal redbrick Victorian-Gothic institutional building, magnificently intimidating but (in my memory always in autumn) charming and a source of pride as the first college ever to award degrees to women. Its founder, Emily Davies, appointed the great Victorian architect, Alfred Waterhouse, to design it because she wanted a building 'as beautiful as his Assize Courts in Manchester'. Girton's corridors of cell-like rooms are endless and its parquet flooring slippery; hence the red sneakers Mary Warnock was wearing, which matched her brilliant scarlet sweater. Her flat is a spacious modern addition next to Waterhouse's chapel – uncongenial from the outside but light and sunny within. We lunched on High Table, my first experience of such elevation; and had pancakes as it was Shrove Tuesday.

Mary Warnock, née Wilson, was the youngest of a large family. They would have been seven, had not two sons died. Her father, a house-master at Winchester College, died before she was born, during the summer holiday of 1924. Her mother was obliged to move out of the school house instantly, so that a new housemaster could move in.

'But she had always been removed from the college in spirit, anyway. She was the complete Edwardian; she wore elaborate hats and long clothes. The idea of ever borrowing her clothes, as my daughters do mine! One hardly knew what her various bits and pieces were *for*.

'Being a widow sort of suited my mother. When my grandfather died she became quite rich, so her expensive tastes could be indulged. My sister and I, when we spend shameful hours reminiscing about our child-hood, always refer to her as "*Mither*". In our house the great cry was "It's different for me." There was Mither's special glass, and Mither's special jam. Mither always travelled first class while we travelled third.

'I really had a childhood such as nobody's had since. It was blissfully happy, and the war simply prolonged it.

'My mother, far from having a career, was totally incompetent; she was the woman for whom the phrase "can't boil an egg" was coined.' (Geoffrey Warnock was once having tea with Mither in her house in Winchester, and the jar of jam on the table was a new one. 'Mither's advice to me,' said Sir Geoffrey, 'was that I should take it out to the kitchen and get them to open it. She was quite helpless.')

'But she knitted and embroidered and in her way she was both clever and independent,' Mary says. 'She was enormously widely read; she had always read more than I had, and would guide our reading. Nowadays, I feel sure she would have reached the top of some university. She came from a very clever Jewish family which converted to Christianity, the Schusters: our Schuster cousins are everywhere. Two brothers Schuster married two sisters Weber and it is still a very close family network.'

There is a large portrait of Sir Felix Schuster, Bart, over Mary Warnock's fireplace. 'A horrible old domestic tyrant, but larger than life. You know the Osbert Lancaster character Sir Otto? My grandfather exactly: very rich Jewish banker, thick German accent. My mother, his eldest daughter, was terrified of him and spent all her time knitting him tiny socks.

'He used to descend on us at Winchester and I remember my mother whispering, "Don't mention the Gold Standard to Grandpapa!" in 1930 I suppose. We were always told he could have been the greatest pianist in the world if he had liked. He indoctrinated us in music, played the piano for us and told us what we might like and not like.

'My mother didn't really care for her Schuster relations, she was much more interested in my father's Scottish family. I see my father as a John Buchan character, somewhat dashing, interested in country sports. He was a rather lazy schoolmaster, I believe: there are still a few of his old pupils around, who remember him with his feet up on a sofa, smoking Egyptian cigarettes.

'I am so interested in the *mythology* of the family. An atmosphere can be created around a character entirely from family hearsay and innuendo.

'Mither was interested in her children but didn't want to see too much of them at any time in her life. My nearest sister Stephana and I were isolated in the nursery with our wonderful nanny Emily Coleman from Hampshire, who could do *The Times* crossword and helped the family until she died at ninety-four. She came to me for the births of all my children and she ended in the house of my sister Stephana, who was possibly her favourite, and who had six children.

'There was no question of equality of opportunity for my eldest two sisters at least; nobody seemed to expect them to achieve much. The two who died were boys, before my sister and myself came along, so my remaining brother Duncan was the only boy. And especially since my father had died too, in an all-female household Duncan was quite a godlike figure: as a child I was frightened of him. He was thirteen years older and was always giving us advice. The one thing everybody knew was that he was terribly clever; he knew everything, and he was good at everything.' (Sir Duncan Wilson became Master of Corpus Christi College, Cambridge, and died in 1984).

'When I went to Oxford I knew that his subject, Classics, was the one for me. I even had the same tutor, who never ceased to compare me unfavourably with Duncan. I worked like a slave, while Duncan was always singing. I even joined the Bach choir to prove that I too could both sing and work.'

Mary had boarded at St Swithun's School in Winchester. 'My sister Stephana and I were lucky in that the climate had changed, in the family, on the subject of education of girls. Dean Inge, Dean of St Paul's Cathedral, was a family friend, and we were taken to be interviewed by him at the home of Grandfather Felix's sister. Dean Inge decided that my sister should be a scientist, and I a philosopher. It was Stephana's misfortune: it was true that at the time she used to enjoy making radio sets from kits, but reading Chemistry at Oxford was a nightmare, she couldn't bear it. She spent most of her time doing music, and came back later to read that.'

Mary read Mods and Greats at Lady Margaret Hall, Oxford, with an interval at Sherborne School in Dorset, a girls' public school, her first experience of teaching, the reserved occupation offered in wartime as an alternative to service in the ATS. When the war was over she went back to Oxford and met Geoffrey Warnock of New College, who seemed remarkable to her because he was so funny. She was outgoing Chairman of the Jowett Society (for the best undergraduate philosophers) and she appointed him her successor. They were married in 1949.

'It was an incredibly different era. Somehow after the war everybody just knew they were going to get married and have children. Among my contemporaries we never questioned it; we never even discussed it. I thought nobody would ever *want* to marry me, but I was quite certain that if I could get married, I would, and that I would certainly have children. To decide *not* to have children was something that I could not have done.'

Here Mary Warnock reflected on the recent arguments about surrogate motherhood, and the need for embryo research in the cause of curing infertility, arguments her committee had wrestled with when preparing the Warnock Report. 'I have tremendous sympathy for the infertile. But the supposition that you must have a child for your own sake is something I do rather worry about. Partly because the people who get obsessional about it tend to forget that children are not babies for ever. Just think of this one child, on whom everything has to depend!'

In academic life the question of working after marriage hardly arises. 'When we were just about fixing up to get married, I was offered a job at St Hugh's as a lecturer and Geoffrey got a prize fellowship at Magdalen, which meant he would be in Oxford too, so there was never any question that I would or would not keep my job. But I was the first married Fellow of St Hugh's. It is almost incredible isn't it, that as recently as the early 1950s there was real dispute as to whether there should be married Fellows at all.

'But Geoffrey never doubted for a moment that I should carry on with the job when we began having children. After Kitty was born I used to get into despair every now and then, and say I couldn't manage and should I give up my job. But Geoffrey's reaction was always "Don't be an idiot, let's spend more money getting more help."

'Finance was one of the crucial things. We were both on tiny salaries, and the girl we first hired to look after Kitty was paid considerably more than I was. But even then, if I said, "We're wasting money, I'm going mad, if the girl gets ill or Kitty gets ill I'm frantic and it's money down the drain," Geoffrey was always level-headed about it.

'In those days a lecturer was paid £250 or £300 a year, on the assumption that you would live in college so it was "all found". As the first married Fellow, if I didn't live in it was just too bad. I did have frightful rows about it. I remember writing a letter to *The Spectator* when someone had made a reference to "well-paid academics".

'Fortunately Geoffrey's father, who was a very successful GP in Leeds with a rich practice, retired that year and gave us his second car and lent us the capital to buy our own house. He was very strict about being paid back, but it meant an interest-free mortgage so that was lucky.'

Why *five* children?

'By the time you've got one, the argument for having more is very strong indeed. When we got to number three, Geoffrey thought that was enough – he very reasonably thought that three was a decent family, and more than he'd come from (two) and it was really all we could manage, and he increasingly disliked the commotion the children caused. But I was by then addicted to the idea of four and desperate to have another.'

(As Sir Geoffrey remembers it, Mary's argument was 'Just think how sad it will be for the third, always to be the youngest . . .')

'In principle I know Geoffrey liked the *idea* of being the father of a large family, he liked the idea of having three children by the age of thirty (he just made it, by one day) but the children do make a lot of chaos and noise and he has always hated the amount of mess I could generate.

'At one stage there were three under the age of six, which does mean there is always a crisis, somebody not wanting to go to school, somebody with a cough, somebody sick and you never know what it might portend . . .

'I was a desperate candidate for pregnancy, sick all the time and permanently exhausted especially when there were other small children around; these were frequently the moments when I did think I must give up work and settle down. My doctor described me as "disastrously fertile". After the pill came in I started to take it but I felt ill, and went back to my old Dutch cap. When each child arrived I adored their babyhood, though it took time to learn this. Each child I liked better as a baby, and I don't remember hating my last pregnancy at all.' ('As you would expect,' Sir Geoffrey says, 'Mary made no great fuss about childbirth.')

'I do so love the moment of giving birth to a new child; this new person, to whom you can attach a new name, it's something for ever, to have fixed a name and possibly a character for the rest of their lives. This is the frivolous view about having children, but my husband always had the highest principles about naming: you may not call a child a name without a reason. You must be able to answer the question, why *that* name?

'Our first child was Kathleen: that was easy, my mother-in-law's name, and known as Kitty like one of my Schuster aunts. Then Felix, after my terrible grandfather but I always loved the name, and Felix is a bassoonist and his name has done him immense good. James was named after my father-in-law, who was at death's door when James was born. "James Warnock" is such a good solid name. Then there was Stephana, known as Fanny, after my sister. The last one I'm almost ashamed to say was Grizel, named after an aunt from my father's Scottish side. I had known a girl called Grizel Anstruther which seemed to me a wonderful name. But I'm afraid she suffered terribly as a small child. She was deeply moved, at the age of five, when Lady Ogilvie, the Principal of St Anne's College, said to her, "Grizel! what a lovely name." But this was the rare exception and she quickly changed her name to Boz, which she has remained ever since.'

Mary Warnock had her five children in eleven years, 1950 to 1961, so the most intense time of child care was in the early 1960s. 'Bozzie started at nursery school when Kitty was taking her O-Levels. Not until then was there a short interval in the day when there was *no child whatever* at home. Unless of course a child was ill – and mine were hardly ever allowed to be, they'd crawl to school on their hands and knees.'

The Warnocks had every form of help: resident granny, resident girl nannies who stayed four years apiece; and dear old Nanny Coleman who came for the birth of each new baby. 'It was an enormous house, and the great advantage was that when Geoffrey's father died, his mother moved in with us and made everything possible. It meant that she was always there, and she had TV, which we didn't, so dropping in on Granny to watch TV became a favourite double activity. It meant that she was never by herself, and never felt neglected, and that the nanny was never alone with the children either. It also meant taking her on holiday with us, when I became very mean and would compare her unfavourably with Mither, who although idle was very well-read; my mother-in-law was energetic and co-operative but read nothing but the *Daily Telegraph* and had very pronounced political views.

'We did very well with nannies. First there was an upwardly-mobile English girl who married from our house after four years, then two Irish Catholics who lived in, loved the babies, and I never had any anxiety about whether they were miserable or had enough social life because they met people through the church. Both in turn got a nice steady boyfriend – it always suited me very well to have nannies who wanted to live their own lives at weekends – and each got married from the house too. The younger one, who married a driver for Wall's ice-cream, I loved dearly. She became pregnant before her wedding, and she came to me to confess and I astonished her by saying, "How wonderful!"

'And then there was old Nan, coming for every new birth. The point about Nan was that she always kept up with what was going on. In old age she became totally gripped by the racing on TV, and every Saturday would place her bet. When I visited her I thought we would be reminiscing about the children but no, she would always ask about public events – had I seen some politician or other?

'I think you have to regard your household as an institution into which you put everything. The people we employed always seemed to feel there was a team spirit, and became loyal to *the institution*.'

In 1966 Mary Warnock moved from St Hugh's College, where she had been Fellow and Tutor in Philosophy – an academic life of writing and lecturing that could be shaped to family needs. She became instead Headmistress of Oxford High School, one of the most academically high-flying girls' schools in the country, which required her presence at school every day from 8.15 am until after six in the evening.

'It did mean that you had to have someone at home who was totally capable and we did: a trained children's nanny who could take the car to be serviced, check that we didn't run out of rice or petrol, take the children to the dentist. Boz had a gammy leg at the time and needed a lot of care. The nanny's name was Biz, so it was Biz and Boz.

'When I think now of feeding nine people every night I can't imagine it but I did. It was one of Mither's habits to read to her children even when we were fifteen or sixteen, and I in turn always read to my children over their supper. The evening meals were in relays: the children's high tea at six, then the nanny's supper, then Geoffrey and I had our civilised supper late-ish, alone. Sometimes I could cook one simple thing that would do for all three, like cottage pie. Geoffrey is unfussy about food anyway and always said baked beans would do for him. He is a man of few demands.

'Over the children's tea I would read to them: *Lord of the Rings* and *The Secret Garden* and *The Little Princess*, and all the C. S. Lewis Narnia books, which in many ways I don't approve of but the rhythms of the prose are so perfect. I remember when we got to *The Last Battle* all of us were in floods of tears including me.

'Recently I was questioning Felix about this and he said he loved our suppers more than anything on earth. I felt very flattered by this and then he said, "Because I never listened to the book you were reading, it was just that nobody could speak to you, so you didn't have to think about anything at all."

'That was one of the rituals I look back on with great pleasure. Another one was Sundays. There was a time when Sunday meant a walk in the afternoon, ironing, listening to "Pick of the Pops", and taking James down to Worcester College choir.'

The possibility of Mary Warnock ever settling down as a full-time babyminder and housekeeper was always obviously quite unreal, in Sir Geoffrey Warnock's view. The nearest she ever came to it was during the long summer holidays, when the Warnocks and granny, nanny, cellos and tubas were transported in two large cars, a Vanguard and an old Volvo, to a house on the coast of North Yorkshire which they owned between 1958 and 1972.

'We went twice a year and we were terribly happy there. Nine tiny bedrooms, and we nearly always had thirteen people in the house – nine of us and four houseguests. Geoffrey and I would take it in turns to have a day working at home while the others went off to the beach. I hated being told it was my day to work and be left in, but I wrote the whole of one book there. I was quite good at working after dinner in the evening in those days.

'We were always ruthless with our children about shutting them away: we didn't have them downstairs after 7.30 in the evening. That was connected with always having supper on our own without them, and the children were very good about observing that rule. For some years our children thought coffee was called "peace", because after lunch we'd say, now the grown-ups want some peace, and they would have to go upstairs for half an hour while we had our coffee. I could not live the way some of my children's friends live now, having their children around all the time, and no set bedtime and so on.

'There is no doubt that, although I think I have been really more successful than I have had any right to be, I do think I have partially failed as a wife, and partially failed as a mother. But the whole package has come out all right. Do I have feelings of guilt about my husband and my children? Yes and yes. The good thing about getting older is that because one's children have more and more definite powers and person-alities of their own, you feel you don't have all that much effect on them anyway. I think their personalities are defined very early in life, and it is in the nature of motherhood to wonder whether, if you'd been different they would have been different. Kitty, for instance, was independent and bolshie even as a tiny baby. She is the only one I still feel more than faintly uneasy about; she had the hardest deal of all, being the eldest, shoved out of the cot for the next one. I always feel I've given Kitty a very hard life. She has been teaching at a Palestinian university, but our children cross continents to see one another. They all flocked to be with Bozzie when she had an operation recently, in a hospital in a most out of the way place. That is one of the things that is so interesting about children: the reaction of the children to one another.

'I always have had a worry list, and the various children move up and down it. Sometimes Kitty's at the top, then moved down in favour of someone else. There was a time when James was going through a lot of awful experiences, like being expelled from Winchester. Felix was a quite horrible bully as a child until he went to the Dragon School in Oxford, where the ethos is that you never bully anyone, you look after younger brothers or friends. Never think that a school cannot have an effect on a personality, because it transformed him, into someone wildly successful, captain of cricket, soccer and hockey but also tremendously kind. He has been a standby to Geoffrey; they're terribly alike. I still, in general, rather regard myself as having a buffer role between the children and their father, to protect them from him.'

Sir Geoffrey Warnock is not, he says, a great fancier of small children. 'I'm a fanatically neat and tidy person' – he sat in his strikingly neat and tidy drawing room at Hertford College – 'and Mary is recklessly untidy. I have a tendency to regard small children as the causes of mess and disorder. My views about children and babies are quite different from Mary's. I find I don't feel strongly about them as *my* children. Increasingly, it is the relationship they have among themselves which is interesting. We originally thought of them in relation to us, but now it is a matter of the quite complicated life they have among themselves, nothing to do with us at all. We ought to have realised that earlier, but one doesn't think much beyond nursery life.'

The Warnocks currently have three homes. Baroness Warnock has her Girton flat, Sir Geoffrey the Principal's Lodgings of Hertford College, Oxford, and their piece of real estate, a brick house called Brick House in Wiltshire. There, Sir Geoffrey says: 'Mary has a little study which is a pigsty, and I have a study which is neat and tidy. In shared quarters, I am constantly picking her things off the floor. But I don't mind doing that.'

I wondered if Mary Warnock would have any advice for a Girton girl who wanted to combine family life with career. 'I can't imagine relying on external aids like crèches or babyminders,' she replied. 'I can only imagine doing it by having somebody based in your own home, as we did, and regarding home as an institution. Partly because of the endless illnesses, and the plumber calling; somebody has to be there. And if there is a baby it means there is always someone to push the pram and do the shopping.

'The one thing women cannot do is seek time off to stay at home because of measles. I have never, ever asked for time off for the children. My maximum leave to have a baby was four weeks, and that was only once. The others were all born in the Long Vacation.' As Sir Geoffrey emphasised, it is crucial to their way of life (and also fortunate) that academics, like writers, can make their own timetables.

'Although we have had problems in our lives about whose job has priority – and I can imagine that blowing up into the most frightful marital disharmony – the fact remains that Geoffrey always had to work, but for me it was optional. And you cannot help being conscious of that, when the going gets rough. I remember once being very bad-tempered with James, wishing he would do something rather than loll about the house, and he said: "You probably feel I should help you because you're so tired, but it's entirely your own fault." He wouldn't think or say that today, being married, with a working wife, but in fact there was some truth in what he said. There was a choice for me.

'There have been crisis periods in our lives concerning jobs. Although always totally supportive about the *fact* of my working, Geoffrey wouldn't have anything to do with Oxford High School days at all. When I became headmistress, he was actually away teaching in America. So in turn he felt terribly guilty when he then became Principal of Hertford and I seemed to be expected to take part in *his* life.'

They are by no means the only married pair of philosophers in the academic world, but they are possibly the most notable couple in the country on the highest parallel rungs of their particular ladder. What kind of marriage is it?

'Whether this is always true of careers pursued side by side I don't know,' Mary Warnock says, 'but our marriage has always run on parallel lines. We've never ceased to get on very well with one another, but it's always been rather like a friendship. You see more of them or less of them from time to time but you catch up with them.

'In a way it's a rather exciting development to be living separately. It means that the weekends are very agreeable when we converge again. Lots of people said, "Are you separating?" and "Funny sort of marriage," etc. when I took this job. I said to Boz, "Everyone will say I've left Papa," and she said, "That's mad, it just shows what a flexible marriage you have."

'I don't think we've had an ideal marriage at all. I think I've been difficult to be married to. And there are ways Geoffrey would drive a good feminist up the wall.

'But I do look forward to life together. We've got this lovely house and I think we shall live a very interesting and fascinating life.'

Margaret Forster

novelist and biographer

b. 1938

m. 1960

HUNTER DAVIES

writer and broadcaster

2 daughters, 1 son

CAITLIN JAKE FLORA

Margaret Forster

%

Margaret Forster was brought up on a Carlisle council housing estate in a family where academic achievement was not taken for granted as it was in so many of these women's backgrounds. She has never had any kind of domestic help, with house or children. Both factors have been very much a part of her public statements and interviews. Indeed, her domestic life with Hunter Davies is one of the most chronicled in the land, especially in the last eight years through Hunter Davies's weekly *Punch* column, 'Father's Day'. (Significantly, when the column became the basis of a Channel 4 sitcom, Margaret Forster's role was altered to that of a non-working mother, presumably to make her more believable.)

But her life has never been ordinary enough for the general public to identify with it. Her scholastic distinction – entrance awards to both Oxford and Cambridge from her state grammar school – followed by early success with her first two novels before the age of twenty-four, were the foundation of an unremitting dedication to a productive writing life: fourteen novels, biographies of Bonnie Prince Charlie, Thackeray and Elizabeth Barrett Browning, and a study of the lives of eight pioneering females, *Significant Sisters*, which ought to be required reading in all schools.

Our first interview took place at her home in North London shortly after that book had been published, and its influence was perceptibly in the forefront of her mind. 'If I had been born in 1838 instead of 1938,' she wrote in her Introduction, 'my lot in life would have been truly appalling. As it was, I benefited directly and enormously from every feminist gain and I am immensely grateful that I did. There is not a day goes by without my experiencing that I have the best of both worlds even if I am also bound to admit this happy state is not maintained without effort. My husband and my children are precious to me but then so is my work. I could not continue to be happy if either were taken away from me . . . I always wanted to be everything – wife, mother, housekeeper, writer. More significant, *there was no role I disliked*. The problem was not choosing but taking all of them on at the same time and surviving.'

Margaret Forster was the second of three children of a manual worker in Carlisle; her mother was the complete housewife-mother. As she describes her childhood home it is inescapably noticeable that her own house near Parliament Hill Fields is also 'immaculate and artistic' like her mother's, but in an identifiably middle-class way. All the details, flowers, colour, light, indicate a pleasure in domesticity; and it is always organised and neat. It is the first and most striking thing about her that she has set this tableau for herself and identifies herself passionately with it, her house.

'My mother, who to me was an intelligent and sensitive person, had a life of drudgery. The typical working-class housewife, in the particular kind of council house, boiler in the wash-house, carting the water in, – the whole D. H. Lawrence bit – an oven that had to be blackleaded, an outside lavatory, an old-fashioned sink and fireplace . . . and in the midst of all this my mother had superbly high standards. Everything was immaculate, and also artistic. There were always fresh flowers in jugs. The furniture was only utility G-Plan, but it was always polished. She had two skirts: one in the morning for working in, and one to change into. She wore her hair in a turban while she worked. She was that kind of mother.

'But she was not a happy person. The strain of the hard physical life, the continual effort that went into everything, hanging out sheets and singing hymns the while, it was dispiriting. Why *did* she have to work so horribly hard? Answer: because she was married and had children.

'I knew no mother of any kind who led any other sort of life. The teachers at school were all Miss. Other mothers were all like my mother. That was my experience of women's lives. All my ladies in *Significant Sisters* were, I found, formed by the experience of their mothers. The thing to do, I decided very early on, is never to marry and never to have children and then you are all right. I was never going to have this kind of life, to look after house and children. I was going to be up and away. Of course they said I'd get married and change my tune.

'Grammar School was the great getaway. I was terrified I wouldn't pass the Eleven Plus. The day the results came, the postman missed our house at first and I remember feeling sick with disappointment. But then my mother came running after me down the street – I'd passed! I burst into tears, I was ecstatic. It was one of the purely happy moments. My whole life seemed at once to change.

'I loved school, hated Saturdays and Sundays, hated four o'clock, hated the holidays. I was the teacher's dream. Nothing was awful, I adored everything. It was quite a snobby little high school and the first week I was there the form mistress asked: "Which one is Margaret Forster?" and I was given tremendous attention. The teachers were keen on me from the start. We didn't have any books at home at all apart from the Bible and a medical dictionary, and I floundered a bit but I soon caught up. I now realise that these women with their hair in buns and their moustaches were taking special notice of me, and I thought they were marvellous. It was they who first mentioned university, who introduced me to writing. But I wanted to be an actress. Home got worse and worse, and school got better and better.'

Getting to Oxford was – even though she has since been often quoted as saying it was wasted on her and that she loathed it – a far more crucial and life-changing matter for Margaret Forster than for those women who waltzed in on an almost predestined course. She chose Somerville rather than Girton, both of which colleges had offered her awards, because gloomy Girton horrified her.

'It seemed cold and austere and aloof and regimented. It made me shudder. Somerville by contrast seemed immediately relaxed, sunny and cheerful with flowers everywhere and people on first name terms, not "Miss Forster". Janet Vaughan, the Principal, had a lovely sunny sitting room filled with flowers. We had a relaxed and happy meal served in scallop shells. It seemed that here everything was free and light. The spirit of Janet Vaughan permeated the place.

'All these years later I was watching Janet Vaughan on the Channel 4 television series "Women of Our Century" and there she was talking about her work in blood transfusion and the metabolism of radioactive isotopes and the treatment of pernicious anaemia, and the liberation of Belsen, and it made me think, *what have I done with my life?* All the while she was Principal of Somerville she was working away at this vital research and she had her two children and would even lend out her house to my friend Henrietta to have parties . . .'

Even if she did not appreciate it at the time, the essential style of Margaret Forster was both strengthened and enhanced by being a Somervillian. She says she loved wearing the scholar's gown, a long gown for those with scholarships, distinct from the short commoners' gowns worn by other undergraduates, and she wore it everywhere. She relished meeting girls named Theodora and Annabel and Henrietta. And she adored, after the moody, dreary adolescent years of sharing a bedroom with her sister, having A Room of Her Own.

'I wanted that room more than I wanted anything out of the women's movement. The room I got, because I was a scholar, was in the library wing and one of the best in the college. Large, square and grand with a big mullioned window overlooking the lawn and the cedar trees. I instantly loved it. That was where I discovered *taste* and realised it had to be developed. I arrived with those 1950s black and green "Contemporary" Woolworth plates, a blue candlewick bedspread and a coffee-table with three splayed legs, and six yards of bright red, yellow and blue material for little cushions to line along the blue candlewick.

'The other girls were all so lovely to me, they looked at my cushions but didn't laugh or snigger. Then I went into Henrietta's room. I saw her gorgeous little antique desk, her beautiful odd cracked and chipped Wedgwood and Spode cups and saucers, her grandmother's teapot, her battered buttonback chair, Indian rugs and an Afghan cover for the bed: a room beautifully littered with mismatched old things. Her clothes, too, were *extraordinary*.

'All the girls – Henrietta, Theo, Annabel Asquith, Anne Summerscales, Tyrrell Gatty the stepdaughter of Lord Balogh, and Judd, Judith Landry, a judge's daughter, saw me as a curiosity. They'd never really known anyone like me before.'

Through these friends Margaret Forster first met women quite unlike her own housebound mother. 'By meeting women like Theo's mother, Jessie Parfit, I saw that if you got married and had children it was still possible to have a career. She was a doctor, lived in an enormous house in North Oxford, her son went to Eton, the daughters to Dartington. I watched the way she ran her life, fascinated. And I came to London with Henrietta and met Janet Adam Smith: another revelation. These intelligent, working women, standing in their kitchens knocking up omelettes: they seemed so happy, with no problems. I didn't know, before then, that you could be like that.

'But I never felt self-conscious or inferior. I had loads of self-confidence. I knew I would do what I wanted to do. But exactly what I would do never gave me a moment's concern. I just saw myself forging ahead at whatever I chose to do.'

All through her Oxford days her involvement with Hunter Davies, who was first at the University of Durham and then working on a newspaper in Manchester, continued. They had met in Carlisle when she was sixteen and there has never been any other man in her life. 'It was Theo who took me off to Dr Helena Wright in Oxford and got me fitted up with a cap. I still didn't see the point of getting married. When Hunter insisted on getting engaged I scornfully agreed.

'We had a nice flat lined up in the Vale of Health, right on Hampstead Heath, to move into when I came down from Oxford and since I'd met all these feminist women who were also married I thought what the hell, it'll make the parents happy and a husband need not be a handicap to having a career.'

But it was her imminent marriage at twenty-two which thwarted at least one job opportunity. Her principal extra-mural activity at Oxford was writing for *Isis* but she also acted in Brecht's *The Caucasian Chalk Circle*. During her last year she was an obvious candidate for the BBC's graduate training scheme which took three men and three women every year. Janet Vaughan gave her a superb reference and she sailed through the first two interviews.

'Then there was the final interview in the boardroom at Langham House. It was going extremely well until they asked me if I had any plans for getting married and I said, "Oh yes, I'm getting married in two weeks' time." And there was complete silence. It never entered my head that that was crucial. I didn't get the traineeship. And I can't remember if it was Janet Vaughan or my tutor who said, "We can't *believe* you told them you were getting married. How thoughtless, how could you have done that?" It hadn't for a moment occurred to me.'

There were other job possibilities. She had written for *Isis* ('A Somerville Scholar Writes . . .') a piece called 'A Woman's Very Own', a defence of women's magazines. James Drawbell, editor of *Woman's Own*, sent her a telegram offering a job. There were champagne cocktails at the Savoy; would she fly to Italy to interview Annigoni? She turned it down. Her tutor called her in and asked her if she would be interested in staying on at Oxford and doing research. 'It was the biggest compliment she could pay me. But I said I wanted to get out of the place. I had no doubt that I would get a job, and didn't ever realise how privileged I was. How lightly I took on that inheritance, not realising what had gone into getting me there.'

She married in June 1960 – no guests, no family present – and they moved into their flat. 'I immediately slipped into the housekeeping role. I loved the flat. It had a gracious sitting room with long windows to the floor, and a pale green fitted carpet and pale green walls. The kitchen was a beautiful sunny room, overlooking the garden and the pond, with bright blue lino and an old deal table. It was six guineas a week and nothing gave me greater pleasure than to clean and organise and beautify it. Hunter did the shopping, I did the cleaning.'

She had already written one novel while at Oxford which she discarded; the next was *Dames' Delight*, about Oxford, which was published. In the meantime she was supply-teaching in a girls' school in Islington, to save money to buy a house. 'I went on resisting the idea of a baby, staving it off by saying I must have my career launched first, and we must have a house. I had always insisted I didn't want any children, while Hunter envisaged a face at every window, at least six, there was nothing he wanted more. I wanted to be a wife and mistress, but I saw with tremendous clarity what motherhood entailed – what my own mother had been – and I knew I wasn't up to it. I was too selfish. I didn't have the temperament. I'm irritable and demanding, not calm and gentle.

'What changed my mind was that I realised how fascinating it would be to create something that would be the product of us, our genes together . . . I played with the idea and began to fall in love with it . . . I saw this child, always as a boy. Hunter kept saying, you'll be a marvellous mother, who needs a cowlike placid mother anyway? It'll make life better. I began to feel perhaps a family might not be all hardship and anguish, it could be different.

'I'd already published *Dames' Delight* and had finished writing the second novel, *Georgy Girl*. When I heard, in April, that Cape were going to publish my novel I gave notice at school at once. And that summer I conceived Caitlin. It was all perfectly orchestrated: the novel would be published in February and the child would be born in March. Wonderful timing and it all went superbly to plan on a hot sunny day. We'd been swimming, we had a picnic in the overgrown garden then we went inside at two o'clock in the afternoon . . . It was an easy, happy pregnancy, I didn't get very big, I was very happy with *Georgy Girl*, and I was writing my third novel.

'And then Caitlin arrived, and instantly the anxiety began. They may cut the cord, but they just don't. This human life, this being, so dependent on me! About whom I was *completely passionate*. I had suspected, correctly, that it would be like this.

'But I kept on writing, in that room through there, every evening, and I didn't see that it ever could be a problem to keep that up. I boasted about how the baby fitted in with my life. And it's true there were no practical problems, the baby was just something else to enjoy organising; she filled my life. But emotionally, it changed me *devastatingly*. We'd got this house and moved in when she was nine months old. The film rights to *Georgy Girl* were sold, and at the same time I became pregnant with Jake. Then it all became pretty difficult. Children did change everything. They changed me.

'They temporarily sapped my ambition. I think if I hadn't had children, the ambition would have been greater and I would have forged ahead more greedily. I might have decided later that I didn't like the career-woman life, but I would at least have tried it. Instead, I chose to turn down all offers, because I couldn't bear to miss a single second. The idea of having someone else look after Caitlin! It was inconceivable. I wanted to do it myself. Nor could I ever bear to have someone else going down on their hands and knees to scrub my floor. That was the beginning of deciding that I would do everything.

'I remember the first time I went out to do major shopping after Caitlin was born, trailing down to Sainsbury's in Kentish Town Road with the pram, just as my mother had always done it – the option of doing shopping in a car never arose – and the first revelation was that I had to leave the pram outside the shop. It was nerve-wracking. Then trudging back, the pram laden. A neighbour saw me and said, "Why don't you leave her with me?" So next time I did. And as I came back down the road I could hear her crying, and the neighbour saying, "Stop squalling you silly little thing." Then, the first time I left her with a babysitter, a lovely person, I came back to her crying and when I picked her up, she stopped. So I found it all very hard. It's shaming but true; I was a slave to that baby, and I wanted to be with her all the time. The blood tie was extreme. She became a rival for Hunter, and I always put the baby first, not him. I could not have endured anyone else living with us, it's such an intrusion; so it had to be me who looked after her. But I found it easy to keep the work going, three hours at a time, three evenings a week, writing my crappy novels. Writing was just playing. I loved it, it gave me energy. It was when Jake was born, two years after Caitlin, that I could no longer boast about how easy it was. Two were *not* as easy as one.'

An interview in *The Times* in August 1967 most typically encapsulates the public image of Margaret Forster at that time. 'This house is my world,' she told Celia Haddon. 'Writing is second. My whole day is a scheme to get time to put my feet up. I can sit for two hours looking out of the window, and because I am efficient and everything is done, I don't feel guilty about it.'

The photograph with that interview is of a woman of twenty-nine with cropped dark hair, sitting in a white broderie anglaise blouse at the table in the sunny garden, smiling towards Jake, aged one, blond and adorable in his high chair, and dark-haired Caitlin aged three, smiling sweetly alongside. Margaret said then, she realised she had become the sort of person who is rung up for articles on 'the new woman'. 'It's rather chuff-making to be on the short-list,' she said. 'But honestly every time they ring up I know they have either just rung or are about to ring Margaret Drabble.' One of the things Margaret Forster has always stood for is formidable forthrightness. Not invariably truthful as she is the first to admit, but invariably direct.

The novel she had just published was her fourth, *The Travels of Maudie Tipstaff*; her fifth was already delivered, her sixth she would start writing the next week. She made it sound effortless. 'Writing is so easy for me that I just sit down and it comes out as if I am talking. There's no hesitation or birth pangs.' Celia Haddon noted the clean, unmessy house and said what an organised person she must be. 'It's awfully infuriating for other women,' Margaret Forster told her. 'They want to be able to go away saying, "She may be a writer, but God her house is a mess," or "Who'd want to be married to someone who looks like that?"'

Margaret Forster now loathes being reminded of what she said in that and other interviews at the time.

In reality and in retrospect she says the first three years of Jake's life were the worst stage of her life, her marriage, and her work. 'Jake was an appalling baby. He howled his rotten head off and caused total havoc. He was like a little gorilla and could swing out of his cot long before he was two. We put netting over it; we doped him with all the things that say on the label "Do not drive or operate machinery" but up the stairs he came; it's not good for your love life and it went on until he was six. He was like a rugby forward and would lie with his head in my stomach and his feet in Hunter's. I was a battered mother. It was not funny, especially if you wanted to make love. I was so tired that the only thing that was attractive to me was sleep. At the same time Hunter was surrounded at the *Sunday Times* on the "Look!" pages with Mollie Parkin and Jilly Cooper who were always pretending to fling themselves at him and telling him what a hell of a fellow he was. Then he'd come home to a grim-faced, exhausted wife and the last thing she wanted to do was cavort in any way. Hunter has always needed me to take a big supportive role, to bounce ideas off, but I was failing. I was still pathetic about going out and getting a babysitter in. Anyway, who would babysit Jake? Hunter would have liked to go to parties occasionally, but I never would.'

While the children were still at this young age the Davieses' life came into a glare of publicity when within eighteen months they each had a novel turned into a film with a glittering West End première – her *Georgy Girl* and his *Here We Go Round the Mulberry Bush*. Hunter also wrote his Beatles biography which made him a great deal of money. The family enjoyed their year of tax exile on the island of Gozo; later, the Davieses gave away earnings from their books to charities like Shelter. (Margaret continues to sign away royalties, most recently the advance on her next biography to the Fawcett Society.) They have always insisted on state education for their children. Caitlin is now at Clarke College in the USA, Jake at Cambridge, Flora still at her girls' comprehensive school.

Flora arrived with a change of gear. 'There came a point when I decided not to play at novels any more. Jake slept, and went to school all day, and suddenly that awful stage was over. I now had the whole day to myself. I had been doing my work while he was at nursery school every morning, but that was only two hours and it was no longer satisfying. Hunter was very keen that I should take up the various offers that still came, television interviewing, or a weekly column: but I turned them down because I knew what felt right. Going out and doing things isn't me, rushing back for the children, worrying about being late. I had my own little empire here at home.

'But I did feel that I had to turn to a different kind of writing, and I turned to my own subject, history, and wrote a list of historical figures who interested me. The first was Mary Queen of Scots but she had already been picked by Antonia Fraser. I chose Bonnie Prince Charlie because nothing had been written about him since the time of Culloden and I could visit the sites and my life would open out ... and in the middle of that, Flora was conceived. I really had thought that two children was just right, especially if you were lucky enough to have a boy and a girl. I thought the child-hunger would be satisfied, but although I hate the phrase "getting broody" I was. The truth is that she was not a planned baby but certainly not an unwanted baby; I knew I was obviously very fertile, but I couldn't resist the idea of another baby. She was born on Hallowe'en, on the day I delivered my manuscript of Bonnie Prince Charlie. She was called "Flora" for Flora Macdonald of course.

'For the first two years she was every bit as bad as Jake, but at least she then settled down. That bit was hard; I was stretched at both ends, in my working life and my domestic life. I began working on Thackeray which took four years. Those were also the bad years with my own mother, going up to Carlisle and waiting for the death scene. From my diary for 1973 (I keep one only every five years, and write only about the children) it seems I didn't get any sleep or rest. Every weekend we went away to the cottage we then had in Oxfordshire, packing up everything and the children every Friday night; I look back now and feel ill just imagining it.

'But I feel my children did me a great favour. I know I could have been good at journalism or television – but I know I'm not suited to team work or to office work. I would not have been able to cope with that; and if I hadn't had the children I might have accepted one of those jobs and it might have taken ten years to discover that I'm really Mrs Tittlemouse and the best place for me is my home. I like the processes of working, but not at the expense of my domesticity. I look forward to Flora coming home, the high point of each day.

'All I want is for my precious domestic life to sail along, which makes me wary of agreeing to anything outside that will involve sacrificing a moment of it. Never a day goes by without my remembering how lucky I am. I appreciate it all: the washing machine, the dishwasher. How easy it is to clean a cork-tiled floor! The Hoover, you just shove it around for a bit! And I can re-organise a room and choose new things for it when I like. I can go out for meals with Hunter at least once a week. My mother, and his mother, never went out for meals all their married lives. I never cease to be grateful for it all.'

Routine is the foundation of her life. No matter what excitements and crises (foreign trips, book deadlines, challenges, involvements that teenage children and aged parents incur, school strikes, illnesses) her life remains fundamentally predictable. There is a clockwork precision about the timing of meals. Every day they both work in the morning (one book every eighteen months from one or the other of them, sometimes both). For two hours after lunch they walk on Hampstead Heath, rain or shine. At four Flora comes home, at five Hunter fetches the evening paper, at six supper is on the table, at seven Margaret is on the sofa in the upstairs drawing room, reading a novel, in peace and silence. Any excitement, even going into the centre of London during the day, upsets her equilibrium. 'I long to get back home. I just can't seem to get enough of my domesticity. I think I've always been middle-aged; I feel more comfortable now that I've reached my natural age.

'It's a question of energy. I need energy to write and if a day goes by without writing I'm distraught. People say I'm amazingly organised but it just takes two interruptions a week and the edifice collapses.'

When we met again she was in the throes of Elizabeth Barrett Browning's life. Having absorbed her diaries she was reading every single novel that Elizabeth Barrett read, comparing their reactions. That day it was Mrs Gaskell's *Ruth*. Researching a life is so enthralling she says she never wants it to end; she feels she should be able to go on 'Mastermind' and answer questions about every single line in her book. A fleeting reference to the colour green, for instance, will have several cross-references in her notebooks. 'It's a complete change from fiction. But fiction takes all my natural abilities, all my curiosity. The thrill is that when you start a novel it's all a magical secret, you really don't know what's going to happen next. I have some vague thing that's hanging about in my head, a sensual feeling, and I sit in that room and have no idea where it will take me. By half-way through, of course, that's gone.'

The effect of writing *Significant Sisters* was to galvanise her into taking direct political action. 'I felt ashamed of never having done anything to change anything. Then the teachers' strike came along and I started writing letters to *The Times* and marching. Nothing had much effect. But the Sisters used to beaver on for *decades* never knowing if there was going to be a result at all. It's still a mystery to me how they carried on.'

'I have had,' she said, 'a hundred per cent encouragement from Hunter. He can't bear me ever to turn things down. He glories in every success I have, and is very proud of the money I make without ever leaving the house. No, it would not have been possible with any other man because I could not have married anyone else. Who else would put up with me? I'm a very difficult person to live with. All I really want to do is read, and I read *all the time*.

'We've been together for thirty years, counting the time living together before marriage, and the sex urge does not diminish. People don't talk about this, do they? If they do, you never believe what they say. Yet it's one of the most interesting aspects. You change a lot over so many years, and love-making changes its nature. Of course it's not the same full lust of the sixteen-year-old when you saw everything in terms of sex, literally everything: I suppose that real hunger and passion lasts about five years. But I've always felt that if there ever came a time when you felt nothing, no desire, it would be just terrible. For Hunter, the need exists all the time: it's exactly like his attitude to food, he'll even drink bad coffee as long as it's there. I like everything, in food and sex, to be perfect. Now, we no longer need to escape from the children to be alone but we do go on these aphrodisiac trips like Barbados when we can sit in the sun all day and get high on freedom. And when you think what our marriage has had to take it's amazing that anything still goes on. But it's easy for me to say this because I've never been remotely attracted to anyone else. I've never felt those physical indications. Across a crowded room I still look at him and think, h'mm, I'm attracted to him. And he's the only person in the world I can talk to without being aware of myself. I can't imagine talking in the same way to anyone else; I have good friends but not intimate friends. He is my only friend. Plus the attraction. As far as living together, we're opposites. If the attraction went, and the talking went, I'd be left with someone whose personal habits are totally different from mine. I don't share any of his interests or his passion for collecting. I fight to keep this house empty, and he fights to fill it.

'He is not domesticated but that is my fault. His mother handed me over a little treasure, who was able at seven to do the potatoes and look after his dying father and his twin sisters, and I let it all go by taking over everything myself. He used to make supper once a week and the children would dread it, toasted cheese again and he'd scream at everyone. He does shop, but I have to write on the list NO BARGAINS. He will do things, but he has to be programmed. He takes no initiative.

'For instance with shared child care, I had to carve out the ground. I had to say things like, "On Fridays, Saturdays and Sundays I want to be able to go into the sitting room at 4.30 for a couple of hours. I want you to take the children out and I want you to put them to bed." He's brilliant with children but I had to insist on the firm schedule. The other thing I invented, when he was at the office and had Monday off, was "Monday is my day". I would go out, sometimes just to go out on my own. I would come back after my Monday and there'd be all the faces at the window, waiting for me. Every day, of course, Hunter's day begins with his coffee and his ironed newspaper on a tray and the curtains drawn back *very* gently. One of Jake's school friends said to him, "How can your mother be a feminist? She waits on your father hand and foot." But long before *Significant Sisters* I realised that that was all my doing. I had a lovely easy husband, but I wanted my space, as they now call it, or solitude as I called it.

'The only serious differences we have had were about children, about Jake's not sleeping and the havoc he created, and about Caitlin's teenage years. The thought of going through that again appalls me. But Hunter will have blacked it out; he blacks out anything he doesn't want to think about, which is *all unpleasant things*.

'What have I not yet done that I want to do? Well, I do still want to write the Great Novel that I myself am enormously proud of, the real contribution to literature. It doesn't make me sad that I haven't yet, but I will know when it happens. I have *great* ambition. Not one single ambition, but a general feeling of ambition, yes. It's a feeling of acceleration, of getting somewhere. I get more ambitious as I get older; I have to work towards something.'

Dr Beulah Bewley

senior lecturer and consultant epidemiologist

b. 1929

m. 1955

THOMAS BEWLEY

consultant psychiatrist

4 daughters, 1 son

SUSAN SARAH LOUISA

HENRY EMMA

Dr Beulah Bewley

Nobody ever challenges a doctor's right to work, and the medical woman's advantage is that this is true even if she has a number of young children. The woman doctor, who used to be assumed to wear tweeds and a moustache, is now accepted without demur in group practices and hospitals, and if she is also a mother her good fortune is to be able to arrange to do clinics and surgeries at convenient times. Beulah Bewley, president of the Medical Women's Federation, is a shining example.

She is Northern Irish, born in Londonderry and educated at Trinity College, Dublin. She has managed a varied career, in hospitals and clinics and in public health, and is now a senior lecturer at St George's Hospital Medical School, an epidemiologist by profession.

I knew, from those who had spoken of her, that she was an exceptional woman, married to a psychiatrist, and that they had five children. When I first telephoned her I was struck by the warm enthusiastic Irish voice. What I did not know then was that one of their children was born with Down's Syndrome, so severely handicapped that she was not expected to live; now twenty-eight years old she lives in the hostel of a mental handicap hospital where the Bewleys visit her nearly every weekend.

I met Beulah's equally busy husband Thomas at 8.15 one morning, in his office at the Royal College of Psychiatrists where he was serving a three-year term as president. I was struck, as on other occasions when meeting each partner separately, by the unity of their views, their approach to life, even the stories they told. Just a few generations ago this kind of partnership would not have been possible. 'Very few things change,' said Dr Thomas Bewley, 'but in the relationship between men and women you can actually measure the change in this century. There's a great advantage if you're both in the same trade. I'm told the lowest level of divorces is among couples who live over sweetshops. We're in the same business together.'

Beulah Bewley was the middle daughter of the three Knox girls, children of an Irish bank manager: Eleanor, Beulah and Maureen, all born within three years. The parents were born from large families: their father the youngest of seven, mother the youngest of eleven.

'My mother never worked herself: the girls in her family didn't. Her brothers had become doctors or solicitors, but you would never have known if the women were bright or not, because they either got married or stayed at home. But I did have one strong, unmarried and rather tiresome Women's Lib aunt. She was adamant that no woman should ever be entirely dependent on a man, and I tended to agree. My father looked at matters more in financial terms, being a bank manager and having three daughters. He would say, "An education is a sound investment."'

Beulah and her sisters were sent to all kinds of different schools because they kept moving house. For a year they had a governess, and for a time they went to a Catholic convent in Kilkenny, despite being Protestants, as there was no Protestant girls' school in Kilkenny.

World War II found them in Dublin, attending the Alexandra School and College – a college where it had been possible, even before women were admitted to universities, to obtain an external degree. Beulah went on to Trinity College to read Medicine.

The Knox sisters were extrovert types, who played a lot of tennis and led gregarious lives. At Trinity, Beulah captained the First XI at hockey and played the violin in the orchestra. 'My social life didn't consist entirely of fellow medics,' she says, but as it happened she met Thomas, her husband to be, when he was in his final year as a medical student. It was at a clinic run by Thomas's father. The Bewleys were a long-established medical family in the city and Thomas's father was a senior consultant; from another side of the family came the famous Dublin coffee-house which still exists, called Bewley's.

She qualified at twenty-three and two years later made the memorable change of name, by marrying Thomas, to Beulah Bewley. They moved about a lot, wherever Thomas had junior posts, working in Dublin, and in and around London. 'I was a bit disorganised about my career prospects,' Beulah says. 'I worked in infectious diseases, paediatrics and did a bit of psychiatry too. At one stage we lived in two rooms in a Limehouse rectory, but we were at home only every other day because of being on duty. When Thomas got a post in the USA, in Cincinnati to do his doctoral thesis, I went with him and did a paediatric residency there.'

While they were in the United States Beulah became pregnant, at twenty-eight, as she had hoped, and they came home to Dublin where Thomas did a locum job and their eldest daughter Susan was born.

They settled in London. Beulah took two months off, but then started to take up part-time posts in Infant Welfare and Family Planning clinics, and also became pregnant again.

A year later the second child, Sarah, was born.

'What happened was that I started haemorrhaging six weeks early. It couldn't have been at a worse time, because all sorts of arrangements had been made to have Susan, the baby, looked after and, when it all happened early, Thomas was on duty and everything went wrong. They thought it was going to be a Caesarean, but then I went into labour. Immediately I saw her I said, "There's something wrong with that baby." I said the same to Thomas when he arrived, and he thought so too . . .

'At first the medical staff weren't sure, and they asked me what I thought – I thought that was horrific – but I had no doubt myself. Then of course there was a hoo-hah: should I breastfeed the baby?'

Sarah was diagnosed a severe Down's Syndrome baby, additionally handicapped with a cardiac problem. She was not expected to live.

'At first Sarah stayed at the Westminster Hospital and Thomas and I went away to the west of Ireland, and walked on the beach a lot and discussed the situation as best we could. When we came back, the consultant paediatrician took Sarah away to another hospital because of her cardiac problem, and later she was transferred to the mentally handicapped unit of Queen Mary's Hospital, Carshalton. Overall, everyone was trying to be helpful and kind, and we were offered masses of advice.

'I didn't like going home with no baby. In fact, for nearly twenty years I never went over Vauxhall Bridge because as we left the hospital I had got so emotional and we had to stop on the bridge. But I think in retrospect life's a bit like a rubber ball; gradually you bounce back, but you don't ever bounce back to exactly the same place, and you are never the same again.'

Sarah is now twenty-eight and lives at Orchard Hill in Queen Mary's, Carshalton. She has a mental age of about fourteen months, and it is hard to say whether or not she recognises her parents when they visit her every weekend. 'For years we did all Sarah's washing, which gave an extra excuse to go down there often. To be honest, I feel that we now go as a duty and would feel guilty if we didn't go. The nursing staff there do such a good job and like to know we are coming, and we can be helpful in other ways.' If Beulah and Thomas are away, one or other of their children go instead.

It is true, Thomas Bewley says, that nobody ever expects anything to go wrong in their own family. And whatever course you take, you are bound to be dissatisfied. There was no knowing, at the time, that Sarah would live so long. No doubt their lives might have been different if her handicap had been less severe and she had stayed at home.

The Bewleys had their next three children within the next few years: Louisa, Henry and Emma. 'I had five births and one miscarriage in eight years, my last child when I was thirty-six. Perhaps it was the affluent sixties,' she says, 'but most of our friends seemed to be having three or four children and we had always expected to have four.'

While all the children were young she engaged an au pair and worked in public health, doing child welfare and school clinics, and a weekly session at Marks & Spencer's in Tooting Bec Broadway, not far from where they lived in south London. 'I had found, at the child welfare clinics, that half the time I was providing family planning advice, so I went to Helena Wright at her clinic in North Kensington to be taught contraception. With her four sons and her formidable pince-nez spectacles she was one of the generation of women doctors who seemed rather frightening.'

Beulah made very specific arrangements to fit in with family life. She would do clinics on Monday afternoons and Tuesday mornings, afternoons and evenings, and Wednesday mornings. Thomas ran a clinic himself on Monday night, but he could be at home while she did hers on Tuesday night. Although they had an au pair, they liked to know that he would be there in a crisis.

They lived inside the grounds of Tooting Bec Mental Hospital where Thomas worked. 'Living in a tied cottage, as it were, was an advantage. Thomas could be reached on the internal phone if necessary, although that only happened once. One of the mental hospital patients used to come every day to help in the house and garden. His name was Charlie and he became part of our family, like a grandfather figure. Our children were known as "Charlie's children", and everybody who came to our house knew Charlie. He'd already been coming to that house every day for thirty years when we got there: they don't have long-stay mental patients like him any more.

'He was a sort of general factotum really: he had a key to the house and grew plum trees from stones, and his own special geraniums. Whenever I brought a new baby home from hospital he would say, "My God she looks small." We were all distraught when Charlie died. Continuity of care for children is very important, and Charlie was part of our continuity, being there for all the babies.'

There was also a series of mother's helps, engaged through the columns of *The Lady*. 'I would always mention "holidays in Ireland" to attract the Irish girls, who liked to get home every year. One of the girls called Teresa stayed for three or four years, and married a male nurse at the hospital.'

It was never part of Beulah Bewley's attitude that work provided an escape from the children. 'I went on working because of my father's "good investment" line; I'd been trained and I felt you should keep at it. Also, my husband was helpful and constructive.

'My career had been in three distinct phases: first in hospitals; then ten years in preventive and occupational health services; and then, since 1969, in social and community medicine.' In 1969 she decided to change course. That year, when the youngest child was four, Beulah had a double laminectomy – i.e. two spinal discs removed. She decided to undertake a postgraduate degree, and at that time the only course available was a two-year MSc at the London School of Hygiene.

'What it really amounted to was starting again in a new field at the age of thirty-nine or forty. Gradually the wheels became oiled, but I remember I found the first weeks exhausting, going back to learning again. Your brain does get sloppy.

'How we managed at home was that Thomas cut down on any additional work to help me. He had a part-time secretary whose son went to the same school as Henry, so he would drive all the children to school and she would collect everyone. We also had a resident mother's help, and we arranged driving lessons for her so that she could help a bit more, and so educationally I pulled myself up by my bootstraps.

'I had to do a one-year project as part of my course, and this I did at St Thomas's Hospital: a study on smoking and health, based on 7000 primary school children. Then I did an MD while I was there, and that was very good for me as an exercise in stamina. It was explained to me that I couldn't be appointed to consultant status without two post-graduate degrees, and I suppose it comes from my Irish background that

I've always got to be told something is almost impossible in order to achieve it.'

That year they also moved to their present house, a 1930s house that could be called the original Wates house as it was built for Mr Wates the property developer himself, with seven bedrooms and three bathrooms. 'By 1973 I was working a five-day week, so domestic help had to be increased. I got a daily who came three mornings a week, and then another who came three afternoons at 3.30 and did the ironing: she would be there when the children came home from school, a sort of surrogate granny who was there to see they had something to eat and to talk to them.

'But with four children, the eldest can help to look after the others, and Susan is quite like me in many ways. Though her education has been more disciplined than mine.' Susan was an academic high-flier, getting four grade As at A-Level and reading Medicine at Brasenose College, Oxford, and the Middlesex Hospital in London.

'I can remember one of the children saying, "Daddy's a very busy man, Mummy's a very busy lady and we are very busy children." When I went back to my studies they all had homework to do and they used to tick me off about not doing mine. Henry was then at Dulwich Preparatory School where you had to sign the wretched homework book every day. We were very much of the school of getting the children to find out for themselves how to approach a subject.'

Dr Bewley plainly inspires loyalty in those who work for her. The same women, a different one for morning and afternoon, have been coming to help in the house for nearly twenty years now. 'They always regarded their jobs as important because "it's important for Mrs Bewley to get her job done."'

She feels she is domestically organised; very neat, her husband says, and full of energy. When he flags in the evenings she can still put in another hour at her desk. 'I make lists and notes and I know that if we don't get the diary sorted out on Sunday night there's chaos. We have three diaries: mine, Thomas's, and the hall table one and if it's not written down in the hall table one it's not official. That's where school terms and holidays were down, as far as a year ahead.'

Staying with friends and families in Ireland was how they usually took their summer holidays when the children were small; then they took up camping in France, where the children would be left with their books in the afternoons while the adults went off to see another château. Thomas

Bewley is the keeper of the family library and is an omnivorous reader himself. 'He has read so much more than I have. Even though I was at the best girls' school in Dublin they actually *locked* the library, and at my boarding school they checked everything you read.'

Thomas Bewley specialises in drug and alcohol dependency and has always worked within the National Health Service: 'My corner is drug dependency,' he says, 'and that doesn't lend itself to Harley Street. But I think the NHS is the best way of providing health care, and there's nothing much I could do for someone outside the NHS that I couldn't do within it.'

Thomas Bewley pointed out to me that most children eventually turn out more or less like their parents. 'You can see marginal differences, which reflect the changes in society: for example my son can sew on his own buttons,' he says, 'and it is unlikely that our children will have large families like ours.' Susan the eldest is a qualified doctor, in obstetrics and gynaecology; Louisa, having taken two years off to go kibbutzing, ranching in California and au-pairing in France, read Biology at York University and is now training to be a chartered accountant; Henry read Physics and Chemistry at Exeter University and Emma works for Grand Metropolitan Hotels.

'You have to impress upon your children,' says Dr Thomas Bewley mischievously, 'that they are *all equally dislikable*.' When there were adolescent arguments, he said, it was useful to be able to say to the three youngest, 'Susan was not allowed to do that, and if we allowed you to do it she'd give us hell.' They all seem to have been affected by their parents' concerns: none of the children smokes and they are all sensible about alcohol, particularly alcohol and driving, Dr Bewley notices. He himself manages to keep within the Royal College's guideline of 21 units a week, which is three glasses of wine per day. The Bewleys are, it should also be added, an extremely sociable and gregarious pair who organise enormous Victorian-style family Christmases with a party for sixty people on Christmas Eve.

Beulah Bewley says she sometimes ponders on whether, if she had not had children, she would have got further in her profession. The only curtailment in her progress was in switching to community medicine, which was her own decision.

'I became an elected member of the General Medical Council after I wrote an article with Thomas about the hospitals' misuse of woman-power and the rigidity in the career structure. We asked: how many women are on the important recognised College Councils, the British Medical Association, the General Medical Council, and the Royal Colleges? And then someone said to me: "Are you standing for election to the GMC? You should practise what you preach." So I did.'

The notion of equality has never been a matter for debate in the Bewley household. 'Thomas's Quaker principles are still there,' Beulah says. Thomas explains: 'I'm an Irish atheist Quaker, a highly select group. The Quakers have always been egalitarian. The present fuss over women priests would not be meaningful to Quakers, who have always had women taking the same part as men in their monthly meetings, and men and women shaking hands at the end, an early example of an assumption that there is no difference between men and women. You can be sure,' he adds, 'that when other creeds run out of men priests they'll be clamouring for women.'

'Women have still got a lot to teach men,' Beulah Bewley said. 'I think it must be very hard to be married to someone who is constantly putting you down. In the medical profession, you have to be prepared to see a lot of rather inadequate men in fairly authoritarian positions. But I've never had any trouble with mature, intelligent men. The more intelligent and mature a man is, the less likely he is to feel threatened by you. It's the ones that aren't who get uppity.

'I think my medical career has been much more flexible and interesting than those of young women doctors today. Surgery, we are told, has to be full-time training, and that is a problem as we are now encouraging young people to share jobs. Some of the young male medical students are realising it's good to be a partner in the sharing and caring of children and instead of struggling up the hierarchy they opt for general practice. It's easier for women now, I think, to get to a consultancy first, say by age thirty-two, and then think about babies – but that has its problems.

'I do career counselling, and I come across what one of my colleagues calls "bio-panic": the "should I have a baby now?" question, and then it's "what about working when the children are ill?" But children don't often get that ill. The clash between family and duty has to be resolved, by careful forward planning and by arranging adequate domestic cover.'

Beulah remembers reading Hannah Gavron's *The Captive Wife* when it came out in 1966. 'It was part of the required sociological reading, and I was fascinated, even though it didn't apply to me. I wasn't a captive wife. I would look at other women and wonder why they didn't get out. I thought some of them didn't really want to.'

Both the doctors Bewley, when talking about their long and successful marriage, used the analogy of the couple living over the corner-shop. 'I'm not like Mrs Thatcher, marrying someone who had already made his pile before he met her; Thomas and I have always been in the same boat, working side by side. We talk an awful lot together; being Irish there's a lot of talking anyway. We have a very strong Irish connection, both being from the same university with overlapping friends. I'm sure it helps to be culturally close and if your families get on well it's more comfortable. We could be competitive, I suppose, both being in medicine, but what it really means is I can push over a report for Thomas to read, and get a different view.

'The very, very important thing is to have a bit of your life that's just you. Can I tell you about mine? In my case it's music. If I could afford it, I'd go to the opera more. That interest started at the age of thirteen when one of my maiden aunts took me to *Madam Butterfly*. Now I have a piano lesson every other Monday night, and it's vital to me. Something quite different, very therapeutic.'

Trixie Gardner

Baroness Gardner of Parkes, *dentist and politician*

b. 1927

m. 1956

KEVIN GARDNER

dentist

3 daughters

SARAH RACHEL JOANNA

Trixie Gardner

'Trixie Gardner believes that commonsense solves most problems,' stated a political handout about her in 1969. It is the first thing that strikes everyone about her: here is a woman of sound sense; a quick mind, and a sense of humour. We met at County Hall in the middle of a vital vote on the future of the Greater London Council, on which she sat as the member for Enfield in north London. Twice she had to go into the Council Chamber to vote against Ken Livingstone.

Baroness Gardner of Parkes, New South Wales, is the most unexpected of peers. It is something to do with being Australian: this makes her quite beyond class. She was one of nine children, in a highly educated family. Her father, Greg McGirr, became Deputy Premier of New South Wales, and her uncle James its Premier. She is by profession a dentist, in partnership with her husband; by inclination a politician, having sat on Westminster Council and the GLC and now in the House of Lords, although the House of Commons eluded her. She is the mother of three daughters. It is characteristic of her that she joined the GLC's Women's Committee, which had formerly been cold-shouldered by the GLC's Tory members. As Mary Stott the journalist says, women's questions bring together women of Right and Left. In a *Guardian* interview Mary Stott said of Trixie: 'It seems absurd to fix the fashionable denigratory label "élitist" on this Australian working dentist. She seems so practical, so straightforward, so politically uninhibited, so unaware of class barriers or class orientation.'

The completeness of the partnership with her husband is also noteworthy: she has always been a dentist in a shared practice with him, so that working together complements family life. When she was a political candidate he accompanied her on campaigns; he even followed her into local politics, becoming Lord Mayor of Westminster in 1987.

Trixie McGirr, as she was born in 1927, was the eighth of nine children in the family of the Hon. J. J. Gregory McGirr. 'My father was an interesting man; he was from a humble country background but he won through the education system and became one of the first qualified pharmacists at Sydney University, then Minister of Health and Deputy Premier of New South Wales – one of the three parliamentary brothers McGirr. My mother was one of the very first seven women at Sydney University, and most of them became fairly famous. She became the first ever graduate high school teacher in Queensland. But she never seemed to be at all distressed by giving up teaching to have the family. I do remember her being asked, "What use was your education to you, when all you do is have all these children?" and she said, "Well at least it gives me something to think about while I'm pushing the pram!" Ha ha!' (Trixie Gardner has an engaging way of bursting out laughing.)

'But she was very much part of the community even though she was never in paid employment – she got the OBE for services to the Bush Nursing Association – and it certainly never would have occurred to her to make any difference between girls' and boys' education. Almost all her children went to university.

'I had done half my dental degree course when my father became ill, and I went home to be with my mother. When he died it was too late to go back to the course so my mother said, "Why don't you learn to cook?" I rang the catering department at East Sydney Tech and they said, "Can you come tomorrow nine o'clock with your apron?" I didn't have time to think, I just went. I think my mother was being quite cunning, because one thing she wasn't was a cook.

'At home we had a marvellous old cook, a man who had been a baker by profession and in his young days he had gone on the bottle a bit. My parents took him on and it gave him a new life. He was an institution; with his long moustache and his lugubrious appearance, he was in our kitchen all the time. He loved being part of a big family. Only a man of his patience would have been prepared to serve breakfast from six in the morning till midday for the various members of our family. He was an element of stability in the household for over twenty years. We never had a nanny but there was a sort of maid, who used to come back after the war once a week to visit, like an old friend really. She left us during the war, when the big house got rather empty, but we were still twelve or fourteen for Sunday lunch. I took over the cooking and everyone was rather pleased. It seemed I might never go back to dentistry. But I'd heard that nobody had ever completed the three-year catering course at East Sydney in the last fifteen years, so I was determined to go ahead and get that certificate, which I did. It was a great help later when I went to Paris and I was able to complete my Cordon Bleu in three months.

'But then I did go back to dentistry at Sydney University and I flew through it. Why dentistry? Oh, because by the time it came to the eighth child, all the other jobs had been taken, it was a case of "you might as well be the dentist". Young people of that age don't have much idea what to do, they get swept along. I already had a doctor sister and a lawyer sister. We were five girls: numbers one, three and five did Arts and English subjects; two and four did Medicine and Science. Most of us went in for large families too: three of my sisters had five, six and seven children – and it was the lawyer sister who had seven. I have thirty-five nieces and nephews, all in Australia.

'There were no jobs for dentists in Sydney in those days; although one friend used to employ me for half a day a week he never paid me. A lot of dentists turned to treading pulp in the paper mills, or bricklaying, or working on the Snowy River scheme. I decided I'd come to Europe and do my cooking. I'd already met Kevin, who was to become my husband. He'd won the prize for dental surgery in our year, and he had a year on the teaching staff. He came to London the year after I did.

'He kept ringing me up and I was always out, which must have made me seem very elusive and attractive but actually I was doing a night typing course at Pitman's because I was planning to go to Canada and I knew I couldn't get work there as a dentist. All Australians at that time wanted to go round the whole world, and if you were a trained secretary or a nurse you could work anywhere.

'At the time Kevin rang, I was just thinking of going off to Scotland on a Lambretta. I hadn't got as far as buying the Lambretta, but I had rung the A A for advice and they told me I'd need a two-piece wet suit; that put me off slightly. Well, Kevin said that by chance he and two friends were going to Scotland by car on a certain day in July. This conversation took place in March. This was quite like Kevin, and quite like him to this day: he had fixed on this arrangement, and there was no question that he might not go through with it. When I'd given in my notice at the practice, I thought I'd better just ring him and check that the trip was still on. Of course it was. That is what Kevin is like: any arrangement is remembered and honoured. He is a fantastically reliable man.

'When we got engaged I thought I wouldn't bother to complete my

Cordon Bleu course in Paris. "If you're marrying me you will," he said so I did, and we got married in Paris.

'It was obvious that I would have to work; the only way we could possibly afford to buy our own practice was on two incomes. We wanted a family but we never discussed how many; we were just disappointed that we didn't have any for some years. After three or four years, I'd gone to attend an infertility clinic and as soon as I was booked in, I was pregnant. It was pretty difficult at that stage because Kevin was teaching at the Eastman Dental Clinic for a year, and I got so large I could only do extractions. In those days dentistry was all standing on your feet, and my obstetrician – who was George Pinker – would only allow me to keep working as long as I promised to rest at lunchtime. Kevin got back to our practice just a few weeks before Sarah was born, but I was taken into St Mary's Hospital ante-natally when toxaemia threatened. Sarah was a big baby, ten and a half pounds, and I had to have a Caesarean which I'd always thought was cheating. In those days only filmstars had Caesareans, it seemed the easy way out.

'So I was very keen to have my other babies without a Caesarean and I did manage to. I must say I'd rather have it naturally any day; the anaesthetic makes you feel so awful and you miss out on the exhilaration afterwards. To complicate matters I developed gastroenteritis immediately and was not allowed to touch Sarah, or go near her. The council sent us a home help who went down with flu, and then another who also went down with flu, and so Kevin had to step in and bottle feed her, which made him immediately closer to her than he might have been otherwise. A lot of men are rather frightened of small babies.'

Their practice was in Old Street, Finsbury, near the City, now part of Islington. 'It was surrounded by 300-year-old houses owned by Bart's Hospital and it was quite Dickensian when we arrived, no running water and a lot of patients living round about who came in carpet slippers and hair curlers. Our building was under threat of demolition for fifteen years. When we arrived there were forty-three small traders in the street including ourselves, and by the time demolition came there were only three of us left. We had to have a sheet of plastic over the roof to keep the water from dripping on patients. "Nurse, fetch the umbrella," my husband would say when we had a downpour. The patients told us, "We come to you in spite of this place." And it wasn't easy to get dental nurses to work in a place like that.'

Sarah was followed by Rachel thirteen months later, at which point the Gardners moved into a newly built house with a garden. 'The neighbours remembered seeing me nine months' pregnant, sieving the soil after the builders had gone. The garden was no more than a pocket-handkerchief but I planted a fig tree – I've always planted a fig in every garden – and espaliered fruit trees: "This one will give you a ten-foot spread," the nurseryman said. I said, "That's all I've got." We were happy there. I got a Spanish mother's help who never managed to learn any English, so I learned Spanish. Six weeks before Sarah was two, we went back to Australia while the girls still cost only 10 per cent of the fare. Kevin had never met my enormous family before; I think he was a bit overwhelmed.'

Three years later another daughter, Joanna, was born and the Gardners moved to a bigger house. 'I'd heard about a big old Victorian place with a large garden, a real family home for children, that might be for sale as the elderly wife was very ill. When Joanna arrived I realised we must look elsewhere and so I wrote to the owner. It turned out his wife had died on the very day Joanna was born and it seemed like a sign. I loved that house. I think Kevin prefers a place that's easier to manage but to me it was the greatest luxury to give the children space.'

This time it was harder to find a mother's help so Trixie Gardner seized upon a solution: she set up an au pair agency in the basement, and ran it for two years. 'It was a fascinating insight into human nature. People would ring up about a job as a mother's help and I'd say, "I'm sorry, it's gone, but there are other jobs; do you want to work with children?" and they'd say, "Oh, no, I *hate* children." Haha!

'If I hadn't been doing that I really would have been tied to the kitchen, with three children under five. That year I took on all the secretarial side of our practice, but did it from home. Then I decided to go back to dentistry; the new high-speed drills had just come in and I did a course in intravenous anaesthesia so that I could do all the anaesthesia and the general dental work. I became the first woman on the Standing Dental Advisory Committee which advises the Health Minister on dental policy in the NHS. I remember I went to one committee meeting a few days before Joanna was born, and then another meeting a few days after, and I thought surely I must look a bit different; but no, they asked me, "Haven't you had the baby yet?"'

The way she entered politics was almost by happenstance; she joined the Conservative Party in the year of the Profumo affair, 1963, because someone knocked on the door, and she supposes she felt a sort of counter-reaction to the general disaffection. She was asked by them to give a talk on Australia; and was asked again the following year. They were clearly impressed because they then asked her to be chairman of the local Conservative women.

'I wasn't too interested, and I said to Kevin, "What do you think about this?" He said, "Give it a try; if you don't like it, you don't have to go on; but you'll never know till you try." And I said, "That makes sense," so I did. And of course once I stepped into the political world I was completely caught up in it. I think they made me a candidate because of my au pair agency: when they interviewed me the chairman asked me what I was doing with an employment agency, and I explained why I'd started it; and he must have decided that sounded like someone who'd been faced with a problem and worked out an answer.' But she soon had to give up the agency because she was needed back at the dental surgery.

Since becoming so heavily involved in politics she has continued to practise dentistry. She was elected onto Westminster Council in 1968, and the GLC in 1970. In 1970 too she fought her first General Election, standing against Barbara Castle in Blackburn. 'Everyone expected the fur to fly with two women candidates. But I liked her very much: a good clean fighter. And I was very fond of Ted Castle. When I later got onto the London Canals Consultative Committee he was my vice-chairman. There was a man proud of his wife.'

She thinks parliamentary life puts an almost impossible strain on women with families. 'The way I coped when I was a candidate and was fighting seats, was to move the family with me. Whenever I went before a selection committee I told them, "If you choose me, you get the five of us." We bought a little house in Blackburn, and Kevin and the children came too; they must have got so tired of my messages blaring out from the loudspeaker over and over. Kevin was marvellous in stepping in to take on the total catering role during the campaigns. I think perhaps a remote constituency is an advantage in this respect: once you get there, you can devote yourself entirely and exclusively to the constituency, there are no distractions.

'When we had Cornwall to nurse, it was exhausting, with a vast distance to cover and a long time travelling to get there. I would leave a car at Plymouth but it was still sixty-five miles further to drive from there. The children loved Cornwall though. The cottage we had there was on a farm and they could stay there with the farm people while we canvassed.'

Trixie Gardner was made a life peer in 1981, when, at the request of Michael Foot, then leader of the Opposition, Mrs Thatcher was consciously creating 'working peers' in the House of Lords. Out of fifteen peers that year, four were women. 'The Commons must be so much worse than the Lords,' she says. 'But the Houses of Parliament are all geared to suit men. I now sit on the Council of Europe Committee for Equality between men and women, and it is so often made clear that we are *the* worst European country for accommodating women in Parliament.'

There has never been a period when Trixie Gardner has not been working. 'While I was at home just after Joanna was born, it was just that time in the early 1960s when the newspapers were starting to say you must not waste your intelligence by not working, so I was brainwashed rather; and once you're back at work you don't have time to think whether you should or not. I've never been terribly good at housework, although I enjoy the cooking side, being so highly trained. And I quite enjoy attacking *major dirt*. I like to spring-clean. But the day to day jobs in the home would never satisfy me; I like doing needlework and tapestry and that sort of thing, but only as a relaxation.'

After Joanna's birth they had an English mother's help who stayed more than ten years. 'I don't know how to advise other people about help, but I do care very much about people and I believe you should show people when you're grateful to them. Perhaps the hardest thing in the world is being taken for granted. I think a lot of mothers' helps quite like being in a house where *more* emotional demands are made on them, so that they are making a real contribution. I think it would be hard to work in a house where the person you were working for wasn't doing anything much. Well, we never had that problem in our house! And our helpers were equal at all times, sharing our lives.'

I asked about Kevin Gardner, thirty years into marriage; she had referred to him already as a marvellous man. 'He's not only such a solid, reliable person,' she said, 'he's very nice too. He's good-looking, entertaining, interested in everything. He's someone I think who has grown over the years, and now he's got interested in politics too. He represents the Lord's ward on Westminster City Council, and he was Deputy Mayor last year so I was able to help him for a change.'

Did he help with the children? 'He's always said that he doesn't really like children,' said Trixie, 'but I find that incredible because he's a marvellous father. I remember asking him, after the third one was born, how many children he would really like, and he said, "Two." And I said, but when we had two you said you'd like just one. And he said, "That's right." Ha! He likes peace and quiet, that's the point, while I like a bustle of people. But he took his responsibilities seriously. In theory I would have liked more children but I always hated that nine months. I found it a long hard time. I adore it if the Australian cousins come to stay and we can enlarge the family that way; once we had two of them for six months and I loved that.'

The girls all went to day schools in London. 'I wanted them at home; I never liked the idea of boarding school. In the last ten years since we haven't had any help, we've all become much closer but I think if you can afford help when they're small, that's everything to you. It also means you don't have to hire babysitters and get the place ready for the babysitter.' All their girls started off at a local convent school. Sarah went to City of London, the independent day school, which she loved and where she was deputy head girl. Rachel went there too but changed to Godolphin, another independent school; she is now a doctor.

For Joanna, the third daughter, the Gardners switched to the state system and she went to Pimlico Comprehensive. 'She loved it and it gave her a lot of confidence. She was elected Head Girl – quite an achievement in a large mixed school.'

Had she ever felt neglectful towards her children because of her work? 'I think they would vary in their answers to that,' she said, 'if you asked them. I know one of them came to the conclusion that they were happiest if you were happy. And one of them, at another stage in life, said she would love me to be there in the afternoons; of course there always was someone there, they never came back to an empty house. Another one said, at another time, we were the only parents she knew who weren't getting divorced, what was wrong?

'I certainly think it was good for our marriage that I was so occupied. When we first got married it occurred to me: what are we going to talk about for the next twenty years? But we've never had that problem. In practice at the surgery, we're good at doing different bits of work in the same place. When we first started together and I sometimes acted as "nurse" I remember handing him a filling and he said, "It's too wet," and I said, "It's not!" and I could see the patient looking a bit anxious, never having heard the nurse argue with the dentist before. Kevin is a clever and direct thinker: he will see straight through a problem and give an answer; it's typically masculine. Lots of minor irritations and disasters he would just let slide.

'I can say that I have never turned anything down because of the family. I've always found having the family an advantage, even if they haven't found me an advantage! I always involved the family in everything, and in my constituencies they always liked the children very much. A politician friend of mine who is a single woman would sometimes borrow our children when she was asked to open a fête. They are all interesting girls. The eldest one has a brilliant personality that sweeps you along with whatever she's doing. She's a keen Brownie pack leader and she aims to improve life for everyone she comes into contact with. My doctor daughter is more quietly confident. She's so pretty and young looking, people keep asking her if she's really qualified. The youngest has just got her degree and is now studying Law.'

Baroness Gardner is persuaded by her experience over ten years as Britain's UN representative on the Status of Women Commission that there has been a change in attitude, and a widening of opportunities for women. 'Maybe it's not been so visible, but there has been a consolidation of possibilities for women. I read *The Feminine Mystique* when it came out, and Germaine Greer of course, who fascinated me partly because of being Australian. My sister, who is something of an intellectual, writes to me about all these books. But my life has not followed any pattern. The point I have to make is that although I have loved my political career and I have loved having all these things, I don't know that I would have enjoyed the achievement so much if I hadn't had the family and their support.

'And I do always believe that although children are important, your husband must come first. My sister and I have often argued about this. But I always felt that, and still do. With my husband, as long as he comes first he's prepared to do anything and everything for the children. But I think if he felt they were rivals for my affection it would be different.

'Kevin and I have been an absolute partnership. The things we did, we did together. The practice, the children, the politics. I think I've been lucky.' Doesn't it make her feel more vulnerable?

'That is the terrible thing of course. Women who are happily married must always face the possibility of widowhood. I know women aged seventy or so who have always been single, and they build up a very happy style of life for themselves. Whereas a widow is bound to be a sad and stricken figure. It's something I'm very conscious of. It can happen to anyone at any moment; I think it's a good thing in life that we don't know, or perhaps we couldn't bear it. I say to my husband and children – they think it's a joke now, I've said it so often – "I want you all to know what a marvellous life I've had with you all." Now they say, "Oh yes, we know!" But the bereaved so often tell me that they wish they'd known that, they feel the guilt of omission. So I say it. I'm very conscious that you can beat everything in life except death. I feel that all my life I've just got by, by refusing to accept that anything is impossible. "Keep Going" – that's my official motto, and certainly my motivation.'

Shirley Hughes
illustrator and author

b. 1927

m. 1952
JOHN VULLIAMY
architect

2 sons, 1 daughter
EDWARD TOM CLARA

Shirley Hughes

❧

Shirley Hughes, married to an architect, mother of three, is an example of how career and family can be combined by never moving outside the home. She has become one of the world's best known illustrators of children's books. Along with a handful of others (Quentin Blake, John Burningham, Helen Oxenbury) she has a style immediately recognisable, and although the black-and-white line drawing tradition to which she belongs rather fell out of vogue during the 1960s, it is now very much with us again. Today she both writes and illustrates her own books, winning awards and striking chords that turn her books into children's classics. In bookshops and children's libraries she draws huge crowds for her personal appearances, a large, plump, motherly figure in a top-knot.

For much of the thirty years she has lived there, Holland Park in west London has provided an ideal visual background (handsome stucco, leafy communal gardens) but now the merchant bankers and shipping brokers have moved in, and for visual inspiration among brick terraces, adventure playgrounds and urban pavements where mothers push prams, she looks further west to the ordinariness of Shepherd's Bush. She works in the confines of the real world, and thinks in pictures.

The view from Shirley Hughes's drawing room, as she talked, was of the communal gardens of Elgin Crescent, one of the great triumphs of nineteenth-century town planning, drenched in twentieth-century English rain.

❧

Shirley Hughes was born in Liverpool and grew up in the prosperous coastal town of Hoylake, Cheshire. Her father, a businessman (of Hughes, the Liverpool store) died when she was four; Shirley was the youngest of three sisters. 'We were an all female family: a widow and her three daughters in a quiet north country suburb. My father had left enough for us to live on and it wouldn't have crossed my mother's mind to work anyway. My sisters and I went to the local high school, West Kirby, which was very good, and we did a lot of playing and dressing up, making up stories and acting them out to anyone who would watch. We drew and we wrote: it was an ideal background for encouraging imagination.' Her mother supplied plenty of well illustrated books (Rackham, Heath Robinson) and when Shirley was nine, and in bed with measles, a pile of old American comics – Li'l Abner, Blondie and Dagwood – opening up other worlds. The elder sisters went off to boarding school but the war intervened and Shirley stayed at home. 'I decided to go to Liverpool Art College. Mother insisted that I should do school certificate first, then I beat it. For a while I worked at Birmingham Rep, because I was doing a theatre costume course. It was a very good art school, but I got tired of living at home and felt I must get away from there. I was sick of the tennis club and being expected to go and secure a young man from a shipping or cotton family in Hoylake. I hated tennis anyway. So I applied to Ruskin and I went.' The Ruskin School of Art at Oxford had a very academic course with no formal training in illustration at all. 'It was a good period to be in Oxford. We were eighteen, and the young men were all about twenty-four; they'd been through the war, and the more intelligent of them were dead keen to come back and get on with things; I have to say that I think they were a great deal more mature in the 1940s than the young men at Oxford with my daughter in the 1980s. I made some very good friends there, male and female. It was a hopeful time. We really thought the Labour government meant immense social hope and would achieve the goals we really believed in and wanted to work for.'

She came down to London and, with letters to three art editors written on her behalf by her tutor, launched herself in the freelance market. Then she came one night to Lansdowne Crescent to babysit for an Oxford friend who'd had a baby, and noted one of the names on the doorbell: VULLIAMY. (It is most famous as the name of one of the great eighteenth-century clockmakers.) 'Whenever I was there, we could hear laughter from the flat above, and tinkling glasses, and girls being ushered through the hall. Then came the day when my friend had a blocked drain and her area was flooded with horrible gunge. The man in the flat above, striding home from work in a smart gent's natty suit and white shirt, nipped down the area steps, removed his jacket, turned up his sleeve and plunged his arm into the drain, instantly unblocking it. So this was John

Vulliamy. Looking back, I feel it must mean that though I was at the time utterly gormless in many ways, I must have known a Good Thing when I saw it.

'He was older than me, he'd already done seven years training as an architect and had been called up in the war although he was a conscientious objector. He'd been a medical orderly, but then felt he could no longer stand back and so he joined the Devonshire Regiment. At this point he'd just started with the firm of Yorke Rosenberg Mardall, which he stayed with always, doing mostly public buildings, hospitals, airports.' They married in 1952.

'It was assumed that I would go on drawing; never for a moment did John fail to encourage me to carry on. In fact he's always wanted me to work just as much as I have. Before you have children, you never really realise what it will involve. What proved immensely important to me were the few years I had experienced freelancing before having the children. They were absolutely vital. I've since advised my daughter to make sure she does the same: get the work experience and establish the contacts, first. The essential thing is to get to the stage where people ring you up and ask you to do jobs. Because once you have a family it's much more difficult to go round with your portfolio.

'I did absolutely anything they offered: educational books, books with terrible titles like *A Madcap Brownie*, all disappeared now I hope. In those days there were far more books illustrated with about twelve black-and-white line drawings. It was excellent training, the equivalent of being in rep. I was not a star, and children's books then didn't command much attention: nobody ever reviewed, or commented on the books or jackets I did. But by doing so many of these line drawings, I worked up a style of my own. Kaye Webb (of Puffin Books) had begun the *Young Elizabethan* magazine, for children, which gave me work, and I was just starting to get more interesting – i.e. well written – books offered to me, William Mayne and Elfrida Vipont, when I decided to marry John. But I already had such freelance connections going that I was able to go into my room every day with some commissioned work to get on with.

'The deadline gives you a terrific drive. I could not have done just the creative thing. I did produce one picture book of my own when the children were tiny, but it was with interpretive drawing that I hung on, fitting into another person's imagination, committed to the author and the publisher who rely on you to do a good job. The first two years after we married were very settled and happy, young love, working like crazy,

John going out every day being the big earner and me staying here being the mini earner. I still remember the wonderful moment when the fee for full-colour jacket artwork went up to ten quid.

'Edward was born in 1954, Tom in 1956 and then a gap before Clara, 1962. They were all planned, and all came more or less at the intended time. But it was an amazing shock to discover how much time a baby took up.

'I thought the baby would lie in its cot while I did lots of drawings; but in fact I used to think, oh Lord, am I ever going to be able to get back to it? It seemed a knife edge every day. I reckoned I needed three hours: if I got three hours I was OK. I do think working at home has its attendant difficulties but it's somehow easier, too, to do concentrated work like drawing. There's no question of needing a nine-to-five stretch: you can't concentrate in that way for more than three or four hours anyway.

'If I got my three hours I found I was happy, and after that I washed shirts and nappies and scrubbed floors and I didn't mind a bit because I had my creative thing. Occasionally I got friends and neighbours to help by swapping children: there was a great deal of box and coxing then, when this area was a lot less posh. The gardens at the back were invaluable, ideal. A lot of my freedom to work was linked with those gardens: our kids knew everyone along there and they were in and out of each other's houses. It was an amusing area in those days for a young couple. Friends from Oxford would visit us, and they'd like the district, and would come and live here too.

'We had very little cash to spare but we did have rooms to spare, so we bartered that space for the au pair. We had the usual series of inexperienced young girls. I thought they were very brave, actually. Whenever a new one appeared, so young and far from home, I would think, Gosh you are brave. They were very useful but not a mother substitute in any way.

'I've also always tried to have two or three hours' professional cleaning every week. When I tried to do the cleaning as well I did get exhausted; this is a large house and I used to long for fewer stairs, built-in cupboards and cork floors. The advantages of this house became apparent later. Good sound insulation, and nothing open-plan, which is death to anyone trying to get on with work in a house with teenagers and their friends and records.

'I always had a terrific determination to be professional and never to be late on a deadline. *No excuse would do*. Not even if both children had measles. I felt you could never risk their saying, "Oh-oh, she's a married woman." I was always ahead of my deadline; that was my great pride.

'I would like to think that women can now say fearlessly to managements, "All my babies have measles." But even now I find I cannot fail to meet a deadline if things are up the spout domestically – because publishing's full of young women with children and I can't allow myself to leave some other mother high and dry.

'There's an immense built-in advantage to being an artist and having children. The actual tactile pleasure I get from my equipment: I get turned on just by seeing my materials, the inks and brushes and tubes and pots and pens: they are a joy to me. It means that if you've got the children off for two hours – to sleep or to playgroup or someone else's house, you can go into that room absolutely cold and you get the juices flowing. This is going to be my best ever, you think. There's such a thrill in it all. It's cerebral, but you can listen to music at the same time. I drew every day. I suppose there must have been days when I didn't manage to get into my room, but I know I hung onto it for grim death because drawing is my joy, and I feel utterly miserable without it.

'There's another very important point. Art, like writing, flows from constant use of hand and eye. After all those years of training it needs to be built into your day. Art has to be practised to flourish; you lose it if you don't carry on doing it. It's very similar to playing an instrument.'

Shirley Hughes's more spectacular success has come later, rather than earlier in life, ever since Dorothy Edwards, author of My Naughty Little Sister stories, and also the late Noel Streatfeild with her Bell family books, chose Shirley as illustrator. The Corrins' story anthologies followed, and also Shirley Hughes's own creations: the Lucy and Tom books, books like Dogger, Up and Up, and Helpers which for anyone with a young family today have become part of the childhood mythology. Significantly, in Helpers the babysitter is male and the mother of the family is a working woman; this was pioneering anti-sexist stuff. Latterly she has branched out with her own style of mixed comic-strip and narrative in the Chips and Jessie books. In her warm, untidy line drawings it is close observation of the children, and her feeling for them (fearful and hesitant in a grown-up world) which lingers. But for a while her style began to seem old-fashioned. 'When I was slogging away in the lower ranks and at my most overworked with three young children under ten, a great change came over picture-books, with the eruption of technique-orientated illustration. I, with my line drawings modelled on my heroes Ardizzone and Shepard, became the reliable old family saloon car, and people like Brian Wildsmith and Charles Keeping were the exciting new Mercedes. I felt terribly outclassed by all these, especially with squabbling toddlers, soldiering on. It was Dorothy Edwards and her *My Naughty Little Sister* books who kept me going; we would tour the old library circuit in areas like Glasgow. All I've ever learned about talking to children was from the time I spent as her sidekick.' Shirley Hughes, a large, comfortable figure, is now a familiar public speaker all over the world, talking to schoolchildren, librarians and teachers.

'The world of children's books used to have a "How sweet" and "Little me" image, to be patted on the head and dismissed. But now children's books are big business for publishers. Illustrating is recognised as a highly specialised skill, which matters even if the audience is unsophisticated.

'Yet for years it was impossible for people even to regard it as work. "You're so lucky!" people used to say, as if it all dropped out of the end of your finger tips. They wouldn't say that if I were a *viola player*.

'I think I had a better academic education at my grammar school than my two elder sisters at their boarding school. But when I said I wanted to go to art school there was a definite attempt to suggest that I ought to go to university. This is assumed to be the only way you can use your brain if you've got one. The same thing happened to my daughter Clara: when she got her good A-Levels, the reaction was, of course now you'll go to university, not art school. But she took a year off to do a foundation art course first, with her place to read history lined up, then she switched to Ruskin to do Art after all.

'For all that's said about the raffish *vie bohémienne* of artists, all booze and having affairs, it's oddly untrue. Your stimulus is all in the eye, and you get it from looking out of the window, and the way people sit round in pubs and in groups, and the way the sky looks. And you see that's all with you all the time, you don't have to travel. This area to me is the most romantically beautiful place, it never fails to thrill me.

'At weekends sometimes I would be desperate to do some drawing and would take off to the room upstairs, and John would take the children off for the day and amuse them. They always liked being with him. Possibly they liked being with him better than with me because they didn't see him all the time.

'Small children hate anything that takes attention away from them. They love activity but they do not like mother to go into a room and shut the door and concentrate utterly on something that excludes them. My view was that if I did go off somewhere else, I would still be able to hear the distant screams. So I always had my work table here in this room. I remembered that Ardizzone had a dais in the drawing room of his big London house, and worked in the bosom of the family. Mind you, he had a wife too.

'There's a watershed with children anyway, when suddenly they're not underfoot any more, but off and away and they are then very relieved that you are busy working on something, rather than breathing down their necks.'

Of the three Vulliamy children only Clara is an artist: she was the one who would rush to use what was left in her mother's gouache palate when she got in from school. Now she is a portraitist and illustrator with a distinctive style of her own. Edward is a *Guardian* journalist; Tom is a molecular biologist.

'I think confidence is a great help in marriage. John is a very confident man who never ever felt remotely threatened by the fact of my working. And I didn't feel threatened by him either, when I was the pathetic earner. He paid for the roof over our heads, and I organised the paying of the bills and I paid for supplementary things, help and children's clothes. My earnings have grown, but only of late, since I started writing. Illustrating is not so well paid, but at least it's a world in which women are equal to men. If you turn in the work, nobody cares if you're male or female. I've never known any kind of discrimination.

'If I look at work, marriage and children, I know that I have needed my work: any confidence I've got comes from it, this one thing I've somehow managed to get quite good at. It was during my Oxford days that I suddenly realised I was getting on well with drawing, and that became my identity.

'I also know that I could not have coped with the solitary nature of my job had I not been married, and I could not have borne not to have children. I feel very sad that such a lot of girls have had a long, academic education and a career ladder to follow which has meant they haven't married, and later they begin to feel perhaps they would have liked children. I would have found it very very hard to choose between one or the other.

'John is a terribly nice man; I mean he's likeable, affectionate and civilised. We have, increasingly, a lot in common. He has retired early, and I'm the one who's earning the money now. He is independent, he has his own money, and he's embarked on a new activity as an etcher of architectural subjects; occasionally he needs a figure drawing to give a sense of scale and there I can help him. It's a case of the tables turning because when we first met, John taught me perspective drawing. My perspective drawing was extremely shaky and his criticism was invaluable. It's such a lark that he's now doing something he's always wanted to do, and I do think it's a tremendous help to our marriage, that we both draw. Now the children are grown up it is the great shared thing. Every year we have a couple of weeks in Tuscany and we take our sketchbooks, and he sketches the buildings and I do the people. I'm short sighted but I've got an eye for the minutiae, I hardly see the larger landscape but I get struck by a little corner of someone's allotment. John sees whole buildings where I see just a part. I have to get the faces and the characters of the people: my one ace card.

'Sometimes I feel I would have liked to try working in a team. You do miss a great deal, I think, by always having to face your problems alone. And, just sometimes, I feel I'd like to be able to play quartets with other people in a way other than social. But that's only a vague regret. By all my travelling and talking I've solved the whole thing of being a trapped face at a window.'

Fay Weldon

novelist and playwright

b. 1935

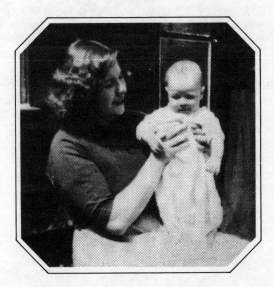

m. 1961

RON WELDON

antique dealer and musician

4 sons

NICHOLAS DANIEL THOMAS
SAMUEL

Fay Weldon

It has often seemed a paradox that, while writing novels which explore women's mad and desperate lives, Fay Weldon herself remains altogether cheerful and robust, married for many years to a husband quite outside the literary world and with four sons aged from thirty down to eight.

Because she is frank and talkative she is frequently interviewed. She keeps two homes: one in a Somerset village; one small terraced house in a fashionably seedy quarter of North London. Members of the family drop in here or there. Somewhere between the two places a prodigious amount of writing gets done: novels, plays, screenplays, biography, criticism. Within the characters in her novels and their elliptical dialogue it is often possible to discern some of Fay's more angry and indignant thoughts, for these are certainly part of her; but in person she is always amiable. She is plump, blonde, and always invigorating company. For the conversation in this book we went to a jolly Indian restaurant.

The following day she wrote to me: 'Dear Valerie, I suspect there is more to be said in defence of the childless than I managed to convey last night. You could even say the having of children is neurotic and craven, and the not having of children is healthy.' Typical Fay; always something more to say. She has discovered the pleasure of talking on platforms. 'Once I was too terrified to open my mouth in public – my heart raced and my voice came out in a pitiful mouse-squeak – but now I enjoy haranguing hundreds,' she wrote in her book *Letters to Alice on First Reading Jane Austen*, a collection of thoughts and homilies addressed from Australia to an imaginary niece.

'I tell you this, Alice, just in case you suffer yourself from that terror of public speaking which renders so many women dumb at times when they would do better to be noisy. If you are in a committee meeting or a board meeting or a protest meeting, *speak first*. It doesn't matter what you say, you will learn that soon enough, simply *speak*. Ask for the windows to be opened, or closed . . . anything.' Like so much she says, it is excellent advice. Her vital contribution is to have helped to give women their voice.

Having heard Fay Weldon's account of her childhood I thought it was perfectly straightforward. Then I re-read some of her old interviews, including my own, and found there was nothing straightforward about it at all. Passport facts (like name, age and place of birth) vary, are given out almost at random according to mood. Was she 'born Fay Birkinshaw?' No, her mother named her Franklin not Fay. She was a child in New Zealand, but was she 'born in North London, a few streets from where she lives now' as in one account or 'born in the tiny village of Alvechurch in Worcestershire' as in another? When we met this time she spoke of her fiftieth birthday a few months before, yet three years earlier when *The Times* (and the BBC) said she was forty-seven, she had told me she was actually older than that; and indeed *Who's Who* says she was born in 1931. I have decided that she must mean 1935. 'It is good to be Virgo-Libra', she said to me once in explanation. 'It gives you a rigorous nature in some respects, and a rather vague one in others.' It amuses her when you say, 'But before you said . . .' expecting her to stick always to the same story. 'What they don't realise,' she said, 'is that my conversation is *unedited*. My novels are the third draft.'

No matter. It seems certain that she was one of two daughters of a doctor father and a writer mother, who emigrated to New Zealand and that is where she lived until the end of the war. Her parents divorced when she was five, and she, sister, mother and grandmother formed a three-generation all-female household, so that she thought the world was run by women. She was therefore never convinced by the women's movement's insistence that it is men who rule the world.

'My mother always worked, supporting us and her own mother who lived with us. At various times she ran a craft shop, was left in charge of a small advertising agency while the men went off to war, and worked in a biscuit factory when they came back. Once she was a housekeeper and we were the housekeeper's children, living in the basement flat. A rat lived there too.

'It never occurred to me that women were supported by men. I had no clear idea of how I would support myself, but I always knew that I would. I would have to.' Her mother's maiden name was Margaret Jepson, but she wrote romantic fiction while they were in New Zealand, under the name of Pearl Bellairs. Fay Weldon is one of those women who has all her life depended on and remained close to a wonderful mother. At eighty, Margaret Jepson is now meticulously rewriting one of her early novels.

'My mother never went to school at all,' Fay says. 'She made a major life decision at the age of five. She was supposed to go to nursery school, and her father, who was a writer, came downstairs in his silk dressing gown and he was told, "Margaret doesn't want to go to school," and he said: "She doesn't have to go to school if she doesn't want to." So she never did.

'My mother's mother and father were later divorced, and my grand-mother left without support. That was really bad because my grand-mother was one of the dependent variety of women; a talented pianist reduced by marriage to being chiefly decorative; and by divorce simply reduced. In deeply conventional New Zealand, we were a unit outside society; decent women were simply not divorced. Nor were they liked for being decorative. Nor did any of us go to church. Outcasts!' She saw her father each summer. But, after the war ended, the womenfolk came to England with the help of a small bequest; her father, having remarried, died in New Zealand.

'We arrived in a very disrupted society. The war had made profound changes in England; not until the middle 1950s did everything settle down again. My mother's family and former friends were no longer there.

'Here was a country in the aftermath of war: food rationing, a flicker of gas for warmth, a glimmer of electricity for light; a dire place to be. We arrived at Tilbury, accustomed to a suburban, island country with greenery and flowers and order, where there was hardly a building higher than two storeys, and here was this extraordinary, grey, ploughed-up, knocked about, soot-drenched ruin that was London! The first night, we stayed with a friend of my mother's. She had the one house left standing in the middle of a bomb site. We slept on the floor, and I woke in the night and looked out, and will always remember the eeriness of the brilliant moon on the rubble; and the shadowed craters, and the high peaks of half-ruined buildings. It was a wasteland.'

They lived for a time in one room in Belsize Park. 'That was the winter of 1946–7, the one which broke all records. I never go past the station without remembering it – or how grateful we were for that blast of hot air which rushes up out into Haverstock Hill when a train goes by. We were good Socialists and read our *New Statesman* and like so many others at that time, looked forward to a better world. I went to South Hampstead School for girls where the state paid for my dinners, as a list on the noticeboard testified, but otherwise I think I was a completely unnoticeable pupil. Stunned by the world and good as gold. But I was always gregarious: I loved my friends and I loved talking: the school served the bright daughters of the North London Jewish community and I felt completely at home. Outsiders all! My sister Jane declined to go to school at all: she did her exams by correspondence course and got to Exeter University with no trouble. She was brilliant and beautiful.' Jane married Guido Morris, a St Ives printer whose works are now in the Tate Gallery: she had three children but died of cancer at forty. Thereafter Jane's children lived with their excellent grandmother, but care and upbringing were shared by Fay. So the cousins have been very much a part of the Weldon household.

Fay went to St Andrew's University and by the age of twenty had her MA in Economics. 'A very odd university; I got through the entire course without talking to a member of staff once. I went to lectures, I wrote my essays and I did my exams. I was perpetually and wretchedly in love with impossible people like the best friend's boyfriend. My mother had gone to live in Cornwall by this time, so from the age of seventeen I was effectively out in the world on my own. And if you don't have a settled family to come out of, how are you ever going to get back into one, which was my ambition? But how could someone like me be seen as a desirable wife by a desirable young man? It distressed me at the time but of course in retrospect it was my good fortune.'

What to do with her life? 'It was an odd world in the fifties for the female graduate; women still didn't really think seriously about careers. I could have gone into the Treasury, I suppose, had I been prepared to sit yet more fiendish exams; or joined Marks & Spencer's trainee programme if I'd been prepared to live in Newcastle; they were very modern and took women too – but what most of us did was shorthand and typing: then we'd be secretaries for a year or two before getting married and giving up work for good. In other words we didn't apply our intelligence to our personal lives. But at least the problem of having children *and* a career, having your cake and eating it too, didn't arise. You were expected to do one or the other. As for me, I refused to do shorthand and typing and so was unemployed, as I deserved to be. I knew a lot about Roman History and how to live in one room and how to get by with no money, but I was completely ignorant of everything else. I knew nothing of the way society worked. I'd done a degree in Economics yet I didn't even know of the existence of *rates*.

'Eventually I found jobs; I messed about. I was a waitress, which I hated. I did market research, going up to people in the street and asking them questions, which I hated even more. I answered letters for the *Daily Mirror* on their problem page. I was their Hire Purchase specialist: people would send in scraps of moth-eaten carpet, wormy chair-legs, with their complaints. There was no comforting them. Then I was a temporary clerk in the Information Research Department of the Foreign Office, writing propaganda. Then I was married, briefly.' This is one of the vague areas of Fay's life. She was married to a schoolmaster, twenty-five years older than she. Her eldest son Nicholas was born in Addenbrooke's Hospital, Cambridge. Whatever the facts of this period they were probably good for her as a writer. Misery and guilt are more fruitful for a writer than married bliss.

'And then things got better: I finally was in charge of my own life. My mother looked after Nicholas for me. He'd had to spend about three days in a nursery and I was so horrified by the awfulness of it – it was a state venture to save deprived children from being thrown into the Thames or whatever – that I rescued him and turned once more to my mother.

'Then I met Ron. What was he doing? Oh, nothing much, like myself. He rode a motorbike around London and painted people's houses and played the cornet at parties. These days of course he paints pictures and plays New Orleans trumpet at proper gigs. He is more genuinely talented than I am; he has more integrity than I have. He is brilliant. But then he was in a state rather equivalent to mine. My poor mother saw me leaping from frying pan into fire; I'd been leaping from pans into fires since the age of fourteen and she was having to bear the brunt.'

Ron and Fay were married at St Pancras Register Office but neither can recall the exact date and they've lost the bit of paper. 'We each had one child: Ron had his daughter Karen and I had Nicholas, and then Daniel was born. By that time I was working in advertising – Crawfords, then Colman, Prentis and Varley, and finally Ogilvy Benson and Mather. And pretty soon I was Superwoman, in analysis and running a home and a family with the help of an au pair and giving dinner parties and going out to work as well. In the sixties it was nothing to be Superwoman. But it made us cross and tired and resentful and we turned into feminists, and started trying to change the world and not ourselves.

'And then I started writing television plays: I'd write them crouching on the floor.

'The advertising agency pretty soon had a lot to put up with. I was a consultant: I reckoned I could do a week's work in four hours if I put my mind to it. The thing about having a special skill of course, as I had, is that people will put up with you calling the tune. And then I've always been basically reliable: I meet deadlines. If I undertake to be somewhere, I'll be there. (That of course is my vision of myself: others may have a different idea.) But I went too far. Copy consultants charge by the hour. In order to make what I thought I deserved, I had to charge for 36 hours a day. After about six months, someone noticed. But by that time losing my job didn't matter. I was earning enough, writing television plays. So I wish I could say leaving advertising was a calculated and moral decision. It wasn't. But I was glad enough to go.'

Fay does not mention at this point, perhaps because for years her name was never mentioned without the tag, that she wrote one of advertising's most memorable slogans, *Go to work on an egg*. It made her slightly famous, and she would frequently be invited to tell how she juggled work and home life. Ron was by now running an antique business in Regent's Park and they lived nearby in what was always described as a cheerfully chaotic household, a new baby arriving from time to time. 'I never registered myself as being successful, ever. I was just fumbling away in the face of adversity and difficulty, working on various accounts like Eggs and Milk and Sewing Machines and Computers, mostly on female accounts which had a vested interest in showing the highest aim of women to be a good wife and mother. And I don't see why that *shouldn't* be women's highest aim – as long as the husband's aim is also to be a good husband and father.

'I can't remember Ron and I ever making any joint decision about anything whatsoever. I think we each try not to impose our will on the other. Which is not to say we don't scream and shout a lot. My first husband had been of the "no wife of mine will ever go out to work" variety, and also, "no wife of mine will ever join the Labour Party". Ron was certainly not like that. We go through life not so much hand in hand but closely parallel. I don't think the children can make it out, even now.'

When I once asked Fay why her four sons were born at such distant intervals she replied, 'I can only wipe one face at a time,' which seemed a reasonable reply. This time she said: 'It was a result of general carelessness and inattention to detail . . . but I was always enormously pleased to have them. I could never have been sterilised. When the last one arrived I was well over childbearing age (their reckoning; not mine) and it was a placenta-previa delivery by Caesarean, and as I went under the doctor said, "While we have you out, would you like to be sterilised?" and I remember replying, "The day you have a vasectomy I'll be sterilised" and passing out, terrified that this *might* be the day he was having his vasectomy.

'The first birth was horrifying. I was very young and totally ignorant, and anyway those were gynaecologically prehistoric days. Nobody even dreamt in those days that fathers would ever be present at anything so messy as a birth.

'The next two were lightning deliveries. Both were meant to be at home, but both babies went past their date. I'd be sent into hospital and the minute I was inside the birth would proceed at speed, in the preparation room or in the wheelchair, and they'd race me down the corridors. "The baby's coming, its head's out," I'd persist. "Nonsense, Mother," they'd say. I never did get inside a delivery room.

'Of course, small children are a nuisance, I'm just attached to them. They're so interesting. Eighteen months or so, it seems to me, is peak age for maternal exhaustion and irritation. The babies are independent and mobile, but have so little sense. The daily wrestling match to get the clothes on! It's rather like the sudden frenzy that seizes the dog when the postman puts the letters through the door – "How dare he!"'

What about motherhood; how does one stand it? I asked. (I was feeling particularly beleaguered that day.) Fay looked at the question obliquely. 'What must it be like, *not* to have any children? Well, the great advantage of not having children is that you can go on believing you're a nice person. You can remain convinced that you are a decent, civilised, pleasant human being. It's when you have children that you realise how wars start. This is the great problem the new mother has, along with all the others: this secret knowledge. It's why she gets into a terrible state. She finds she would rather sleep, and just let the baby cry. And this is what it's like ever after: you don't sleep, because the baby needs you. You are not full of pure love after all; it is mixed with resentment.

'But it's very odd, isn't it, to meet the childless, people who can suit themselves, who don't have all the bother and paraphernalia of children in their lives. I suppose it will happen to us again when they've gone; but if we are lucky or sensible enough to have our children late, we will be OAPs before we totter off around the world alone.

'Of course there are other advantages to the having of children. It is a training in diplomacy, in keeping the peace. And with what pleasure and relief you can turn back to your work. When you think of the life-and-death decisions a mother makes every day – are they going to have bicycles, can they go to the shops, can they cross the road? – and she has only her own judgement and knowledge to go by, and the decision takes her about five seconds. Yet if she worked in a vast company she wouldn't dream of making such a recommendation without memos and meetings and serious deliberations, with experts, and statistics to back her up, and paid holidays to allow her to recover from the strain of it all.

'When I was a young mother I was very conscious of how children simply stop you from getting on with your life, but the older I get the more I feel that children are just as good company as adults. It's to do with sexuality, I suppose: the conflict between the erotic and the maternal. You do have to choose, but as you get older it causes less of a conflict.

'But at least children are now seen less as the mother's sole concern. You *never* used to see men carrying their children round supermarkets, or holding their hands in public. Ron is more conscientious than I am with Sam. He feeds him and clothes him and sees he gets to bed on time. I tend to let Sam wander round all evening, putting off going to bed, but Ron looks at the clock and says, "What's he doing up?" and then Sam comes down in the morning after a good night's sleep, to a laid table for breakfast.

'Ron is now more of a feminist than I am. It's been a long and difficult path. He runs the household. In middle life, without even discussing it, we have somehow switched roles. I used to cook; I used to be a phenomenal cook. Now I can't cook at all, because Ron does it.'

She pondered on what was the essential ingredient of being able to handle a marriage and family and work. 'I think the most important thing is energy and health. Too many headaches, too much introspection, too much consideration of the self, and the domestic confrontations are just about all you can manage.

'I also think long years of education help. Having the mind developed in some way. Academic training does keep the mind and body separate. One may be physically and emotionally tired, but the brain is not, and understands what its function is. Without education, this may be harder. This is the advantage of the educated woman. The other great truth is of course that money helps.

'At first there was just me, the house, the family, guests, and a full time job. It was a traditional marriage, Ron didn't do much in the house: he was running an antique shop: it meant long hours and hard work. We had various forms of help but it was always quite hard to find people who'd put up with our requirements. For example, the coffee had to be ground from beans, not instant, and there could be no culinary short cuts. It is the endeavour that fulfils you; grinding the coffee, not drinking it; that's what it's all about. Now what practical person is going to be sympathetic to that? And the help's perfectly sensible instinct may well be to throw away every chipped vase she comes across, without realising that it's Liberty 1905, or polish away a hundred years of pewter patina in five minutes, and I was always reluctant to interfere with the help's self-determination.

'However, admirable people did turn up and we'd all get on well. And after I'd started writing television plays, and become subversive and frivolous, as the times demanded, and so got fired from OBM, my time was my own and writing is the kind of occupation which fits in very well with having babies – unlike serious employment.' Twenty years later she has written twelve novels, many stage and radio plays, screenplays and reviews.

'The having of babies is good for creative work. It may simply be an influx of oestrogen, of course. I *like* getting up in the night; I *like* having my dreams disturbed, my thoughts not my own: it keeps everything in the unconscious stirred up. I wrote *Puffball* immediately after Samuel was born, thinking I must write down all the mystery of the unborn and just-born child before the memory of it had gone; as it does go.

'And that of course is something that people without children *don't* know about. I enjoy pregnancy, too. You don't have to achieve anything: there can be no sensation of wasting time because all your time is being used up by the baby. So perhaps it's a particularly enjoyable time for people with restless super-egos, because they can have a rest. Nine months off from calculated achievement and self-improvement.'

Life is too full of paradoxes for comfort, Fay says. One of these is the professionalism of Fay as writer alongside the apparent scattiness of her homelife. One day I arrived at 4 pm to be told: 'There's no milk; so you will have to have either wine or Cup-A-Soup.' Another day I went to interview her and found her submerged in the pink sheets of her double bed, in a small bedroom grandly papered in gold. She said she had mild bronchitis. But when the telephone rang and the caller asked how she was, she said, 'I'm extremely well, thank you!' breezily. She said she enjoyed spending days in bed being slightly ill, while life continued all around. And continue life did: small son upstairs, larger son going back and forth arranging a party for a departing nanny; new nanny serving lemon tea; secretary Jane in delicate correspondence with the word processor while the fast printer machine-gunned on; washing machine and drier whirring and spinning and rattling away somewhere beyond. 'I am obsessed by consumer durables,' she said. 'If washing machines had registration numbers like cars, I'd buy a new one every year. Having spent my young womanhood unencumbered by labour-saving devices I now think dishwashers, electric carving-knives, toothbrushes, can-openers and so forth are wonderful. I can sit and watch them working instead of me and thinking up excuses to buy new ones. Ron finds my attitude to the material world reprehensible and he is right. It is my vice.'

It is part of her image that she loves being at the kitchen table with her children, 'especially on Saturday mornings, having breakfast with the radio on, when the week's over but it's not yet Sunday . . .'

The four sons are Nicholas, jazz panist and composer, Daniel who studies film at Goldsmiths' College, Thomas who is doing O-Levels at Millfield School in Somerset and Sam at the village primary school. Where the children go to school is where home is in Fay's view, so home is now Somerset. She used to be provocatively optimistic and defensive about London, no matter how littered and desperate her area became; the local ILEA primary school educated her children, and they went to Somerset at weekends. Then she reversed the situation when Thomas went to Millfield, and took to Somerset life, which she had formerly affected to despise. Where once she said: 'Country living is so much effort: you spend your life chopping logs and traipsing to far-flung shops; friends stay around for days revealing their true natures,' now she said she'd done her bit for the middle-class investment in urban culture, and retreated to rural peace once more. The truth is it is a blessing in life to have a bit of both.

'We are not,' said Fay, 'I suppose, a conventional family. Living in two places is not a good or restful idea but it becomes an advantage: if only because when in one place you would always rather be in the other. It does you no good to be placid and satisfied. And of course British Rail benefits greatly.'

What did she feel she had left undone in her life? '*Everything*. I always rather liked the idea of running a factory – a Yorkshire clothing mill, perhaps. Or a large international corporation. I just want to be in charge of *more*. That's why I like writing for television so much. The audiences are huge. The responsibilities are enormous and unrecognised. I spent my last birthday in a television studio and didn't begrudge it a bit. It's so animating.' (They were taping the four-part series, *Heart of the Country*.) 'It's animating because it involves so many skilled and gifted people, who work out and follow through *my* ideas. It is an extra-ordinary sensation. What power!

'Of course you can have a family simply to exercise power, but it is not advisable. You can say to small children, "You must not touch electric plugs," and they won't. But say to them when they're bigger than you, "You must not stay out all night," and all they do is hate you, and quite right too. There is great legitimate satisfaction in simply bringing everyone safely to the close of another day. I remember feeling that particular sense of contentment on the camping holidays we rashly took through the 1970s. Having faced adversity, weather, snakes, hornets, the very lack of a home all day – here they all were safe and snug under cover: there was great satisfaction in that. I still like going up to bed later than everyone else, when there is nothing going on in the house except a great deal of young peaceful breathing: a houseful of sleeping people is mysterious and wonderful.

'Having had several children gives you a useful kind of confidence. You've seen it all happen before, and they've somehow survived. They go through bad patches and good. They've stayed out late and they've come back, eventually. You know that whatever they may be like at one stage, they will change yet again. And that they will eventually return to the temperament they revealed in the first few weeks of their life, which is what seems to happen. That's why new babies are so interesting.

'I knew from a sonic scan at seven months just what Sam was going to be like, even before birth: reasonable and inquiring, with a light, faerie nature. Thomas is most like me in temperament. He was an amazingly beautiful baby, a sort of golden colour. Daniel was just extraordinarily charming, but very private. Nicholas, the first, was magical because I hadn't somehow realised what a baby *was*. He could read fluently when he was three. I thought all children were like that, the apples of their teacher's eye. I was wrong.

'The fact is that women have the number of babies they can afford to have, practically, emotionally and physically. None or one or two or three or four or more: it's a question of her circumstances in life. But on the whole women end up with the right number of children for them. Not to *want* to have babies at all I do see as a deliberate limiting of life, but that's me, speaking out of my generation. If a woman wants babies but can't have them, she may be very sad but she has not deliberately limited herself. The benefit to her is in the *wanting*, not the having.

'I do think my children have always been singularly independent. There was a great deal (before Ron took over) of my putting plates of food on the stairs for them to take back to their rooms, which they seemed to prefer to enduring our company or our nagging, our getting in the way of their private thoughts and their TV programmes. I had to forget all preconceived notions of what family life was and so, poor things, did they. It was no good reading books on how to bring them up: it just didn't seem to apply.'

Fay Weldon was one of the few women I interviewed who had, or who admitted to having, tempestuous periods in her marriage; she had actually separated from Ron when she went out to Australia a few years ago for instance, but then he had come out to join her there. All seemed calm again now. 'I see marriage as a self-imposed journey of self-discovery,' she said. 'Children also oblige you to make this journey. Perhaps there is an inbuilt pressure that doesn't just require but enables you to stay together longer for the sake of the children.'

Jane Wynborne, Fay's secretary and the decipherer of her much-amended handwritten manuscripts, imposes efficiency on her life. 'Correspondence is no longer a problem. My mind is sifted free of all the heavier guilts and burdens, because instead of never, never answering letters, including the ones I'd put aside to answer and never did, these days Jane gathers them up and they get answered. This keeps one on better terms with a good many people. It also multiplies the volume of correspondence because, of course, people then write back.'

One of life's pleasures for Fay is company; she shines at dinner parties, holding tables in thrall with her racontage in a deceptively soft whispery voice. 'It's argument I really absolutely enjoy. I like overstating cases, which some people misunderstand. They think that if you put forward a point of view, it's your fixed and permanent opinion. I am worried if I am taken too seriously. It constantly astonishes me that someone as fundamentally silly as I am can have achieved a state of being thought to be intelligent and mature.'

Re-writing is preferable to writing ('you come fresh to the first draft as if it had been written by someone else') and both are preferable to publication: 'The more successful the book the more depressed I feel. If the reviewers say it's good I feel they have no judgement, and if they say it's bad I just hate them. You have to be your own critic: and a very severe one you find yourself to be.'

She says her novels are chiefly about women because she is one; she understands them and they interest her. Her characters are wives and mothers and daughters; they get pregnant, are betrayed, are victims of their biology, of each other, and of ill-chosen males. Sometimes she is accused of lack of sympathy for her male characters. She says she simply observes them as they appear to her to be. The difference between her male and female characters is, she says, that she can invent women, being one, but only describe men, not being one, and invented characters are more fictionally vivid than described ones. She adds that those who believe there is no difference in the natures of little boys and little girls, other than that dictated by environment, are deluded by wishful thinking; and all mothers know it.

I have always found it consoling that Fay Weldon's view of men is blunt and scathing, but that she never for a moment wishes not to be in their dreadful company. This does mean Fay is regarded by some as a betrayer of the women's movement. She has even acknowledged that men are as much victims of human nature as are women. And that without men, one would miss the richness of life.

I did observe Fay one evening at a Women in Publishing meeting, when she was talking on the subject of 'How Women Write About Sex'. There seemed to me a lack of common ground between the earnest audience and Fay on the platform, fulsome and free-ranging in her thoughts. Like so many of those who pre-date the modern women's movement (when she wrote *The Fat Woman's Joke* in 1967 she wasn't even aware that there was such a movement), her ideas on sex and men were not originally inhibited by mistrust and low expectations.

Fay Weldon says she admires the dedication of radical separatist feminists as she does anyone who manages to live by their principles and not just talk about them. But she lives now in an all-male household – the opposite of the one she grew up in – and is content to do so.

'I wouldn't describe myself as having a career,' she told me. 'What I do, it seems to me, is an activity, an extension of my human nature, in the same way as getting married was something I just fell into. Choice in these major matters seems not to operate. What I did, what I do, appears not as a decision but as the only possible course to take. Not a bit like, shall I take the early or the late train?

'Women who get on well in the world in a career, and forgo marriage and children on its account, have perhaps chosen to live what we see as a man's life with all its advantages, but alas never have the *opportunity* of having a wife. The male executive may talk to or see his wife and children very rarely, but at least he has the privilege and comfort of having them.'

Dr Elizabeth Shore

doctor and civil servant

b. 1927

m. 1951

PETER SHORE MP

*Labour Member of Parliament for
Bethnal Green and Stepney*

2 daughters, 2 sons

THOMASINA TACY PIERS (*d.* 1977)

CRISPIN

Dr Elizabeth Shore

Elizabeth Shore, I had heard, was the only woman in the Civil Service who had reached Deputy Secretary rank *and had children*. She was interviewed along with other 'Mandarines' in the *Observer* magazine in June 1984 and was quoted thus: 'At [job] interviews, men ask questions of women that they certainly would not ask of men. We should ask everyone, not just women, about their domestic commitments.

'What I would like to see would be both men and women being offered the chance to work a four-day week. That would give a real opportunity to anyone with children to have a career and find time to involve themselves with their children's lives.'

There was no indication, in the article quoted above, that Elizabeth Shore was the wife of Peter Shore, the Labour MP and former Cabinet Minister. That had been a stipulation without which the interview would not have taken place. 'I was reticent,' Elizabeth Shore told me, 'partly because of the fact that I am married to a Labour MP and serving a Conservative government, and partly because I'm sick of the "Oh yes, you're Mrs Shore" attitude. I didn't get there because I was Mrs Shore! From a career view, my husband has been a ball and chain round my neck.'

By the time we talked, Elizabeth Shore had left the Civil Service and taken up the post of Dean of the North West Thames Region at the British Postgraduate Medical Federation of the University of London.

She has extremely short curly hair. She is full of energy and enthusiasm and a tireless talker. We met at her office, at the end of a day's work before she went off to dine with one of her daughters.

Elizabeth Shore, née Wrong, comes from one of those families where all the children are destined for Oxbridge as a matter of course. In such an academic family, to want to be a family doctor, as she did, was considered the humblest of ambitions. Her grandfather was a Canadian, a professor of history in Toronto. Her father, Edward Murray Wrong, was sent over to Balliol College, Oxford. Her mother, Rosalind Grace Smith, was a history graduate of Girton College, Cambridge. They had six children of whom Elizabeth was the youngest.

When Elizabeth was six months old, her father, an Oxford don, died. 'Knowing he had rheumatic heart disease, he had saved money and invested it, but it all got lost in the slump. So my mother had to go from a big house in the Banbury Road, Oxford, with domestic help and living quite decently, to being without any home of her own and staying in a house with her eldest sister.'

The three eldest children, all under ten, were sent away to school, and the three youngest were shipped out to Canada. That is how Elizabeth came to live in Canada from the age of three to ten, while her mother took up supervising undergraduates and teaching. 'When we met again, she was a total stranger to me. She had fought like a tiger to get us back, and so we were moved from a large house with servants in Canada, and brought to a small terraced house in Oxford. One curious fact is that the woman who travelled out to Canada with us married my widowed grandfather; and some years later my mother re-married; so I had the experience of attending both my grandfather's and my mother's weddings.'

Canadian relatives paid for an educational trust which provided for all the children to be packed off to boarding school, so Elizabeth went to St Swithun's at Winchester (the same school as Mary Warnock) until the war came, when St Swithun's closed down and they were all sent off home. 'I'd hated it there anyway. For three years I went to Oxford High School as a day girl and then, because I wanted to read Medicine and my mother could not afford it unless I paid my way, my sister – by then at Lady Margaret Hall – had a look to see which schools were getting scholarships and the family decided to send me to Cheltenham Ladies' College. Oxford High had been lovely; Cheltenham was something out of the dark ages. They tried to stop me from doing science and switch me to arts, but I hung on.' She won scholarships to Oxford and Cambridge. (The six Wrong children all went to Oxford or Cambridge.)

'Although the scholarship to Oxford was a major one, and the one to Cambridge only minor (my mother sent me a telegram saying, "Never despise honest cash"), I chose Newnham College just to get away from Oxford since that was home.

'I was very happy at Newnham – liberated after Cheltenham. I met Peter at a May Day party in my first year. He was a former airman reading History. That summer, we went to Italy because he had a scholarship from the British Institute in Florence to go and look at art, and we got engaged the following March.

'I decided to do my finals in two years instead of three, so that I could go to St Bartholomew's Hospital in London and Peter and I could then leave Cambridge at the same time and marry. A drawerful of letters arguing my right to sit Cambridge finals ensued. In the end I had to do both Cambridge and Conjoint finals in order to get qualified. The whole of my last year, Peter, with his Arts degree, was looking for work and not succeeding, and we couldn't marry unless he had a job. Then we found two rooms off the Caledonian Road in North London for £1 a week. So we went home and got married in St Giles, Oxford's cathedral, and I started at Bart's [St Bartholomew's]. Oxford City immediately cut my student grant to one third its original level, even though we had no regular income.

'There were only five women out of sixty students in my year so you got a disproportionate amount of attention, and had to know things and be on your toes. I remember one consultant asking me, "Is your husband dead?" These men had never *seen* women medical students before.'

Thirty years later, when the Equal Opportunities Bill came in in 1975, Elizabeth Shore, working at the Department of Health and Social Security, discovered that there had always been a female quota at most of the London hospitals. 'I thought it odd that there seemed to be the same proportion of women every year – about 20 per cent, never varying, which the legislation has now made illegal. This had kept the numbers of women students down artificially for years.' Cambridge and Oxford ran a quota too. At Oxford, women had to attend a special 'quota interview', as they only took 10 women medical students a year.

By a failure of family planning, Elizabeth Shore had a baby in May 1951, and took the two separate sets of medical finals in June 1951. 'Bart's was very understanding about it, and allowed me to work on the wards right up to the time my daughter was born. I had to get back straight away to work as we had no money: nor did either of our families. But I had never doubted I would work for my living. My mother had always worked, because she was a widow with six children and otherwise you starved. My three sisters all expected to work and have in fact done so.

'Fortunately, there was a girl living opposite our family in Museum Road, Oxford, who adored babies and had been to help my sister, the LMH don, with her new baby. She took our baby, Thomasina, back to Oxford for two months, while we moved to a house in Highgate. Meanwhile I had met an anaesthetist who had a Finnish au pair. The au pair came to inspect me, and agreed to write to her friend Helga, so the next thing we knew we had this marvellous au pair. We also found lodgers who paid a nominal rent. The arrangement was, anybody who joined the household must agree to babysit, so that the au pair could go to her evening classes. It was a complicated ménage, but nobody new could join it without some babysitting. Peter was then working at Transport House, the Labour Party headquarters, and shortly after-wards he had a constituency to nurse as well. And I became pregnant again – again by mistake.'

Dr Shore had to resign from her residential job at the North Middlesex Hospital and there was an awkward patch when she was out of work and had no income. She did a series of locum jobs, surviving with the help of au pairs, and did a year as a trainee general practitioner in St Albans until she had her second child, Tacy – a Quaker name. 'Then I heard from a girl I'd been at school with that if you went to work in Harlow New Town, the development corporation would rent you a house and I might be able to get into a doctors' group practice. So we moved up to Harlow and I worked in Welwyn Garden City, driving 40 miles a day, until our third child, Piers, was born.

'Those days were not easy. I remember moving from Highgate to Harlow while both the babies had whooping cough: I'd been advised not to give them the vaccine because of the side effects. And although I wanted to be a GP, I couldn't put my plate up because the Development Corporation owned all the houses and wouldn't allow anyone to run a business from one. And the GPs in Harlow would only recruit men: the last thing they wanted was a woman doctor who was obviously very fertile.

'Our third and fourth children were both planned. By this time, I had gone to Hornsey Town Hall and sat at the feet of a great guru in contraception and earned a Family Planning certificate. But the only job I could get was in an old London County Council clinic in Paddington, so I used to drive in all the way from Harlow every day.' Finally, they decided to move back to London. They managed to buy a big house in Putney, where they have been ever since, with their children and a succession of lodgers and au pairs.

'By the time our fourth child was born, I'd reached a steady working point; I did an evening Family Planning clinic, a ten-till-four mother and baby clinic – a comfortable niche in Community Health which fitted in with school hours – and locums for Putney general practitioners. But it was intellectually stultifying. You can do infant welfare standing on your head. I worked for the LCC for seven years, telling women about feeding and child rearing, all the things I was doing at home anyway, and then I reached the age of thirty-five. I'd had four children in eight years and I promised myself that when the last one was five, I'd do something different. Saying the same thing to patients over and over again gets boring. Our youngest, Crispin, was now three so I started to look around.

'One day I sat in the clinic and nobody came because of the rain. I read the *British Medical Journal* from cover to cover and there I saw an advertisement for doctors to join the Ministry of Health. I didn't even know they employed doctors! But it was a better pay scale than I was on, and Peter was working in the Transport House Research Department, which in those days paid their staff very badly. He took my job application very seriously and went to the House of Commons library to get out the Annual Report of the Chief Medical Officer, expecting me to read it before my interview.

'That's how I came into the Civil Service. The medical profession regards not doing clinical medicine as admitting defeat. They consider medical Civil Servants are the enemy, though I often find myself telling young doctors how interesting and varied life is in the DHSS. I stayed there for twenty-two years, ending up as a Deputy Secretary.

'Peter meanwhile became MP for Stepney. He had contested several elections before that – St Ives, Halifax. I would go and speak on his platform. Before I married, I hadn't been interested in politics, but I made myself interested. At first, I'd sit in the kitchen because I couldn't bear that timbre of the political voice, arguing, but then I realised that I couldn't exclude myself from something so fundamental to Peter. You have to take an interest in each other's lives. He was adopted for Stepney very late on in 1964 and I remember Tony Benn had to help me to get him to the adoption meeting because he was walking with a stick, he'd been very ill with viral encephalitis . . .

'Of course I had to carry on with my work. I had studied all those years from the time I was sixteen when I decided to read Medicine. That investment of effort wasn't going to be thrown away. Also, we needed the money. We couldn't have raised four children on what the Labour Party Research Department paid Peter.'

The children all went to local state schools. 'There was no question of a Labour Cabinet Minister's children doing anything else, and we didn't want to, anyway.

'In those days everybody believed in comprehensives. We had quite deliberately bought a house within the LCC area and we were determined to use the LCC comprehensives. I had had a private education, but Peter had gone to Quarry Bank High School in Liverpool. I know the state schools have been damaged by cuts and industrial action now but I would make the same decision again, although I would probably agonise over it more.

'Having the family and the job was exhausting but it had the advantage of being two things which were totally different and rewarding in quite different ways. When I was at the DHSS, I tried not to take work home and was always determined to keep the weekend free. But that meant I might work really late, until 9 or 10 pm, to avoid taking papers home. If you spend all weekend doing office work you're still tired on Monday.

'On my journey into work my mind would make a click as I began to think about what awaited me and on the way home that night another click to plan what needed doing at home. By Friday evenings, I'd be exhausted and I'd feel the DHSS had had everything they'd paid for out of me, but I could still spend all weekend cooking and taking the children out, living in jeans the whole weekend. One weekend we calculated we'd provided 87 separate meals, when various children had had friends in.

'We used to run a late breakfast in those days because Peter was always so late the night before at the House and we were both still tired out in the morning. The children used to churn off to school sometimes without seeing me and if there was a letter to be signed they would tell the teacher, "I haven't seen my mother or father," and they wouldn't be believed. On Sundays we'd lie in till about eleven and I remember the bedroom full of children . . . Once a GP came because one of the children was sick and he *reeled* at the sight of our bedroom with all the nappies and little vests and chocolate biscuits. Then we had the stage of doing mince pies and tea every Sunday for an entire football team: but that's teenagers.

'When we gave up having au pairs altogether, when Crispin was eleven, we divided and priced all the household jobs under proper Union principles. I did ironing and the shopping. Tacy did the evening meal. Crispin did the stairs. They could withdraw for O-Levels, and the Union re-negotiated wages regularly. When I gave up the au pairs, our agency said, "You'll be back!" but we managed without because the children were so helpful.

'I remember the children nagged and nagged not to have school dinners, and I finally agreed that they could come home for lunch but they'd have to cook it themselves, so they did. Now I'm delighted that Crispin is domesticated when I see him and his girlfriend cooking together. I wasn't consciously raising him to be like that.'

In 1977 the Shores' third child, Piers, died of a heroin overdose at the age of twenty. The coroner recorded a verdict of drug addiction but the family belief is that he was not an addict, just terribly reckless. 'He had driven a car while under the influence, there was a court case coming up, and he had some girlfriend trouble, but he was living happily at home at the time. So I do believe that it can happen under your nose and you do not realise what is going on. We knew he was going around with a mixed-up crowd but if we had known then what we know now, I think we still wouldn't have known what to do about it.

'When you're unhappy, it comes in waves. You don't share unhappy thoughts because the other person might not be on that wave. If you're thinking about Piers, the last thing you do is talk about him. At the time, we talked for a week. We didn't go to work, the whole family was there including my son-in-law; after that we all went back to work and got back to family life. I remember stumping round Putney Common with Peter asking, "How did this happen?" For a while I had to talk about it the whole time.

'Peter has found it much more difficult to talk about until very recently. He once asked me, "What do you say when people ask how many children you've got?" and only lately has he started being able to say, "Do you remember when Piers was a baby . . . ?"

'I know grief can be destructive. You can't share grief the way you can share happiness. I know my daughter next to Piers in age has never spoken about him to her husband at all.

'When we remember Piers it's always with his father, because they had a special relationship. The rule we had was that Peter took charge of the next-to-youngest, the one who needed a fuss made of him because there was a new baby. Instead of feeling squeezed out, the next-to-youngest would be taken off to do things with Peter, and Piers was of course the last one to have this treatment, when Crispin came along.

'Peter was marvellous when the children were little. He used to cook and shop, and I remember seeing him reading a White Paper while feeding a baby with a bottle. He got de-skilled when he became a Cabinet Minister, and now he does expect me to get supper. I feel that women can always fit in several things at once and it's men who miss out on the rich variety of day to day life. Wherever you are going you can think: if I go that way I'll pass the butcher and pick up a chicken. In fact, for a time I took over everything at home: paying the rates, etc. Our marriage has *evolved*. When I needed it, Peter did everything; and when he was a Cabinet Minister, I did everything. Even now, I do most of the garden but I leave the trellis to him.'

When arranging to see Dr Shore, I discovered that she had an unbreakable rule. If Peter Shore is at home, she does not go out. If he is out anyway, then she allows herself to go out too. But this means she cannot organise her diary until he has filled his, usually one week in advance. This way all free evenings are shared.

'We do rattle a bit in such a big house. But there's usually someone staying even though all the children have gone.' (Both daughters are married and each has children; Crispin has completed a PhD and is at present working in Italy.) 'Just after Piers died it was a very disrupted period and we had them all staying with us again for a while. Occasionally still the lodger's flat is in use by one of them avoiding a bridging loan when moving house. But every time a room becomes vacant Peter fills it with bits of paper.'

Staying married is in Dr Shore's view a matter of inbuilt temperament. 'I married the sort of man who stays married. We've looked with increasing incredulity at friends whose marriages have broken down. I have seen a marriage destroyed by a single infidelity. I don't accept that you can be sexually unfaithful and stay married.

'We ask ourselves, how do we differ from other people? It's like when your son dies: you ask, why should your family differ from others? He wasn't emotionally deprived, he wasn't outclassed by other members of the family . . . Then you ask, why should I think I'm charmed? I've built my life on a rock that might be threatened, just like everyone else. We had a very bad patch of five years when Piers died and two daughters' marriages broke down, but that's in the past.'

Dr Shore says that when she applied for her present job she wasn't at all sure that she was a marketable commodity at the age of fifty-eight. 'You mustn't think I was still ambitious,' she said, 'I wasn't. I am working so that I will have a better pension in the long run. Ambition dies overnight when you have children. You don't stop being competitive though. And I don't think anything that's happened had anything to do with my working.

'I really only ever wanted to be a GP. My mother was élitist, and frowned on Second Class degrees. In her view it was the stupider members of the family who became doctors; in a fiercely academic family you were regarded as a failure if you didn't win a scholarship and get a First. Being the youngest, I determined to play it cool. I didn't want to be *top*. I wanted to learn something that would give me a skilled craft and a lifelong livelihood. And I spent nine years battling to get into general practice.

'Now I keep meeting young women who have waltzed into general practice and met no prejudice and no immovable objects. For those of my age group it really was a handicap to be a woman, especially a woman who was intent on having children. Yet I know that the patients enjoyed it when I brought the baby with me in the back of the car.

'My advice to women doctors would be they should never give up; they have shown they have the energy and the staying power. When it comes to promotion, it's the steady-as-you-go types who get there, those who are consistently reliable. If they can possibly work whole-time, they should. It looks better; they'll be consultants at thirty-seven instead of forty-seven. And they lose confidence in dealing with patients otherwise. So many people destroy their careers by emotional inadequacy. In medicine, a lot of your work is based on your own personal experience, helping people to run their lives. Running a house isn't all that difficult nowadays; there are devices for not being there and the house goes on running. It does work; it can be done. I never took a day off for the children. If I was late I'd say it was the car. Always give the man's excuse, never the woman's excuse.'

The Shores play a lot of tennis (the previous week, Dr Shore had beaten her husband 7–5 6–2 when he was exhausted after a long day in the House) and one of their hobbies is 'swimming in rough seas' (*Who's Who*). They have a flat in St Ives near a surfing beach and their holidays consist of fanatical surfing six times a day which is Dr Shore's idea of a great time. 'We tried camping once,' she says, 'and gave up after one night.'

'Life is full of variety,' she says, 'and always interesting. You bring up your children and let them try all sorts of things, as long as they are sucking life to the full. Years of swimming, a house full of pets, and music lessons which they hated.

'What I like now is getting home a bit earlier. I might have time now to master the Magimix; I've never had time to read the booklet yet. When Peter ceases to be an MP, and I stop doing this, I'd like us to live somewhere like Chichester or High Wycombe. Then I'll be totally domesticated, and spend my time cooking, gardening and having the grandchildren around.'

Barbara Mills, QC

barrister

b. 1940

m. 1962

JOHN MILLS

businessman and
city development consultant

3 daughters, 1 son

SARAH CAROLINE LIZZIE PETER

Barbara Mills, Q C

Women in the legal world who have large families are extremely rare. There are one or two women judges who do have children, but as judges they are not permitted to be interviewed. Mrs Barbara Mills is a successful barrister who in 1986 became a Queen's Counsel. (Out of fifty new silks, only five were women.)

Like Mrs Thatcher, Barbara Mills sat for her Bar exams in the same year as having her first baby. But Mrs Thatcher, having had her twins, went back to work and sent her children away to school. Barbara Mills pursued a more exacting course. She went on to have three more children – all four attending the local state schools – and never relinquished her legal career. The law is particularly demanding; few women intending to be mothers even attempt it. The court sits at 10 am and the days can be long. No concessions are made to the mothers of small children.

I interviewed Barbara Mills at her home in Camden Town, north London. She lives in a long street once described to me by the socialist and CND pioneer, the late Peggy Duff (who also lived there) as the street nearest central London with a real social mixture of people, because it contains gentrified Georgian terraces (like the Mills' house), council dwellings, and private lodgings.

On each occasion I visited her, Mrs Mills was in the middle of long, difficult cases in court (as I knew from reading the newspapers) but there she was at home in the evening, with domestic life shipshape. Her great skill, she says, is organisation. Her husband is the former Labour leader of Camden Council, and – not to distinguish him from the other John Mills, but just because she prefers the name – she calls him by his middle name, Angus.

Barbara Mills (née Warnock, but no relation to Mary) was a bright, academic child at St Helen's School, Northwood, Middlesex, an independent school. She won a place at Lady Margaret Hall, Oxford, to read Law and while there won the Gibbs Scholarship, the major law scholarship, and was made a college scholar too.

Her parents had separated when she was about twelve, and after that her father played no particular role in her life. She was the elder of two daughters, and her sister went to London University as their mother had done.

'My mother has always been very proud of us, and helpful when we've been on our knees – "Can we send the children to you this weekend?" – but going to Oxford and then becoming a lawyer was an independent decision on my part. My mother was very much of the generation who did not work after marriage; she was always there.

'At Oxford I met Angus. He was doing PPE at Merton, but he was older than me, being one of the last post-National Service intake. We got engaged as undergraduates, but we were a rather unpromising combination with no visible means of support. What actually happened was very tightly timed. The day fixed for our wedding was the same day as my viva. I got a Second; I'm not First material. My talents are more organisational than those of the gifted academic.

'I had a very gruelling interview with the Principal of Lady Margaret Hall when I told her I wasn't going on to do a Bachelor of Civil Law; they didn't envisage people having *careers*.

'We married on 28th July 1962 and I was pregnant by the end of September with my Bar exams still to do. And then I had the prospect of my pupillage. So feeling sick as a cat and trying to establish myself in our small flat, I then found that I'd selected all the wrong papers at university and I was quite unprepared for the Bar exams, but somehow I scrambled together and in the end I did my exams on 15th May and had the baby on 8th June. So I was called to the Bar with Angus clutching the baby outside.

'Then I found out what a problem I had: no visible means of support, small baby, nobody will take me seriously. Angus was setting up his own business. So I did part-time lecturing and in the meantime had our second daughter, Caroline. Once you have one baby you might as well have a second. My husband is from a large, close-knit family with 100 second cousins, and he always said he wanted us to have six children. So with two children under two I started my pupillage, two years behind my contemporaries who were soaring ahead. How we managed was by buying this house as a wreck, the year after we married. We lived in the basement and ground floor and let the top two floors. As our finances gradually got better we moved upstairs and even built an extra storey. And when I started my pupillage, we got a nanny in.

'But how it really worked was this. The Morris family next door had six children, and they ran a nursery school in their basement. Well, my nanny didn't seem over-employed so we said why don't we take the Morris nursery on, as it was about to close. We got a Camden Council licence – we were very strictly inspected – and it grew to a class of 24 and took up the whole basement. We always employed nursery nurses as nannies, because getting that NNEB certificate proved they had gumption, you knew they could stay the course. You must have a nanny who can change a wheel and mend a washing machine, someone with practical brains. We also employed a cook in the nursery for the lunches, and a daily cleaner every day. The nursery never really paid its way, but it was almost self-financing while I wasn't earning, as a pupil-barrister, and it took an enormous load off us. All our children started life in our nursery. It folded when Peter, our youngest, started school, and then somebody else took it on.

'When I was pregnant with Peter I had quite attuned my mind to having four girls; they would be *The Mills Girls*. I think youngest sons in female families tend to be spoiled, or just a bit different.' (At this point Peter, then aged thirteen, came into the room. 'I'm going to make another cake. Do we have any cocoa?' he asked. 'I haven't the faintest idea.' 'We're out of eggs.' 'I have some at my chambers.' Peter then roller-skated off into the night to buy eggs.)

'We had four children in eight years and I would have gone on, because Angus likes children so much, but honestly we could not face the sleepless nights any longer. For ten years there was not one unbroken night. The law is harder than almost anything else to combine with being a mother because you simply have to be there, at the Old Bailey at 10 am with your head screwed on to your shoulders and quite unemotional, and if your child is being operated on that day that is just hard luck.

'At the same time it is easier because you switch right out of home gear. You just don't think about it. You leave it all behind from nine to 6.30, and lead a completely separate kind of life. In a way it is easier than trying to work at the kitchen table. If I were here, I would know that someone would expect me to deal with problems.

'We had altogether five nannies, if you count the one who lasted only three weeks because she kept saying "That's not my job." It's impractical to have people around who say, "That's not my job." They all had every weekend off, and use of car.

'The nanny and I never overlapped. When I got back I picked up the reins. She never worked in the house when I was there: her rules and mine were not the same, and could not be. I would have none of the "But Elizabeth lets me do that . . ." business from the children. No playing one off against the other.

'At weekends we used to split our duties. Angus took Saturday afternoon and Sunday afternoon, and I did the mornings. It worked awfully well. It meant if you felt dead beat you could go to bed without feeling guilty and no hard feelings. I'd go flopping into bed and he'd take them off to the park or Bethnal Green Museum of Childhood; we saw a lot of that place over the years. My husband's pretty hard to beat but sometimes he had to be galvanised. His idea of a wet winter afternoon activity sometimes was to sit and read *The Economist* and clear up the mess afterwards. But every third weekend we'd take off to my mother-in-law's. She has thirteen grandchildren whom she never tires of seeing, and a large house where the whole family converges all the time. She is a splendid person who would always take the children if we were a bit distrait.'

Was she ever in any doubt about not staying at home herself? 'I wish that I were a different kind of person, in the sense that I know I would not myself be happy at home looking after children. And I don't think the children would have liked it either. But it would be nice, I think, to *be* that sort of person.

'The fact that my husband was at home made quite a difference. I rarely get home before seven, and it's nice to know he's here. And the fact that he was running a business downstairs' – years ago he started an import–export company which he still runs there today – 'meant that there were always a number of people around who would rally round in a crisis. This was always very reassuring, if you leave home for the day.

'I also have a genuine daily who comes in every day from 8.45 to 11.45 and lives opposite. She's as honest as the day is long and she's been doing it for ten years and that makes a huge difference to life. She also cleans downstairs, which is my study by night and Angus's office by day.

'I certainly felt that the number of children I had were not of much assistance at the Bar. I would emphasise the real physical strain it puts on you. I liked the idea of having six children – because, as a working mother, I wanted them to be company for each other – but when I'd had four by the age of thirty-one, I did not feel physically capable of going on. I stopped from exhaustion.

'Mine is a ladder career, and you lose such ground by taking time off. Fortunately I had three of my four children in May or June, so I could go off from April to September. This fitted in neatly with Bar terms.

'It is all a juggling act, and it depends on energy and good health. I have twice overworked and been laid up as a result of not going to bed. A barrister is allowed to be ill between 4 pm on Friday and 10 am on Monday, but I had viral pneumonia and then drove myself and everybody mad having bed rest. I'm not a Margaret Thatcher: in the normal course of events I find lack of sleep very debilitating.

'When we had all four of them at home we seldom got up before eight in the morning and there was a mad scramble to get everyone ready with their lost plimsolls and their sudden announcements that it was the school play tomorrow. Fortunately they didn't have far to go to the local state schools, Primrose Hill primary school and Haverstock Comprehensive.

'This house had proved wonderfully flexible. You would never know there was a business going on downstairs and I always look forward to coming back to it: there is so much going on. I would hate to come back to an empty house.'

The second time I visited the Millses I was again struck by the cosiness and extreme tidiness of the house, a peaceful centre in two busy lives. Barbara Mills had been in court all day and was making a casserole in a le Creuset pot. The telephone rang and rang; there had just been a controversial programme on television about Docklands in which John Mills had taken part. The family was absent, but two of the children were at their hospitable grandmother's and the Millses were about to dine with John's brother.

'I do think if you're contemplating my kind of life you need a husband who positively wants you to do it. Not just a man who doesn't mind it, but one who can take the rough side of it, helping you if you're tired after a rugged day, or if you have to have a very heavy evening at short notice. The sort of husband who is genuinely prepared to shoulder domestic burdens.

'We have our carefully demarcated duties. I cook and John doesn't and I'm glad because I couldn't stand to have him in the kitchen. But I don't expect to have to deal with the drink. Money, drink and the rubbish are his concerns, that is how it has worked out, and everything to do with food and school are mine. Each expects the other to be completely competent: he sees to it that we never run out of drink, and I don't expect ever to be unable to create a meal. I am pretty efficient. It would grate on me not to be able to run an efficient household. If we ran out of loo paper I'd never hear the end of it.

'We lead very separate lives. John became a councillor of Camden Council on the day Peter was born, in 1971, and that involved a lot of evenings and committee work. My life is non-political and it has to be, and I don't pretend I never groused about his political work. I have very seldom heard him make a political speech and I think he has only been in court on three occasions when I've been there. It's not lack of interest, it is just a matter of having separate interests and separate hobbies. I have a whole range of friends whom he doesn't even know, and he has the same. In fact our lives are so divided that sometimes we get to know the same people independently of one another, and they never realise that we are married to each other. We converge only domestically. For twelve solid years after our marriage, I had small babies around. Then there is tennis: I play every weekend, with friends he doesn't even know, and he flies aeroplanes. We do go to the cinema together a lot, and we join in the splendid big family gatherings and we get on very well together. But he doesn't play tennis, and I have come to realise that it is vitally important to have a bit of time to myself completely outside the three lives of barrister, wife and mother. For me, it is tennis.'

The Millses do share their rather dramatic holidays. John Mills had been in the Fleet Air Arm and the RAFVR and acquired a commercial pilot's licence, so he could rent planes and fly the family to the Caribbean, South America, North Africa. Barbara Mills would organise itinerary, maps, hotels, visits to friends en route; John Mills, as leader of Camden Council, would use the trips for political purposes, observing different types of régime (Cuba, Jamaica, Grenada, Puerto Rico, Haiti) looking at inner city regeneration and urban policies. So the family flew over Angel Falls in Venezuela – twice the height of the Empire State Building, and only otherwise accessible from a base-camp two weeks' trek away. They reckon it worked out cheaper than six commercial air fares to such distant places. John Mills says Barbara is just the sort of woman you would go into the jungle with. 'And I have,' he said. 'She is an extremely well organised woman.'

I asked each of them what the essential facts were in the working out of their lives. Both replied (on separate occasions) with numbered lists. She said:

'1. A husband who expects and wants you to work.

'2. Enormous good health: your first obligation is to keep going in your job.

'3. Enough money to live in relative comfort. You need two cars. You need, if given a sudden day to spare, to be able to buy all the clothes you'll need for six months, that free day. We struggled our way up to this point, but it would be exceptionally difficult even to contemplate it if you were never going to earn more than £100 a week, however hard you worked.'

He said:

'1. My wife is such a good organiser. Hence the arrangement with the nanny running a nursery school in our house.

'2. Barbara is much nicer to live with when occupied than when under-stretched. It was always clear that Barbara would have a career. My own mother must have been one of the last of the generation who were highly qualified – she read Chemistry at Oxford in the 1930s – but then had a family and never earned a penny in her life.

'3. Two incomes are better than one.'

'We've hardly ever spent a night away from each other in twenty-four years,' says Barbara, 'but when he went away for ten days recently I was very dreary and rattled around the house. I don't think we have changed much in character since we first married; only our eccentricities have become more so. We are, I should add, *very* fond of each other.

'Most marriages hit the buffers when they see too much of each other, or one of them gets boring because they haven't enough to do or one has too much to do so they feel hard done by; that's a very destructive feeling. Suspecting that one is taking more than a fair share is a feeling that must be kept out of a marriage. When you're both working very hard – and Angus is a compulsive worker too – the risk is that family life consists of friction rather than relaxation. What we've found works for us – and perhaps *finding what works for you* is the ultimate factor – is that we make time for each other every evening, but not till late, 10 or 11 o'clock. Before that, he'll pack up at 7.30 and pop in and say, "What ho, have a drink," and then he works on while I prepare some sort of meal, and if I'm working I rush through it and then we sit down to dinner at

10.30 or so. It's a very nice relaxing time. And we're very careful about not boring each other about our work.

'Every Sunday night we have a session with our diaries and sort out the coming week's timetable. The week starts, for us, at 7.30 on Sunday evening, and I am the original Filofax woman, even though my working life is quite unpredictable: if a jury is out, one does not know if they will return today; I may suddenly have to go to the Court of Appeal tomorrow.

'The week finishes with predictable regularity at 7.30 on a Friday evening when I get home. We used to have family supper on Friday nights, which was very cosy and successful for about two years but then it started to be "I'm going to a party, Mum, do I have to come?" Now that Sarah is moving out and Caroline's away at Bristol University, that discipline is beginning to break down and Sunday lunch is more the focus. It may all sound frightfully over-organised but it's worked for us.

'I've found that though my work load has got consistently heavier, life itself has seemed to get easier. Four small children were more demanding than anything, and if you've spent fourteen years never actually having one uninterrupted night it is bliss when it stops.

'Our profession is very fair. If you are working level with a man, you get paid level. If you can get the work, you get paid the money. And there are so few women in the law that women get noticed: you can't just sink back, you do stick in people's minds.

'I meet dozens of girls who want to become barristers. I start with a bucket of cold water. If you don't want to do this *passionately*, stop now, because there are many heartbreaks ahead. You must know with a deep certainty that if you didn't do it by sixty you would feel you had failed. And girls may not appreciate the problems of combining it with marriage and children. But if you are *absolutely determined*, you have to be prepared to watch men you know aren't as good as you, getting further ahead. And then there are financial problems at first, and emotional, mental, and physical problems. You have to be tough in the broadest sense to do it.

'I think I am harder on the women in my profession than on the men, simply because I know what it all means and if they aren't tough they won't survive. It has never crossed my daughters' minds that they won't work for a living. I do feel a bit guilty that they might think they've taken second place, but I've talked to them and said, "Have I made you feel in second place?" and they said, "No," and I think they mean it. Would they have liked a different upbringing? They don't say so, and when I hear about other families' problems and I reflect that we have had, as yet, no drugs, no drink problems, not even a smoker among them, I realise we're very lucky. I did always tell them that because of my position, if they ever did get into trouble there'd be a hell of a ballyhoo, but they've had a lot of freedom about going out, always leaving a phone number, and they've all been very independent. It might be a bit oppressive to have a successful and well-known parent. But the only rules we have made is that, one, they do something; and, two, they do something that fulfils their talents. If you don't cling to them, you don't alienate them. They all still want to come on holidays with us.

'A large family makes life more interesting; they are as different as can be, and they team up in different ways. I do know I would have found it very difficult to cope with a handicapped child and a profession. So we've been lucky. They have had their ups and downs but they're all well adjusted, in rude good health and have plenty of friends.

'I still have one or two unfulfilled ambitions. I'm a historian manquée, and I have thought of trying to write a legal history book. So many things are taken for granted in the English legal system; the right of silence, trial by jury, etc. I should like to take the six or eight most important things and tell how they became part of the system.

'I don't want the pace to slacken off at all. I don't think I shall ever retire. I can't see myself in the granny role. Those who have a lot to do, do an awful lot.

'Nobody has ever been able to say of me that I could not do something because of my children. I have made it my business to put in 105 per cent of effort in this respect; you cannot fail to turn up in court because your child's not well. You can't bring a trial to a halt. I've hacked out an unusual role, because there are not that many women at the Bar with children. I think I may have contributed to a change in attitude; I hope I have. It cannot be said, any more, that a woman will be needing time off for her children.'

Anne Blythe Munro

journalist

b. 1905

m. 1938

NEIL MUNRO

journalist

4 daughters (2 sons by previous marriage)

AILSA BLYTHE ALISON MARSAILI

Anne Blythe Munro

'I'm probably the oldest journalist you'll meet,' said Anne Blythe Munro, 'because I was eighty last week.' She is lively and spry, and hardly draws breath, talking in rapid-fire Scots, always with a very proper concern for the economics of life. 'This house,' she said immediately as we went into the sitting room of her Hampshire home, 'was bought entirely from the proceeds of freelance journalism. This five-acre field cost £500, and we built the house for £4500; even our dearest friends hate us for it.' A photograph on the table showed her ('probably in a skirt made out of furnishing fabric') with her bicycle and her four daughters in the late 1940s.

Anne Munro left school in Glasgow at the age of sixteen at the height of the Depression on Clydeside and had to find her own way into journalism and her tenacious approach to her work continued through forty-eight years of marriage. She told me how she was to be found sitting up in her hospital bed typing, hours after having a baby: 'What's this?' cried the ward sister. She was writing a short story for *The Lady* about having a baby. The children, she said, were both a source of copy and her great escape from one world into another. She described to me how she juggled her double life and made the emphatic point: 'It is no use grumbling. You just have to get on with your life: you selected it! Nobody made you have all those children *and* agree to do that job! So you're an awful fool if you take on work you can't cope with.' When working at home she would shut herself in a hut in the garden and trained the children to understand that if she were a doctor, and seeing patients in her surgery, they couldn't come in and say, where's my red socks, could they?

While we talked, Anne's husband Neil was in the next room listening to one of the Talking Books for the Blind. He was a tall, handsome, courteous and gentle man, who had supported her to an exceptional degree all her working life, even looking after the family at home while she worked during the week in London. The next time I spoke to Anne – a few months had elapsed – Neil had died, after a short illness, at the age of eighty-five. At first she hesitated to remain in this book. Then she wrote: 'My objections have faded because he would have laughed at the very idea. And I don't feel like dying at the moment.'

2❧

'I was the eldest of four,' says Anne Munro, 'in a very typical Scottish family where the boys had careers but the girls had nice ladylike jobs, but only until they married. To talk about being a writer was considered rather fanciful. I'm sure my parents hoped that I'd soon grow out of it.'

Anne was living in the Glasgow suburbs and at a fee-paying school working for her Highers (the Scottish equivalent of A-Levels) when the engineering company where her father was manager closed down. So her father was unemployed. 'There was no unemployment benefit for managers, and when the savings were exhausted and the silver sold off, it was time for anyone who *could* get a job to take it. I got the offer of one, as office girl and junior cost clerk, in a local motor works; the company secretary was a friend of my father. Salary nine shillings a week! It was a terrible comedown after being at the high school. Costing time-cards – awful! There was I, tall and slim and smart and making dresses out of old suits, and my passion was turning things into words. But I hadn't even a typewriter.

'Then this secretary man had a problem; he had to write out the minutes of the monthly board meetings in a huge minute book and his handwriting was poor. So I was asked to do it for him. They gave me a small office *with a typewriter* and a drawer full of paper, two days a month.

'So two evenings a week, on the Albion Motor Company's typewriter, my ideas turned themselves into bright newspaper and magazine articles on "How to make an evening dress out of Granny's shawl" or "How to keep a husband's love." I posted them off on the way home and of course some of them came back, but not all of them. I studied my markets at the public library, discovered the Writers' and Artists' Year Book, and found my way into the local newspapers, the women's magazines and the trade journals.

'I did this stolidly for more than two years until I was able to buy my own second-hand typewriter for £6 and I doubt if anyone on that firm ever suspected me.

'When I reached the stage when I was earning 23 shillings a week as a junior typist and around £2 10s as a spare-time journalist, my parents agreed that this writing business was worth a chance. So I wrote a nice little letter of resignation.

'"What folly is this?" protested my boss. "A precarious thing like journalism when she could have a nice steady job at 25 shillings a week until she marries!" My mother said that perhaps I could have a more interesting career as a journalist. "*Career?* But she's pretty enough to marry!"

'Up until then I had never met another journalist. But within a month of starting to work at home I had a letter from one, Mrs Marianne Hunter, Women's Page Editor of a Glasgow evening newspaper to whom I had sent an article. She asked me to call at her house and over tea asked me to write a regular weekly feature, "Corner for Girls", at 15 shillings a time. It was just what I needed and I was actually working on it next day when the news came over the local radio – the old cat's whisker set – that Mrs Hunter of the *Glasgow Evening News* had suddenly died.

'I didn't know what to do. But I put on my best coat and hat, found my way to the *Evening News* office, and knowing no better, asked to see the editor. And there was this good-looking, grey-haired man and a colleague, standing in considerable dismay. What I didn't realise was that these two men, having lost their Women's Page Editor, were left with a great gaping hole on page 2. When I appeared, and said I was the journalist engaged by Mrs Hunter to write regular features, they fell on me. They said, "Can you write?" I said, "Yes" and flourished my fistful of cuttings. And before I quite realised it I was on the staff of the *Glasgow Evening News* at 7 *guineas* a week – and had met my future father-in-law. That good-looking, elderly editor-in-chief was the Scottish author Neil Munro, Neil's father. Actually, I didn't meet the younger Neil until some years later; he had already moved to London where he was picture editor on the Northcliffe provincial press.'

For the next few years Anne Blythe, as she was then, did every female job on that Glasgow paper: edited the women's pages and the Saturday Supplement, the gossip columns, and wrote three signed features a week. She learned to write fast, straight on to the typewriter. She was at Glamis as a reporter when Princess Margaret was born.

Her name, Anne Blythe, made such a good by-line everyone assumed she'd made it up. 'The film star invented it,' she says. 'It was *my* own name.'

In her early twenties she married a journalist on a Glasgow morning paper, but kept on her job and her name until their two sons were born. 'Then it was back to freelance writing, and luckily too, because when that marriage ended I was financially independent and able to earn my own living from almost any point on the map.' They were divorced, and the Scottish court appointed tutors-at-law to be responsible for the sons, one of whom was Anne's father. 'After the boys went to school in Scotland, I moved to London and made contact with old Glasgow colleagues who had reached Fleet Street. One of them was Neil Munro.

'We were married in September 1938, and as we were both freelances and war was looming, we came down to Hampshire looking for a cheap place to live. We found a cottage for £40 a year, furnished it with oddments from our families and began bashing away on our two typewriters. It was an awful gamble. Neither of us had a regular income and until the month's cheques came in, we could be very hard-up indeed. But we kept at it and the children arrived; Ailsa in 1939, Blythe in 1941, Alison in 1943 and Marsaili in 1944. Neil went off to a war job in Dorset but came home at weekends. We managed some trips to Scotland for holidays to see the boys, but for most of the war we were stuck in that tiny cottage with hardly room to swing a cat, far less for a mother with a red-hot typewriter.

'People used to say, "What are you two, Catholic or careless?" But I was already thirty-three when I married Neil, and when you want a family at that age you have it quickly. It didn't matter to either of us that they were all girls. To Neil and me they were all beautiful and great fun and an endless source of copy. I was a regular contributor to *Mother* magazine and did radio broadcasts on "Having a baby in Wartime" on the old Kitchen Front programmes.'

In the early years there was usually a young girl from the village who could come in to help with the nappy-washing and the pram-pushing. 'But I always felt that so long as the children were well-fed, warm and clean before they went to bed, and so long as I could walk across the room without breaking my neck, I was winning. "Keep the centre of the floor clear" is still my recipe for family sanity.'

While the children were still young enough to go to bed early Anne Munro turned to writing romantic serials for the women's magazines. 'It proved to be much easier than the factual argumentative articles I was doing, and the method of payment was marvellous. You get paid as you write. The cheque comes in for instalment one on Friday and that's the carrot. You press on with instalment four. I got to the point when I was writing two instalments a week, of different serials. One heroine was married and one single. Another time *Woman's Weekly* started publishing one of my serials when I hadn't yet written the ending. It was very lucrative but nerve-racking.

'To ease the space problem we got the local builder to put up a beach hut affair in the garden for £40 and here I bashed out my romantic fiction and kept all my clutter. I could shut the door on it and the children were not allowed to come in. I was writing for the women's magazines under several different names: Anne Blythe in *Housewife*, Linda Charles in *Everywoman*, Alison Keith in *Mother*, Anne Galloway in *Good Housekeeping* and Blythe Munro in *Woman's World*. Neil could never remember which was which.

'With so many magazines for women and so few for men it was inevitable that a woman writer should earn more than a man writer, and we accepted that as a fact of the market. But other people didn't see it like that. The local bank manager was very impressed by my earnings when we talked to him about buying or building a new house. But he insisted that any loan or mortgage must be in our *joint* names because in law Neil was liable for my debts and my income tax. The same crazy rule applied when I tried to open an account at John Lewis', and when I had my fallopian tubes tied. In each case they had to have *his* signature first. Body and bank balance, a married woman still belonged to her husband.

'Among family and neighbours, especially other mothers I met at the girls' school, there was also the suggestion that being a working mother wasn't quite *nice*. Obviously I must neglect my children and they were very sorry for my poor husband.'

When Anne was approaching forty-five and the four girls were at a day school in New Milton, she had an offer of a part-time job as Home Editor of the monthly magazine *Everywoman*, with a very good salary and all expenses paid. Neil was already working with a London publishing house from Monday to Friday and living very uncomfortably and expensively in lodgings.

'We knew it was a chance I shouldn't miss. Romantic fiction was beginning to bore me. We thought about moving the whole family to the London area, but house prices were appalling and we in the rented cottage had nothing to sell.

'Just then we had another lucky break. A five acre field on the edge of the village suddenly came on the market because the farmer who had planning permission to build a house there couldn't get a housing licence. In those post-war years a licence was given only to those in *need* of housing; planning permission was merely the environmental side of it. We had the need all right; the cottage was almost criminally over-crowded. The children had started drawing on their bedroom wall and they'd reached the ceiling. So we bought the field for £500 and were able to build a four-bedroom house for £4500. It took almost a year to build, and during that time I took the *Everywoman* offer, and Neil left his publishing job and took over the garden. The land had been registered as a smallholding, so he invested in poultry, sowed the field with grain, and became – in a small way – a farmer. His kitchen garden fed us luxuriously for years, and when my work kept me away overnight from Tuesday to Thursday, he took over the household as well.'

With the aid of a couple of small legacies and some royalties, the Munros paid off the mortgage. But it was an unusual ménage for the 1950s; Anne, who seemed to have candid friends, says she was often asked if she didn't think it wrong to sacrifice her husband's career for her glamorous job in London.

She travelled to London every week in a first-class compartment regularly shared with Lord Mountbatten or J. B. Priestley. Edmund de Rothschild once gave her a Stock Exchange tip, and Mountbatten would be doing his homework on the South East Asia Command. Anne wrote a paragraph in *Everywoman* about a moth-hole in his sock: 'So levelling, a moth-hole in a famous sock.' She stayed overnight at the Cowdray Club, lunched at the Savoy or the Dorchester. She had exciting trips abroad – to America (tea with Mrs Nixon at the White House), to Paris for a press show. But at the office her work consisted of unglamorous skills: organising colour photography and room settings, subbing copy, forward planning; as well as checking facts and keeping deadlines, the two laws which rule a journalist's life. 'I made sure the children didn't imagine that their mother had a *glamorous* job.

'I lived a kind of double life. From Thursday evening to Tuesday morning I was a country housewife, washing, mending, and cooking meals with occasional dashes into my hut (we brought it with us from the cottage) to finish off a romantic instalment. Then up with the lark on Tuesday, into my London suit and off on my bicycle to the station while Neil got the girls breakfasted and off to school. Once in town I worked quite long hours, but with my free evenings I could take on the late appointments for colleagues who had to get home to their families. If you haven't got to think about cooking meals and getting children to bed, you can get an awful lot more done. I became chairman of the Women's Press Club of London, and served on the council of the Cowdray Club. Then I was appointed to represent other women journalists on a quango, the Metrication Board Committee. With my Scots blood I remember asking the necessary question "Why are we paying for this?" when they wanted to produce special leaflets for everyone.'

When *Everywoman* folded in 1966, Anne's contract was transferred to *Woman* where she was furnishing editor until she retired ten years later: meanwhile domestic life under Neil's supervision continued efficiently. 'At home Neil was very happy working out of doors. And for the girls coming home from school it meant there was always a parent to provide food and help with homework. At weekends all the family helped to clean the eggs ready for the packing station van, and if I rang to say I couldn't get home until Friday, nobody complained.

'One of the advantages of being married to a journalist is that he understands the demands of the job. He knows that a deadline is a deadline, and you get down to it – all night long, if necessary. Many a time when I have been out in my hut struggling to get the opening line, Neil has come across the garden with one or two typed suggestions – "Just to see what a fresh mind can do." But beyond that he never interfered or criticised, and although he read most of my articles and listened to my broadcasts, I know he never read a word of my romantic fiction. And I preferred it that way.

'The great snag about journalism is that it *looks* so easy from the outside. Everybody can write and the tools of the trade are in every household. Every writer has been irritated by the acquaintance, usually a woman, who says, "That's the sort of job I'd like to do if I had time" – as if time was the only requirement. But unless you can write *well* and can do it on any subject at short notice, you fail. You must set yourself high standards and stick to them; it's reliability and tenacity that brings in the cheques. You also need cast-iron health, and a large handbag.'

All the Munro girls did well at their day school, Fern Hill Manor. 'We had years of rationing and years of frugality, passing on the Camel Hair Coat and the Party Petticoat. And by the time the last one was out of nappies, the eldest had pictures of pop stars all over the wall.

'They tell me now,' Anne says, 'that they had a particularly happy childhood, with slightly eccentric parents but a specially good father. They remember him producing strawberries when their school friends came to tea and cooking giant omelettes if a boyfriend stayed to supper. Their mother's weekly trips to London seem to have left no impression at all. Compared to other families they considered that Neil and I were "happier than most", and we didn't give them any trouble.'

Of Anne's six children only one has become a journalist. Her elder son, now Professor of Education at Glasgow University, has written a couple of scholarly books, and the younger became a graphic artist. Ailsa went to university, Blythe into nursing, and Alison after a spell on *Woman* and the *Sunday Times* is now director of a Public Relations company. Marsaili was a secretary in PR. They all married in their twenties, and although scattered across the world, they come home in droves to the house in Hampshire. 'What is fascinating to us is that of these six young families, five of the wives have careers of their own – and nobody thinks it odd.'

She misses office life. 'I miss the conversation and the other women. Of course there is always the company of Women's Institute women, and shopwomen, but I mean intelligent women. I miss the perks of office life, having Robina or whatever her name was saying "You've got five minutes to powder your nose, Mrs Munro, the taxi's on its way." I still hurtle around the village on my bike, but I do miss the opportunity to move around to other places. And I did always enjoy having money of my own. I couldn't imagine not earning my own living.'

One of her last working trips abroad was to a conference on women in Washington. 'Here I discovered the importance of semantics. The delegate from the Philippines said: "My country will accept the diaphragm and the condom and the rhythm method, but not Birth Control." What did she mean? It turned out that they had always equated Birth Control with Abortion. So you see, we should never say "Birth Control" when we mean Conception Control, or Family Planning. It's the "Birth" in *Birth Control* that is so emotive to the anti-abortionists.'

Neil Munro told me that their children and ten grandchildren were his chief pleasure in life. At eighty-five he was still handsome and elegant, but almost blind. When I arrived, he was listening to the tape of James Cameron's autobiography *Points of Departure*. After his years as a writer and publisher, it hit Neil particularly hard to be unable to read; nor could he do the garden himself any more. 'One of the points about our marriage,' he told me, 'is that my wife is a complete extrovert and I'm entirely introvert. She has enjoyed going out and meeting people and I've been perfectly happy staying at home and growing things. I think we have been very lucky in lots of ways, and I'm glad our daughters have inherited bits of both of us.'

Her one regret, Anne Munro said, is that she has never painted a good picture (she did all the drawings for her book on soft furnishings) nor written a really good novel. 'They were all such potboilers, my books, written purely for the money to keep the family and pay for the central heating, the motor plough, the second bathroom. Maybe they gave pleasure to somebody, but we laugh now when the girls hide them at the back of their bookshelves.'

Pramila Le Hunte
teacher and former Parliamentary candidate

b. 1938

m. 1959
BILL LE HUNTE
marketing planning executive, IBM

3 daughters, 1 son
ARJUN ANJALI ASHIKA ABHA

Pramila Le Hunte

Pramila Le Hunte was selected by the Tories for the Labour-held constituency of Birmingham Ladywood in 1983: it seemed a good idea to have an Indian-born, bi-lingual and bi-cultural candidate. She lost – but she has not ceased to apply for seats. She has always been fiercely ambitious.

When we first met she was head of the English department at North London Collegiate, the London girls' school, but she was also active in borough affairs in Richmond, Surrey, and directed the local Shakespeare Society's productions. She was constantly flinging her energy into other challenges like sailing, microlite flying, and film-making.

The first time I saw her she was still teaching, while beginning to fight her parliamentary seat. The second time, we met in the National Theatre café: she had been ill, and her marriage was plainly not very ideal, but she was continuing to rehearse two plays at Richmond (one political drama, one Ayckbourn) and she wanted to emphasise the tremendous battles she had had to fight to get selected as a political candidate and to reach a senior position at her school. No other woman I interviewed ever had to contend with the question of race.

The week the first edition of this book came out, I heard that Pramila Le Hunte's marriage had ended, and later that she had lost her job teaching English. The next time we met, it was clear that she had had an embattled year, 'a De Profundis year', she called it. She had been a member of Sir John Kingman's Committee of Inquiry into the teaching of English, which reported in April 1988. This had been a fascinating and fulfilling experience. But at fifty she has to face life without a husband, her family grown up. It is a dilemma that faces many women, so I have kept her story in this book.

Pramila Le Hunte was the only child of an engineer father from the Punjab: he was an Anglophile and a graduate of Bristol University. She was brought up in Bihar and Orissa, north-east India, a beautiful jungly area where there was no school. Her mother, herself a graduate, taught Pramila until she was nine and could go to school in Delhi.

'My mother was basically a clever girl who had read Philosophy and Politics, and found herself stuck in remote places with her only daughter and the servants, while her husband was away on business; so I had her undivided attention. I was not an easy child to teach and she was very strict with me. I remember gruelling grammar lessons, and the maxim that you cannot do anything until you have done your work. I learned about self-discipline fast. She brought a master in to coach me in Maths, and I suppose sensing the political changes about to happen in the 1940s, she got me a Hindi master too so I would have a good working command of Hindi.

'We moved to Calcutta and I got my English degree there by the age of seventeen. But long before I had left school I had fixed my mind on going to Cambridge: I went to the British Council library and wrote away for information myself. Eventually, my father supported my decision at the crucial moment, but by and large it was all in the teeth of opposition. They didn't want me to go away from India. But I longed to sit at the feet of Leavis and C. S. Lewis and E. M. Tillyard.

'My mother did want me to get a degree, in India, and I suppose she would have liked me to become a doctor or a lawyer, but she would have then fixed a match for me and I would have married and had a part-time job perhaps, but I would have stayed near her. It was my father who stepped in to support me. When Cambridge came up he said all right, take the exams and if you get in I'll help you. So I took them and got in to Girton. That very year, the foreign exchange regulations came in and then my father really had to move quickly to release the money to pay my fees. He made strenuous efforts for me.'

She flung herself with typical industry into university life, playing in the table tennis team, sailing, rambling, reviving a defunct debating society called the Girton Cabbages, helping to run the Indian Society and the UN association. She joined not one but several religious societies, just to find out about religion in England. She also met her English husband, Bill (Le Hunte is an old Essex name) in her first year. He was reading English at Christ's College. It was hell, she says, facing the strong opposition from her parents and his mother, to the idea that they should marry.

But they married while still at Cambridge, finished their degrees and after the first baby, Arjun, was born, flew to India where Bill had a job with IBM in Bombay, in marketing. In India the next three children, Anjali and Ashika the twins, and Abha (all girls) were born. Pramila worked for J. Walter Thompson as an advertising copywriter. 'I wasn't going to give up work until the day before the second baby was due, but the birth was six weeks premature and turned out to be twins. I'd flown over to Calcutta to see my mother and she said, "Come and see my doctor. Just to put my mind at rest," so I did, and that doctor discovered the twins. I remember Bill meeting me at the airport, and breaking the news to him. Then we had the fourth one just two and a half years later – which meant we had four children under the age of four. That was hilarious. But you mustn't forget, you get domestic help in India. It means you can enjoy the babies more, because the time you have to spare you aren't washing nappies.'

At this stage she went back to Orissa to help her father with his iron and manganese mines. 'Perhaps it would have been better for him in his business to have a son, but he never said so. He introduced me to the business, allowed me to make decisions and to manage engineers and even the garage with its fleet of lorries carrying ore from the mines. I made it financially more viable; I wasn't going to muck it up, I wanted to earn his trust. In my twenties that must have given me confidence.'

While she was there she also decided to do something about the fact that there was no school in Orissa. Her son was now two and needed a school, so she would build one. In this respect Mrs Le Hunte resembles her Victorian predecessors. The founder of her present school, North London Collegiate, was the formidable Frances Mary Buss, who started her own school because she believed young women had to be educated if they were to find a new role for themselves in society.

Pramila Le Hunte started by having the land bulldozed. Residential accommodation was given by S. Lal and Co, the family mining business; she persuaded various mine-owners, including her father, to organise bulldozers to level the site for playgrounds. 'I also encouraged firms to provide carpenters, electricians, to create furniture and fittings as there were no shops to provide them. I got some female labour and trained them myself as children's ayahs. S. Lal's accountant, whose son attended the school, offered his services free. I got a headmistress who was training with me at St Bede's College, Simla, and I taught there myself for three years. After the first thrust it became self-financing. We added to the classes year by year as the children – Indian, English and Japanese – grew. I remember Arjun was two years and nine months old when he started and soon afterwards we had a concert on the back verandah, and the programme reads "Songs by A. Le Hunte". He sang "Twinkle, twinkle little star". He also held the cushion for Cinderella's slipper, this little mite in wig and eighteenth-century costume.

'When I left I gave the school to the local church, and it has become a flourishing high school. I went back and visited it a couple of years ago, and it has grown so large they've had to build a college for the children to go on to. In a quiet way I have a sense of warmth and achievement about it. We started with 25, and now they've got 400 and a quad and playing fields. All it took was someone to do the spadework. For years everyone had said, "My God we need a school here," but someone had to do the spadework.'

Back in Calcutta after that episode, nursing the smallest baby for nine months, she lectured at her old college, Loreto, where she had done her first degree. 'The nuns were very accommodating: I would always lecture at 9 am, so that I could feed the baby during the second session.'

She also wrote for *Femina*, the Indian women's magazine, and opened a small boutique called Tivoli, just to see if she could do something practical. It was the organising side of it she liked. 'Once I'd planned it and created it, I'd just pop in after college to see how it was going. My customers were the same age as my students so it was a nice corollary. It wasn't a financial flop; I came out evens in the end. But I look at that life now and I feel I couldn't do as much again.'

In 1968 the Le Huntes brought their family to Richmond. Bill got a staff job with IBM, first in marketing, then in IBM's sales training programmes, and Pramila went back to her studies. 'The first few months we were here was my longest ever period of unemployment, but my father had said, get yourself qualified in Britain. I did already have a teaching diploma from Simla, but it seemed likely that that wouldn't count. I know we were both still under thirty then, because we went on under-thirties mini-trek holidays to Turkey and Greece and Yugoslavia.' Since the youngest was then four and about to go to school, she had time to do a Diploma of Education and a basic teaching diploma during the day. She also started an M. Phil., researching along the lines of the

Schools Council Project on 'Children as Writers', run by Dr Harold Rosen.

She taught English at Godolphin and Latymer, another academic girls' school in Hammersmith, before going to North London Collegiate. But before she left Godolphin, and as soon as her youngest daughter had finished her O-Levels and could therefore be left to organise her own studying, Pramila Le Hunte entered politics.

'I just rang up the local party in Richmond and said I wanted to help. I said no, I didn't want to organise bazaars, and no, I didn't want to deliver envelopes. I wanted to do committee work.' She became the candidate for Richmond Town ward. Tea and cakes with local residents on Thursday afternoons, she said, was an excellent antidote to the pace of school life. Within four years of that first telephone call she was adopted for her first parliamentary seat. Since then she has been short-listed again, but is now only interested in winnable seats. Meanwhile she sits on the National Advisory Council on the Employment of Women – which is looking at, for instance, how to encourage women to train in electronic engineering – and on the advisory group on race relations.

Feminist books have never interested her in the least. 'I suppose they must have had some impact on people who were *not* achieving. I never felt tied down. It might have been different if the women's movement had hit me during my teens, when my mother was so strict and I did feel frustrated: if I had pursued my dramatic interests at that time my mother would have kyboshed it, in case I came into contact with men . . . I notice that my girls at school have picked up the word "sexist" and they use it a lot. But I think you've got to have unfulfilled needs to let it worry you.'

'Since living in England I had no help in the home at all; never have. I don't think I kept a very immaculate house, but somehow we managed. When they were younger we had a rota for domestic jobs which changed each month. One washed up after meals, so that they didn't all feel pressed into washing up all the time; one was in charge of keeping the house tidy. One did the hoovering; one helped me with the laundry. The changeover day was Saturday and the union rules were very strictly observed. It went on until the age of fourteen or so and eased off for exams. Of course they're all bone lazy and undomesticated now.'

Mrs Le Hunte refers to adolescence as 'an untidy time'. The test is, can you let go? 'I thought I was letting go, but I still got, "Why do you want to know where we are?" I tried to show that I wasn't interested in morality questions, but in the safety angle. I'd say, instead of coming home at unholy hours, I'd rather you stayed the night.

'Last term, I taught Blake's "Innocence and Experience", and tried to adapt it to the girls' own lives: why you have to be lost in order to be found. We debated it over and over. They wanted to be able to explore, yet they wanted their parents in the background. Would they feel excited or frightened to be out on their own? They said they weren't ready to leave home yet, at fourteen or fifteen – that's the parent-bashing age. And I said, but how many of your parents stop you from thinking for yourself, developing your own ideas?'

Mrs Le Hunte said she had no recollection of ever finding the children were too much, or got in the way. When a baby cried nearby as we talked, she said: 'Remember you have double that noise with twins. I got used to it.

'I know I might not have been able to do so much with my life if those critical first years, until the eldest was eight and the youngest four, had not been spent in India, with a living-in ayah. I didn't want to give my full-time attention to the children; that's what my mother had given me. I wanted to do the important things, not the unimportant things. I did the contact, not the maintenance. My memory is of spending quite a lot of time with the kids. I used to come back from lecturing or afternoon classes and play with them or take them out. Even the Indian women who didn't have jobs used to spend time away from the children at coffee mornings, and having their afternoon siestas. I wasn't sleeping in the afternoon, but working. I think my contact-hours with the children, or whatever you call them, weren't too bad.

'The children still remember India very well, and they know their relations there and go back often. They like the better life out there: it's very indulgent for them when they stay with my mother, ordering their breakfasts from servants.'

On the subject of marriage, Mrs Le Hunte was contemplative. 'If you accept the rules of the game and if you marry when you are both kids, particularly when you've been under the constraints I was under, you grow up differently. Bill and I have developed quite differently. He distances himself from my interests; he likes walking and I don't, he's not interested in politics or the theatre. Once I dragged him to a Tory selection meeting, but only once.

'We used to do shared things with the kids, going camping, once a month we'd take off for the New Forest or somewhere in Europe, and for a time we had a house in Wales for weekends. Although I enjoyed the children, I think perhaps Bill enjoyed them more. He was a buddy, he played with them. Discipline was left to me. He was an indulgent father; the twins are particularly close to him.

'I've always thought we ran along on separate parallel lines. We've been doing our own things for fifteen years, almost since we came back from India.

'No, I never did feel trammelled by being married. I did quite a lot of things because I had a secure home base.'

She wanted the children to be as active and independent as possible, encouraged all the usual activities like Brownies, Guides, music, choir. 'I don't think my daughters regard me as a model at all. People say they are like me, they look like me and they laugh like me. Anjali is a workaholic like me and has ambition. The lad is a well balanced chap. On occasion they have all helped in my stage productions. But I don't think they have yet found their reality. In their twenties, they seem much younger than I was at the same age.'

Abha, known as Bem, the youngest daughter, is recently down from Cambridge. 'She sits and evaluates me,' said Mrs Le Hunte. 'She said to me, "One danger of being successful is that you always want *more* success." I thought that was pretty perceptive for twenty-one. I love her aphorisms. She also said, "They say behind every successful woman there's a man trying to stop her."

'My husband never stopped me, but he only supported me by neither objecting to nor interfering with what I did. Which meant I had the space to develop myself despite family commitments.

'When we first came back here, and I had no friends or contacts here and he was out at work all day and would come back quite late, or would go out with colleagues in the evening, he said to me, "Why don't you join the Richmond Shakespeare Society? That's the kind of thing you enjoy, do it." So in a way he encouraged me.

'I think underneath it all he is a traditional man who would have preferred to have someone waiting at home, and not getting cross or bored waiting there. I used to ask why he didn't bring people back home in the evening but work is something he has always kept separate. I'm sure I'd have created trouble if I'd actually been stopped from doing anything.

'I don't consider myself successful. It's a wide brief I've given myself. Maybe I've spread myself too thinly. I know I wanted to be a success like my father, but not to be just "Mr Lal's daughter"; I wanted to be me. That was the first booster rocket, wanting to develop the mind.'

Seeming so very self-sufficient and organised, did Mrs Le Hunte feel she had missed out a bit on sympathy? 'Yes. It is lonely,' she replied at once in her rapid-fire way. She supposed she had had less of a social life over the years, but she had kept up very good friends. Last year she had suddenly become ill; her doctor told her she must slow down and find some interest that was relaxing, that didn't involve rushing about. She took up the harp.

'I asked the harp teacher at school, "Is it barmy to want to learn at my age?" and she said not at all, so I do that every Monday, and it is something I feel will last. It is hugely therapeutic. Just the beauty of the sound is so important. It soothes me. And – this is important – it is also a new challenge. I have tried other artistic challenges – painting and pottery and jewellery-making, but they're not me.

'I do feel I have slowed down and I did feel it was time to re-think myself. I didn't like the emotional side of the menopause at all. I've never been a depressive. But I started to think about what I should do with my life now. I bought a word-processor as an investment, and began taking stock. Should I have developed my artistic side more, or my dealing-with-people side more?

'Sometimes one wants to express things in dramatic ways and that's why I've taken up writing. Last year I did a production of *Peer Gynt*, and then the Tony Harrison version of *Le Misanthrope* for light relief, and now I've nearly finished writing a play of my own, based on Blake and inspired by the series of child-battering cases that coincided with the Tottenham riots. I'm using Blake's image of the sick rose for the inner city, the worm and the decay at the heart of the rose.

'I would have liked to have a job that involved travelling. That is one area that I feel you can't combine very well with a family. Does any woman travel round in her job and bring up a family? Lots of men do it, *and* they leave working wives behind. How do they manage? Lately Bem and I have done a lot of travelling, Central America, Haiti, the Caribbean; we were in Guatemala in the middle of guerrilla warfare.'

In retrospect it should have been obvious to me as we talked that Mrs Le Hunte's marriage was not going well at this time, as there seemed to be little common ground. In the week this book was first published, I heard that the marriage had indeed ended. Later I learned that Mrs Le

Hunte had also lost her job at the school. It had, she told me, been a stressful year, a quite horrible time. They were divorced on Leap Year Day, the irony of which did not escape her. 'It affected my amour-propre disastrously,' she said. The Kingman Committee of Inquiry into the teaching of English had been a lifeline. But she had spent her holidays looking for a new career in her fiftieth year. She had taken a Cordon Bleu cookery course and was thinking of buying an old manor house and starting a guest-house, possibly with a small theatre attached. 'All my life,' she said, 'I have had plans and projects. I've always taken risks.' Only now, like so many other women, she is doing it all alone.

Elizabeth Longford

Lady Longford, *writer and historian*

b. 1906

m. 1931

FRANK PAKENHAM

Earl of Longford, former Leader of the House of Lords,
social reformer, writer, public man

4 daughters, 4 sons

ANTONIA THOMAS PADDY JUDITH
RACHEL MICHAEL CATHERINE (*d.* 1969) KEVIN

Elizabeth Longford

~

Elizabeth Longford is probably the most distinguished materfamilias in Britain apart from the Queen. As a historian she would have been famous anyway; as the wife of Lord Longford she would have had a curiosity value even if she had done nothing at all. But as a celebrated biographer, as the mother of eight children and grandmother of twenty-five who has always preserved, in print and in person, a gracious and life-enhancing vitality, her distinction is unmatched. ('Queen Victoria had one more child than I,' she says, 'but a great deal more help in the home.' To everyone to whom she is talking she manages to convey the impression that that person is the cleverest and most interesting in the world. The Longfords do not stand together at parties; each darts gregariously around, talking to as many people as possible. Each regards the other as exceptionally good company, and they are both unswervingly certain that they would rather be with each other than with anyone else. 'I think it would be very difficult to become bored with Elizabeth,' says Frank Longford. 'No one else has ever been.'

We met for this interview in the Longfords' flat in Chelsea.

~

Elizabeth Longford was the eldest of five children, born at 108 Harley Street, London, in 1906. Her father, N. B. Harman, was an ophthalmologist and lived above his consulting rooms. Her mother, Katherine Chamberlain – niece of Joseph, the Victorian statesman – had just qualified as a doctor at the Royal Free Hospital, then an all-female medical school. She pulled out one wisdom tooth for £3 and never practised again, but married instead. 'My father assumed she was going to practise, and there was a room in Harley Street for their work room, but that became *his* consulting room. I assumed it was his fault; she had her first two children eleven months apart, just as I later did. On the other hand she had such a fleet of servants, I can't really understand why she could not have worked. She was a feminist, and made a lot of snide remarks about the way women were treated in the hospitals.'

Elizabeth's brother John still practises in the same house and her parents' portraits still hang in the waiting room. Her childhood was entirely under the supervision of a Cockney character called Nurse Robins, who taught her the splits and did all the things Dr Spock expressly forbade – smacked, had favourites, failed to keep promises. Mother's role was to read the classics to her children every day of their lives, a ritual Elizabeth carried on with her own children. 'I think my mother gave me only one piece of advice about life, and that was not to take up acting,' said Lady Longford.

But she was destined to shine. After schools in London (Frognal, and Francis Holland) she boarded at Headington School, Oxford, where she won every prize. She went up to Lady Margaret Hall at Oxford as a scholar in 1926, to read English, but switched to Classics in her first year, determined ('an academic snob') to mingle with other scholars.

'I loved drawing and painting and had at first thought of the Slade. But it was not unusual in our family for girls to go to university; two aunts had been to Newnham. My father believed that men were superior to women, and being inordinately proud of having been at Cambridge himself, he decided that his three sons should go there, and that Oxford was good enough for his two daughters.'

At Oxford she found herself invited everywhere, extremely popular and widely adored. *Isis*, the undergraduate magazine, made her one of their Isis Idols, when this accolade for a woman was almost without precedent. 'May she live long in the great tradition of British women,' they wrote.

She mixed with David Cecil and Osbert Lancaster, Evelyn Waugh and Randolph Churchill; she met Lord Alfred Douglas ('Bosie'), Auden and Spender. 'Oh, you were one of the aesthetes' molls,' the poet John Betjeman later told her. When Miss Harman was awarded a mere Second Class degree instead of a First she had forty-eight letters of condolence. But she had already fallen in love, a compensation.

She first met Frank Pakenham, as Lord Longford then was, early in her Oxford days. 'He was one of the bright young things, and I was just one of the young things.' At their first encounters he seems always to have been asleep (to this day she says he cannot lie down without sleeping) and her first sight of him was of a Greek god with brown curls, on whose sleeping brow she bestowed a kiss.

They became engaged in the winter of 1930 and her first glimpses of her future husband's family were of a series of dotty eccentrics. 'Who is that woman? I didn't invite her here,' Aunt Caroline aged eighty-nine kept saying at the dinner table, occasionally removing her false teeth and having the butler whirl her chair round to put the teeth in again.

'To me, marriage held no terrors whatever and not a vestige of doubt. It appeared perfectly right and obvious; I hardly thought about it, except to get the home ready,' she has written.

'To Frank, as to many males, there was something faintly tyrannical even about the generous way in which his mother-in-law provided us with household goods. "Does he like a very rough bath towel?" she asked me one day in a shop when we were choosing linen. "Most men seem to." When I passed on the question he was appalled. "Certainly not; as soft as possible," he snapped, clearly affronted by the sudden revelation of what a husband might be expected to be – an alien, abrasive creature measuring up to some myth of bullying masculinity in which he had never believed.'

They married on 3rd November 1931, the wedding having been postponed a week because it clashed with the formation of the National Government. It was a day of glittering autumn sunshine but with a tremendous wind, so that the bride's veil flapped like a ship's sail. The wedding was at St Margaret's, Westminster, the reception at Grosvenor House, then off to Euston Station for the night train to Liverpool, en route for a honeymoon in the wild west of Ireland. At Euston, no booking could be found in the name of Pakenham. They wandered disconsolately up and down the platform until a carriage was found, mislabelled Buckingham.

'I assumed I would carry on working. I had been lecturing for the Workers' Educational Association – at Frank's suggestion I had presented myself to the Oxford Summer School of the WEA, after which I became an English and politics tutor to the WEA in North Staffordshire during the hungry winter of 1930–31. I had been swept up into the working-class struggle to keep above the poverty line both in material and spiritual things. I had never done any teaching before but I really enjoyed it, and although I had a small but adequate allowance from my parents (£300) I wanted to earn more. We had £1000 a year and it seemed enough to live on. I must have assumed that I would have children too, but I remember Frank asking me when we were still at Oxford whether I wanted to have a family and I said no, certainly not straight away. I was in a groove of what were considered advanced women's views in those days. I thought I had no maternal instincts; I thought I was going to have a career in Parliament. Yet immediately I was married, I proceeded to have a girl and boy as quickly, in the same order and as close together as my mother had had me and my brother.

'In my experience the first child is not necessarily due to maternal instincts, but to the wish to reproduce the loved one. We'd been married nothing like a year when Antonia arrived – just ten months after the honeymoon, for the worst or perhaps the best possible reasons. I used to have appalling periods, of agonising pain, and someone had told me it would be all right after the first baby. Well, the period I had in Connemara, on our honeymoon, was quite the worst I had ever had, so I was determined it would be the last.

'I'd been to Dr Helena Wright, the wonderful gynaecologist, before our wedding because she was a friend of Naomi's [Mitchison] and she had told me all the necessary things about marriage. Funnily enough my parents, though both doctors, had told me nothing. I was in fact a virgin on marriage and so was Frank; he went to Helena too. We were her pupils.'

It was Dr Wright who told the Pakenhams, when they had the first girl (Antonia, their 'wonder-child') followed by Thomas the first boy eleven months later, the great secret of how to pre-determine the sex of one's child. 'I had great confidence in her,' says Lady Longford drily, 'because she had four sons.' A mild alkaline douche – a dessertspoon of bicarbonate of soda dissolved in a pint of water half an hour before sexual intercourse – was Dr Wright's simple prescription for a son. (When Elizabeth Longford vouchsafed this to me, I was the mother of three daughters. But I never got round to trying out her formula, because quite inadvertently I became pregnant very shortly afterwards, and had a son anyway.) 'Much more difficult to produce girls,' Elizabeth Longford said, 'because if you try to increase acidity you can instead produce sterility, temporarily at least.' But for boys, it worked every time for her. She says she used the formula between the births of the girls, who came naturally, as a means of evening up the sexes. Although with hindsight she stresses that it is not necessarily the sex of children that makes them different from one another, it is the individual personalities. All Lady

Longford's eight confinements were at home, including the last at forty-one, 'which would certainly be frowned upon today.'

'As soon as I had my pigeon pair, as they used to call one-of-each, I returned to my old love of being a Labour candidate. There was nothing but encouragement from my husband (who was then a Conservative) and no difficulty about leaving my two children, aged one and two, with their nurse on an evening when I drove over to Cheltenham for a meeting and back the same night to our home in Oxford. Nor did anyone in the constituency doubt that a woman candidate was just right for a hopeless seat. I based my campaign shamelessly on mothers and children themes, making special play of the fact that my two children drank in milk alone the whole dependant's allowance of a man on the dole.'

Elizabeth Pakenham, with two children under two, did rather better at Cheltenham in the 1935 election than her male predecessor had, but Cheltenham ('home of lost colonels') was unwinnable. Her next seat was in industrial Birmingham. 'I had told the selection committe at Cheltenham that it was possible I might have a third child; by the end of 1944 I had six children and was still going strong. During those years there was nearly always a baby or a half baby, and I breastfed them all, usually till they were fighting for a bottle, at nine or ten months. For a time we had a marvellous nanny, Jean Birch, who was then called up into the Wrens (it was wartime) and then we had part-time people, and daily people, in Oxford. Then suddenly everything was transformed. An old great-aunt of Frank's died at ninety-six, and her old lady's maid-cum-housekeeper came to us, to be a kind of marvellous grandmother to the children. She could make stews out of nothing. And her niece came as well, as children's nanny, and she was good with a sewing machine. So really, this meant I could go about making my speeches whenever I wanted to. I managed quite well ferrying to and fro between Oxford and Birmingham, where the baby of the day would lie in a carrycot at the back of the hall waiting for the next feed. We had no feeding on demand in those days; only a stringen Truby-King' (the current child care guru) 'régime of four-hourly feeds modified – greatly daring – as occasion arose. This basic discipline, applied to my very amenable babies, helped me to combine motherhood and politics for a time.' She even convinced herself that a young, female candidate ought to base her chief political interest on The Family. 'It could give me more authority, or at least mutual fellow-feeling, with the mothers of King's Norton.'

'But I retired from being a candidate, partly because of the war and partly because of the babies. There was a small clique in the local party who, when I must have just had another baby, put up a motion at a meeting: "We congratulate Mrs Pakenham on her fifth child, and we hope it will be her last." I was so angry I said, "I'm sure it won't be the last, I hope it won't." The rumblings of criticism in the local party grew. Each child was assumed to be the last. Rachel was hard to explain; then in November 1943, the twelfth anniversary of our wedding day, Michael Aidan was born.

'I had given a great deal of time to the constituency, but I realised they doubted my ability to represent the seat in Parliament while burdened with a young family of six or more. Added to this was that Frank had been adopted as Labour candidate for Oxford City. I had to face the fact that after the war was over, my Birmingham seat would swing over to Labour in a big way. But Frank's seat was more dubious. My feminist ardour suddenly fell apart. I just could not see him keeping the home fires burning while I set the Thames on fire at Westminster. And there were the difficulties of always having a carrycot in the back of the car – there was no heating then in cars – on the journeys to and from London. There was the petrol shortage, and leaving the children. It was one of the major decisions of my life. When Michael was two months old, I resigned from a seat which was won for Labour a year later with a thumping 12,000 majority.'

When the result was announced, the Pakenhams felt 'forlorn, out in the cold'. As a recompense, Elizabeth says, Nature allowed her another daughter and another son.

'There is no moral, either feminist or anti-feminist, in this success/ failure story . . . if Frank and I could have gone to Westminster together, I think we would have done so, and I'm sure I could have managed even with six pairs of pattering feet at home. We would not have been the first husband and wife at Westminster (there were Sir Oswald and Cynthia Mosley); we would have tied with Aneurin Bevan and Jennie Lee; but I doubt whether our last two children would have been born. And though it would have been fun, it *would* have been incompatible with our family lives.'

Elizabeth did stand once more, for Oxford in 1950 (the only mother-of-eight ever to fight an election, it is believed) but she knew she would be defeated. 'The fight would be a "propaganda" one; my family would not suffer and I would discharge my political debt.'

After the war ended, the time for nannies had passed. 'We had a series of foreign girls, and all except one were extremely nice and they all stayed longer than a year; one for two or three years. All my daughters and daughters-in-law today have help: the only difference is that their nannies call them and their husbands by their Christian names; mine never did.'

When the scientist (Lord) Solly Zuckerman came to lunch at the crowded family house in Chadlington Road, North Oxford, he recalls Frank saying, as he opened the door, 'Come in quickly or they'll all fall out.' It is interesting to note, however, that the quantity of babies was not a result of her being a Catholic, for at the time she was not. 'I believed in contraception and family planning up to the birth of my sixth child.' Elizabeth had even spoken rousingly for contraception in a debate at the Oxford Union, supported by Max Beloff and Bertrand Russell, 'and all eight of our children were wanted. It was after the seventh was born that I became a Catholic.'

It is one of the interesting parallels of the Longfords' marriage that she turned her husband from a wavering Tory into a Socialist, to become First Lord of the Admiralty under Clement Attlee, and she followed him into the Catholic Church. She had been an agnostic with no interest in religion; she had always left Baby Jesus talk to the nanny. But Frank Pakenham converted to Catholicism in 1940, and deeply distressed and shocked Elizabeth by not telling her about it. A few years later, she began to feel it was essential to find a philosophy of life and death. 'Now I firmly believe in immortality,' she wrote to her mother in 1944. That year, she miscarried twins. 'My anger with the Church showed how near I was to devotion and trust.'

After a brief period in the Anglican Church she was received into the Roman Catholic Church in 1946, just after her daughter Catherine was born. The infant Catherine was baptised a Catholic, with Evelyn Waugh as her godfather.

Did she enjoy having so many children?

'I have an unfair advantage: I never find the company of small children boring. I like my grandchildren to ask questions all the time because I like answering questions. And if they don't ask, I put things to them and interest them in new ideas and test them out next time I see them: how many flower names do they remember? And with my own children I did that even more.

'I didn't really begin to put pen to paper until Kevin was three, so it wasn't until the family was complete and most of them were at school, the elder girls boarding. So I wasn't in the least guilty about starting to write then, and the children didn't seem to worry. They took a certain amount of interest when I quoted their cute little sayings in my column in the *Express*.

'The two things Frank did were to introduce me to politics, which was not in my life before him at all; and secondly, to give me tremendous encouragement.' It was he who insisted that she needed a room of her own where the children might not enter without permission. 'When I first had the vague idea of writing an article, he would say, why not a book? then, why not write three? It all really started through him. Journalists were always on the telephone, ringing up for my views – having so many children they thought I would have views, which indeed I did. Then the features editor of the *Daily Express*, Tony Hern, said I ought to write my own views, in a short weekly article. But we'll have to get it past the Beaver first, he said. So then I met Lord Beaverbrook which was great fun. Frank and I went down to Cherkley for a day and a night, and I had to write three pieces to show the kind of thing I would do. One of them was on children's imaginary companions: both Antonia and Kevin had them.

'There was still rationing when we went down to Lord Beaverbrook and as we were leaving he said to me, "I suppose your children eat?" I said yes, they eat whatever they can get. "Well wait a minute," he said. He pressed a button and a screen rolled back revealing shelf upon shelf of tinned food. "Fill up the boot of Mrs Pakenham's car," he ordered, and a footman piled the boot with tins.'

Lord Beaverbrook later told her: 'You are now practising the Black Art,' meaning journalism. 'No one who practises the Black Art can ever escape.'

Elizabeth Pakenham's column, 'Women and Children First: A Daily Express Family Page' ('by Elizabeth Pakenham, the mother with something to say') began in 1955; later she continued writing for mothers in the *Sunday Times*. 'Which parental virtue do I find it hardest to practise? Patience. Which do I rate the highest? Patience,' was a typical opening. (Rightly, Elizabeth Longford had concluded that in people who are known to have a 'way with children' 90 per cent of that 'way' consists of patience.)

Is it worth it, making your child do his piano practice? Does the enthusiasm for children's activities wear off after the first baby? What do you do if the baby climbs out of his cot every evening and makes a grand re-entry into the living room? ('Pick him up promptly and return him to bed. There must be no lingering downstairs until he feels tired.') Lady Longford advised showing love above all things (only twenty years before, as she emphasises, parents had been *discouraged* from kissing and fondling their children too much) but also commended discipline. 'Before marriage I was an ardent believer in absolute freedom for the child ... The arrival of two and more taught me that unlimited self-expression is bedlam in a family.'

By 1960 she was reporting in 'Mainly For Mothers' in the *Sunday Times* on the recent increase in the number of married women going out to work and she was obliged to state where her own priorities lay. 'This generation, in fact, wants to have its cake and eat it. This is an operation demanding immense determination, energy and knowledge of how to do the job most efficiently. (By the job I mean of course motherhood.)'

That she valued the children above everything was never questioned. 'One day after the birth of Antonia I was saying, never again. But that feeling soon passed and I became so interested in the business of child-rearing, fertility, sex determination, the whole science. Birth is simply the most exciting and enthralling event. The endless speculation, for each nine months, about what it was going to turn out ... afterwards one does feel flat. One gets very excited about a book and how it is going to turn out, but you have all that excitement with a baby and it's not in your hands. It's a complete surprise, a birthday present.'

Compared with the children, the books for which she is now best known played a minor role in her life story for a long time. *Victoria R.I.* was an immediate bestseller and won the James Tait Black Memorial Prize; it sold even better in the United States where it was re-titled *Born To Succeed*. As light relief, she had also contributed to a 'Pakenham Party Book' featuring all the Pakenham females. She offered a copy to Evelyn Waugh who by now had six children himself. He wrote: 'Thank you for your charming letter and the promise of your Party Book. Laura has never given a children's party in her life. Pray God it does not move her to do so.'

It was always exciting, she says, to decide on the names. 'Antonia was named after *My Antonia*, by Willa Cather: at that time there were no Antonias, and for years people called her Antonio. Thomas was for Frank's father, killed at Gallipoli. Paddy, because we were both tremendously interested in Irish history and politics. Judith and Rachel were because I like old names, I suppose I must wish we had Jewish blood. Michael was nearly Aidan, but we decided perhaps it was too unusual, so became Michael Aidan; then Kevin John Toussaint: I'd become a Catholic so I thought I'd have a Catholic saint and one patriotic in the struggle for Irish freedom; Toussaint because he was born on All Saints' Day.'

Their youngest daughter, Catherine, died in 1969 in a car crash. That year had begun memorably. Five members of the family published books, a fact celebrated with a Foyles' literary luncheon. In August, Elizabeth and Rachel were visiting Michael in Warsaw (where he was Second Secretary at the British Embassy) when they heard that Catherine ('funny, pretty and popular') had been killed in a car crash at the age of twenty-three.

'This was an appalling black, slippery rock suddenly outcropping on my pebbled shore,' wrote Elizabeth Longford in her memoirs.

'I am sometimes asked whether faith helped: belief in immortality and a personal resurrection. My answer is that nothing lessens the pain at the time.' But she added: 'Faith saved me from asking the terrible questions, "Why? Why her? Why me?"'

Several grandchildren – two or three families' worth – always come for Christmas at Bernhurst in Sussex, the Longfords' country house, where traditionally Lord Longford dresses up as Father Christmas and falls flat on his face with the weight of his sack. 'It once really happened,' says Elizabeth Longford, 'but now it's an act.'

By all accounts she is an exemplary grandmother to her twenty-five grandchildren, very much the pivot of the whole clan. There is one grandmotherly skill she feels strongly about exercising. When telephoned about a grandchild's problem she generally counsels: 'Please do nothing.'

'I'm a tremendous believer in not taking urgent steps,' she says. 'The reason I feel so confident is that I can think of so many cases where things have worked themselves out. So the terrible depths of blackness and alarm are not justified. An apparent non-interest in school, a sudden onset of naughtiness – I think it's very comforting to be able to recall parallel cases. One gives the wisdom of the ages: I've been here before, it's going to turn out all right.'

She does not see her life as a three-dimensional achievement. 'I could not be more pleased with my marriage or my children. But with the writing I used to feel that if I'd started sooner . . . I wrote the *Jameson*

Raid in my fifties, and *Queen Victoria* came out when I was fifty-eight. Today I take a different view. If I had started sooner I would have written more books, but not necessarily *better* ones.'

In her autobiography Elizabeth Longford wrote: 'Those who can divide themselves between husband and children on the one side, and government and academic assignments on the other, like my friend Mary Warnock, have all my admiration and envy.'

She played it differently. 'The children were never rivals to my writing. When the time came for having leisure to write, nobody needed me to do anything else. It is possible to have too much leisure. I like being forced to write against the demands, that feeling of having to use what time there is. If there's no tension, I can't really begin.

'When they were small they were always busy doing things and I would simply remove myself. If I look back to working when they were all still around, I see it always as summer. I picture myself sitting in an embrasure of rhododendron bushes and that's where I wrote my *Daily Express* articles. So I could still be part of the family, or at least within earshot.

'I've never been worried about interruptions. You've got to make up your mind that you will be interrupted all the time, and not mind. I do know that if you're going to be cross it makes it worse. I never wanted to be shut completely away. And the children soon got into the habit: I've often heard a younger one say, "Let's go and ask Mummy to play croquet," and an older one saying, "No, Mummy's working, you can't."

'The only time I can remember working in complete solitude in those days was when I was still living in Oxford and the whole family went away for three days and I began thinking the world was at my feet, nothing to do except what I wanted to do. And after a very short time I felt I'd been tugging on a tug-o'-war rope and had let it go and had fallen flat. Only when they came flocking back did life resume its nice energetic pace.

'But all these things only work if you like all the aspects of your triple life. And I did.'

The Longfords, now long past their golden wedding, and both eighty-one, have often been asked about the key to a happy marriage. 'We are active comrades,' Lord Longford has declared. 'I never think about our marriage at all. It's rather like asking myself how do I manage to breathe or how do you get off to sleep?'

Lady Longford told me: 'The first essential is to find the right person. I weave all sorts of mystic stories about that, which I believe.

'The other side of the secret is to be a marriageable person. Some people are and some are not. You might be unlucky and marry a black card. Two black cards can't marry. We were two white cards, so it couldn't help but work. If you look back to courtship, you think of amazingly lucky moments when you felt predestined and meant for each other.

'The old adage about marriage, that your joys are doubled and your griefs halved, is true. The pleasure of a very long marriage like ours – fifty-five years, which although I am very old, is a large portion of my life – is the enormous background of jokes, anecdotes and analogies, like when some extraordinary thing happens in politics that also happened twenty years ago and makes you roar with laughter. Also, you know each other so well you can't conceal anything. I think I find Frank funnier than he finds me.'

Lady Longford memorably describes her husband's eccentric character and appearance ('high domed forehead, monk-like tonsure, round gold spectacles, spade chin which have made life easy for the caricaturist') and his crusade which gave the press an ideal cause for caricature: pornography. She writes graphically of his hopelessness in all practical matters (he used to have to get his mother's butler to sharpen his pencils) and his total lack of interest in appearance or material possessions. But this made him easy to please domestically. 'Never a complaint about food, drink, cold or indeed any creature comforts. And there was not a dull moment in his company.'

She says they would discuss the children over pleasant matters but it is the mother who remains more protective over difficulties, even when the children are middle-aged.

'The large family is a special satisfaction. When we had two boys and two girls, I remember feeling "Now we've got a real family." What I didn't realise at the time was how it multiplies to the most wonderful number of grandchildren. I have one of our Golden Wedding family portraits hung in the bathroom and I look at all those rows of heads and think, well, who could have thought they'd all be here? Without us two they wouldn't.'

Was it ever a big decision to put the children before an outside commitment? 'Many years ago it was suggested that I might do a job that I could have given some thought to: running an Oxford college. We talked about it and really it was the same as when I gave up politics, or the thought of getting into Parliament. But I don't regret it. I never feel, when in the House of Commons, I wish this were my home.'

Mavis Nicholson

television interviewer

b. 1930

m. 1951

GEOFFREY NICHOLSON

journalist

3 sons

STEVE LEWIS HARRY

Mavis Nicholson

~❧

Nobody can interview people on television better than Mavis Nicholson. You know beforehand that the questions will be intelligent enough
to make her subject think, and that she will listen to the answers. This
alone would distinguish her from most practitioners of the television
interview; but there is also the fact that although she is *a woman* and
appears on television, nobody discusses her clothes or whether she ought
to wear earrings. They are too interested in what is happening on
the screen: a small, quick, dark-eyed Welsh woman making Kenneth
Williams unbend, or David Bowie sound intelligent, or Prince Philip
deeply sympathetic.

The Mavis on screen is very like the Mavis who used to be a lively,
talkative mother of three sons before she was, literally, discovered at the
age of forty. In this book she represents the woman who stays at home to
bring up her children for a decade and then emerges from domestic
boundaries to take on the world at large. Before having children she was
an advertising copywriter, as was her husband Geoffrey. Since Thames
TV offered her the role of frontwoman on their afternoon magazine
programme, 'Good Afternoon', she has done many series of interviews
and talk shows, and has written for magazines and newspapers.

What is it about her that makes people want to talk to her? Even
before she went near a TV studio she was the sort of person who couldn't
take a train or a taxi without returning full of bizarre life-histories. In
those days, instead of chat shows she would have supper parties, at
which to hold the table enthralled. Now that she has the attention of an
audience of millions her manner is much the same: a level eye on her
subject, by turns friendly and beady; an original line of questioning – a
searching one followed by a sympathetic one; endless curiosity to the
point of downright nosiness; frankness about herself; warmth, sense,
and a zest for stories.

When she first went into television her stories were no longer about strangers on trains, but about the celebrities in the studio. I think my favourite is from the early days of 'Good Afternoon' when Mavis found herself interviewing Mary Stocks, the economist and educationalist. Baroness Stocks came into the studio wearing a trouser suit, and when she sat down it became clear that the flies were undone. Mavis leaned forward, *sotto voce*: 'Lady Stocks, I'm sorry but your flies are undone.' The lady looked down unperturbed. 'Oh,' she boomed, 'I suppose everyone was expecting a penis to pop out.'

Before she moved onto the screen Mavis wrote about people's homes for *Nova*, the innovative women's magazine of the 1960s. She wrote chiefly of how people gave their homes their essential character. In those days her own kitchen was an early example of what became fashionable: nothing flash or streamlined, but a cosy place with a mock-up Welsh dresser, mismatched plates, a round unpolished mahogany table where people sat and talked when they dropped in. Now the Nicholsons divide their time between a real old Welsh farmhouse outside a village in Powys, and when in London, a rented flat above a hairdresser's.

⁊⦁

The really lucky thing about her life, Mavis Nicholson says, is that things happened to her at the right time. 'I would not have been a good mother if I had had my babies earlier; and I could not have been a good mother if work had come along when I was at home with the children. I could only do one thing at a time.

'I married at twenty-one and didn't have the first baby until I was twenty-seven. Which meant that I had a little peep at work, enough to realise that I didn't want to go into an office every day, so that was out as a career. But because I'd had my look around when the children arrived, I didn't feel I was missing too much.'

She was born in Briton Ferry near Swansea in South Wales. 'When and where I grew up, mothers lost their figures early and gave up a lot of their lives to their children, and looked as if they weren't going to do anything again, ever.

'I never thought that would happen to me, partly because my own mother was a complete character who stayed quite intact even though she had a drab domestic life in an overcrowded house. She was hard-working, but never lost her spirit. She sort of wanted me to be a teacher, as she had wanted to be: she thought if you were educated you could be something other than a housewife, and that you could *travel*, that seemed to be important. And a non-traveller I have turned out to be. But I never thought that I wasn't going to do something, even though I didn't know what.

'I knew that women were held back, and that it wouldn't be easy, but then it never seemed to me that my father had an easy life either. Working as a crane driver in Wales in the 1930s wasn't easy.'

She was the eldest of three. 'I had five years as an only child, before my twin brother and sister were born. "You were never out of somebody's arms," I was always told. The house was full of family – uncles and grandparents as well as parents, and I was cuddled and loved to distraction. Which was the only thing I ever wanted. I'm not ambitious you see: the only thing I'm ambitious about is to be loved.'

They were so overcrowded in the three-bedroomed house that Mavis slept with her grandmother in a big brass bed until she was seventeen. 'That was very odd; necessary though,' she says. 'I never saw myself in a mirror either, hardly. There was one mirror on a wardrobe door in one of the bedrooms, that's all. That's how I got so confident. No bathroom, so I never saw myself naked either. Quite interesting, that. My grand-mother was the wonder of my life for a long while. She took me off for treats in her fox fur, while my mother looked after the twins which took a hell of a lot of doing in a house without hot water.

'And I never thought that men didn't work in the house, because my father would come in, having worked a two-till-ten shift, poor bugger, having cycled ten miles from work, and he would then clean out our one living room. Somebody had to do it and he never seemed to object, and I didn't think it odd that he did it.'

Her grandmother was one of nature's raconteurs, always a teller of stories. 'She would tell me stories about a little girl with black hair. And I knew it was me. This little girl would be sent out to do some shopping and would be tempted by a little old woman, who was really a wicked witch. And I would say, "What was the little girl's name?" and she would say, "It begins with M . . ." and the little girl would be taken prisoner, and would escape, and the little old woman would chase after her and would be run over, and it was the little girl's fault. Those stories tantalised me as you can imagine.

'I was the whole of my grandmother's life. She'd had a really rough time with my grandfather, who was a drinker. He lived with us but nobody talked to him; I didn't until I was seven, and then only outside the house. He'd come from a farming community himself and didn't speak English. I'll tell you what I did have, early on. A great instinct about people, and knowing why they behaved as they did. And I really understood from the beginning about my grandmother wanting to be my mother.

'As I got older I became very religious because social life was centred on the chapel, and I became immersed in chapel life which seemed full of bright people. And my poor grandmother realised the bird had flown.'

There was a schoolteacher who became her beloved mentor. 'Eileen Sims was Welsh, unmarried, with black hair and a double First in Latin and Greek but she wasn't allowed to teach in grammar schools because she was a conchy, a conscientious objector in the war. But she took me every Saturday morning for Latin. She said to me one day: "You're going to be famous in some sort of way. You're not going to be content with what I've been content with. You're going to fly off." And I thought, yes, I think so.'

Mavis went to Swansea University, still living at home at first and travelling there on the bus, but then moving into a women's hostel in college. At the end of her second year she met Geoffrey Nicholson. 'It was quite romantic. He was a year older, having done his National Service. I was going to the Birmingham Arts Festival, to play Mrs Dudgeon in *The Devil's Disciple*. He was going as a reporter for the college paper. His girlfriend, Norma, said, "Do look after Geoff for me when you get there." It was New Year's Eve and we'd all gone to various parties, and as the clock struck twelve, Geoff walked towards me, very poetic-looking, very thin, long hair which no one had then, and red shirt which no one wore, and said "Happy New Year" and kissed me.

'I'd been going round with the catch of the sixth form, Ken Jones, tall with green eyes and long lashes, the one everyone wanted. We had planned our first child – who would be called Steve – and when I got to Swansea I broke off with him I'm ashamed to say very roughly and cruelly and I never saw him again till years later we bumped into each other in Piccadilly, when he showed me the pictures of his children in their garden with the swing and the apple tree, and Geoff and I were still childless then so perhaps it was sort of "see what you missed . . ."'

Mavis did not get her degree because, unaccountably, she walked out of her Economic History paper. 'To this day I don't know why. Geoff and I had swotted the night before, and every question that we'd prepared came up. He stayed, and passed, and I went out and walked round the grounds. It's like a blur. My tutor asked me afterwards, "Why did you do it, Miss Mainwaring? You'd have got that one." It's still a mystery today. For ages I believed I'd failed, and I used to dream about failing the exam until quite recently when Geoff put me right about it: "You didn't fail. You didn't take it." But I can't explain it.'

It was at Swansea that she and Geoff met Kingsley Amis, who has remained a lifelong friend; when Kingsley Amis won the Booker Prize for *The Old Devils*, set in Wales, his companion for the Guildhall dinner was Mavis Nicholson – who as it happened had interviewed him the previous week on her TV programme, 'Mavis on Four'. It was also at Swansea that a professor informed her that her name, which she had always pronounced Mainwaring, should be pronounced 'Mannering'. Never mind; she was shortly to become Nicholson anyway.

After university both she and her husband-to-be won Edward Hulton scholarships to train as advertising copywriters in London. Mavis lodged, at first, at Geoffrey's mother's house in the suburbs of south London. 'I was quite impressed by his home, having a phone and a car, but I knew claustrophobia would set in rapidly so I got a flat with two girls from college at Emperor's Gate, Kensington, and Geoff would visit me there and walk home to Norbury, late at night in the dark and cold. I thought then nobody could love me so much as to do all those miles of trudging, night after night.'

They married at Kensington Register Office on either August 16th or 26th, they never remember which. 'I wanted chapel but I'd already lost my religion. Geoff wasn't religious, even though he'd been a choirboy and once wanted to be a vicar. I rather fancied the idea of being a vicar's wife, of a sort, at one point.'

They both carried on working at the advertising agency and lived in an unfurnished flat in The Cut at Waterloo. Their first two sons, Steve and Lewis, were born there. Mavis left the agency to have the children; her last account, she remembers, was for Knight's Castile soap. Geoff's was the slogan 'Hey, fella – Fruit-tella'. 'We soon realised there was nowhere for a child to play, and no schools, so we moved to a mansion block in North London, a lovely flat three floors up with a Pither stove, lent to us by friends, in the living room which made a cosy warm heart to the place.

It looked like a Russian room. We had no car and no money, but we had a lot of friends and I was really happy with life.

'I would take the children out *every* day, because I thought you had to, to Waterlow Park or to Kenwood House on Hampstead Heath, tobogganing. I adored the changes of season and the way you notice it more with children, the leaves falling and the mittens in the snow. It's such a pictorial time. What I liked was that the children took you back to your own childhood (and now I know that grandchildren take you back to your children's childhood, and I adore that too). You have the time to see it through their eyes. I wouldn't have wanted it any other way. I had very long black hair, to show that I wasn't really a housewife, I was really Juliette Greco. I could wear it in a plait in the evening, over one shoulder, or long and down for a party when dancing into the night, or in a bun when I wanted to look like a business-woman . . . We had tons of friends and were very sociable, and once the children went to school we had even more.' Their third son Harry was born at this time.

'I didn't have a huge idea of myself as a Fulfilled Mother. I never had a great craving for bay-bees, or stared longingly into other people's prams. I really liked them when I could draw with them, because I still really felt I could have been a teacher. I never missed my life in the ad agency, not for a second. Geoff was working at home, too, which made a difference: I wasn't isolated. But it also meant it was difficult to keep them quiet so that he could work. I don't think I was as sympathetic as I might have been, to the difficulties of his working at that time. He had to help me: we both shopped, being on the third floor with no car. Luckily there was still a local grocer – Welsh – who delivered if any of us were ill. What absolutely never occurred to me was the alternative of handing over your child to a seventeen-year-old au pair as other people did. At seventeen I didn't know the arse of a child from its elbow.'

She acknowledges, in retrospect, that she must have started wanting to do something creative when Harry, the youngest, was about four, and she began to be envious of Geoff's life. He was then a sports reporter on the *Observer*. 'You want to go to Birmingham to a football match in the rain?' he'd say. But she started taking photographs. Someone gave her an enlarger and she printed her own photographs of people's children. An architect friend asked her to photograph the conversions he was doing, so from the proceeds she could sell her first camera and buy a better one. Just at that time Peter Crookston, a former colleague of Geoffrey's who was now editing the magazine *Nova*, invited Mavis to come along and bring some ideas. '*Nova* was a brilliantly outlandish magazine full of women wearing shawls flung over their shoulders and skirts with their pettis showing. I became their Home Editor, not writing about consumer goods but more about the feel of a home and how you make it your own.

'By then we'd moved to our own house. We got the deposit because Geoff was editing a new magazine called *Now*. It folded before it ever came out and he got paid half a year's salary which was £2000, just enough for the deposit. I set up a column called "How?" on *Nova*, which was practical advice on how to find out about everything: how to change doctors, how to detect someone on drugs, how to get children looked after. There was someone to do the research and I worked at home, but when I went in to deliver copy I had that rare treat, lunch out. Once a week we had Nell to come in and help to clean, and she would look after Harry if I went into the office that day. Geoff was wholly in favour of my doing it because he wasn't affected, and nor were the children because I could give them all the time they needed when they came back from school. To have been out between four o'clock and seven would never have fitted in for me at all. I wasn't the kiss-you-after-you've-had-your-bath-darlings type. Nor did I have a burning vocation. It would have been very different if I had. I'd have had to manage to fit in a home and job as so many women have had to.'

Mavis's job in television arose directly from her involvement as a parent with Steve's school in the borough of Haringey. The issue was the bussing of immigrant children across the borough: 'It was a very racist idea: only the immigrant children would have been bussed.' Mavis and a councillor appeared on the Eamonn Andrews 'Today' programme on Thames TV to put their case. The parents were a high-powered group, all of whom have gone on to do other things. There was Naomi Mackintosh, who later went on to a post in the Open University and then to Channel 4 (as Naomi Sargant); and Nicky Harrison, who went on through local government to become chair of education in Haringey. As for Mavis, when the 'Today' programme was over Eamonn Andrews told her: 'You ought to be on television,' and she said, 'I think I ought.'

Very shortly afterwards she was offered the chance to join the new afternoon programme, along with Jill Tweedie, Mary Parkinson, Judith Chalmers and others. Jeremy Isaacs said to her: 'Will you come on television and not change? Promise me you won't change.' 'And of course I did change,' Mavis says, 'and became more natural on television than in real life.'

She has often told how she used to have childhood fantasies of stardom, and that when her face became well known after the age of forty she discovered she wasn't really so enamoured of the star aspect at all. She thinks the word star should be banned anyway. 'When I was younger, to have been recognised in the street would have been enough. Now I'm much more excited if people remember what the programme was discussing.'

She says she was not too old to make this fresh start; she was just old enough. 'Lucky old telly, I thought, a bit.

'I felt at home with television at once. Yes, I had wanted to be an actress, really, as a child. A film star. But by the age of forty – and if you don't know yourself by then there's not much hope – I knew enough to know it wouldn't take me over, it wouldn't go to my head or anything. I was dead scared, of course, at first. I remember Jill Tweedie and I agreed that neither of us slept the night before our programme, *at all*. Now I think ooh lovely, three million people watching. Once I grasped how lovely that was, I loved it. I've been doing it for sixteen years now. "The able veteran" the *Sunday Telegraph* called me the other day.'

During the times she is not doing a weekly programme they retreat to Wales, where they are near their son Steve and his wife Jane, who run a pub in Shropshire, and Mavis's first grandson Ben: 'heaven on two legs' in her view. Of sharing thirty-five years of marriage, Mavis says: 'It's very handy to be married to your best friend. That's luck, really. If you choose someone who grows up with you at an equal-ish pace, and you have a good sex life so you don't need to wander, and you don't get bored with each other . . . perhaps if only one of you leads an exciting life the other might get a bit fed up and disagreeable and jealous. Geoff had years of introducing me to his office friends; he always seemed to like them to meet me, which is most flattering. Then he had to cope with me becoming a publicly recognised face and him being the anonymous writer. "You're Mavis Nicholson," people would say, and he's generous enough to see that that's the way it's fallen this time. Rivalry never came into it for some reason. And money is a silly vanity: you're sharing everything anyway. You've got to share money completely, without a doubt. Very important that is, whether one of you is earning or not.'

For a while the Nicholsons worked together on a new venture, a children's newspaper called *The Tuesday Paper*: it would be fun and informative without being a comic. It was a huge success with those who bought it, but it never made it to the mass circulation of W. H. Smith's. And it had to end.

'I think I've leaned on Geoff terrifically for intellectual backup. He's more thoughtful than me and better informed. He can give me a great deal of help, and I can give him something extrovert perhaps. Maybe opposites live vicariously through each other. Neither of us has been involved in hierarchical careers, I'm glad to say. He's always been very affectionate and very critical. I do depend on him. The only fear in a happy marriage is that you depend too much.'

She regards herself as belonging to a fortunate generation who were allowed to stay at home looking after children, as she wanted to, and then to reappear while still young and energetic and choose what they wanted to do. 'I don't know whether it's class or education, but I was convinced that there was no question of my being covered up by the debris of motherhood. I did have a little help in the house, and I think that's where there is a need for help. I think there ought to be opportunities for working-class mothers to get jobs again after the children have gone to school, and for them to have the further education they might have missed. Middle-class and educated women can do pretty well what they want anyway, if they have the nerve.'

She had once told me that she rather wished she'd had more children – she liked them so, and truly enjoyed bringing them up – but now she says three was the perfect number, it's given her time to do other things. 'And now that I'm a grandmother it's another source of love and affection. I'd have hated not having children at all; I wanted more people to love, and more people to love me.'

Children who reproach their parents for adolescent misunderstandings get little sympathy from Mavis. ('You know you're a terrible bully don't you?' she told young Adam Nicolson, the writer, when he and his father Nigel appeared together on her programme to talk of the book they had written exploring their relationship.) 'I've decided that children really can't go on blaming their parents for things. Mostly parents try their hardest, and then I reckon it's up to the children to have the responsibility to disentangle themselves. All I hope about my children is that they like me, as a pal after the mother part of things isn't needed any more.

'I do think that I would worry, if I hadn't spent all that time with them, that I had missed too much of them. It's something you have to be watchful about in marriage too, being ready to give the attention that's necessary.'

On feminism, she said: 'I always used to feel I lagged behind Jill Tweedie, when I worked with her, on feminism; I had a bit of catching up to do in a sense. I've certainly always thought that women weren't where they ought to be: a fact of life that had to be altered. I would always want to go on fighting on behalf of other women. I don't say, "If I can do it, you can too, kids." If there's any help to be dished out, I want to be there dishing it out.' (Mavis was the chief signatory on a *Times* letter opposing the threatened amendment to the 1967 Abortion Act, in 1980. Her name headed a list of prominent women in the media voicing their resistance to any plans to make abortion more difficult.) 'But I don't see,' she added, 'that women can get very far if men don't change their lives too.'

Last year she had broken her foot very badly and had been suddenly rendered quite helpless. 'Geoff had to do everything for me and he waited on me hand and foot. I said, "You've been so nice to me and looked after me so well," and he said: "I suppose I like knowing exactly where you are." It's so much easier if there's someone at home when you are busy. I can see there's a lot to be said for that, the Mr and Mrs Woodentop set-up. But somehow we luckily recognised that if every husband needs a good wife, so does every working wife.'

Dr Wendy Greengross

General Practitioner and counsellor

b. 1925

m. 1949

ALEXANDER KATES *d.* 1982

orthopaedic surgeon

3 sons, 2 daughters

NICHOLAS HILARY TREVOR

RICHARD POLLY

Dr Wendy Greengross

Dr Wendy Greengross was first of all a voice: a distinctive voice full of commonsense and understanding on that much missed programme, 'If You Think You've Got Problems' on BBC Radio 4. She was particularly good at discerning the problem beneath the stated one. Her name would later often crop up in the context of organisations which helped people, marriage guidance, advice to youth and so on. I knew she was a practising GP and that she had five children; I was fascinated to read, once, that her husband thought three was enough but told her if she had any more she would have to support them: so she did. Then a friend of theirs told me: 'No, the truth was that Alex Kates, Wendy's husband, would have liked *six* children but he'd read somewhere that every sixth child in the world is Chinese . . .'

When I wrote to Wendy Greengross asking to meet her she replied, hesitating on two counts. The first was that she had tried to remain fairly private about her personal life. The second was that her husband had died three years ago. But if I still wanted to talk to her I could contact her later 'by which time I may look on your venture a little more optimistically'.

I dwelt on this. Widowhood is the most threatening factor of married women's lives: most women end up as widows, and all you can hope is that it happens later rather than sooner. Who better than Wendy Greengross, famous for her sympathetic advice, to represent this huge category of women? Would she speak differently from the other interviewees about what she had achieved in her life, in the context of widowhood? When we met she had just moved out of their large family home into a smaller house, with her dogs, and agreed to be interviewed in the midst of her still busy working life: writing, teaching and lecturing. Dr Greengross was also on the Warnock Committee, one of the two who were doubtful about the proposed 14-day limit on embryo research.

When Wendy Greengross became a medical student there were already thirteen doctors in her family but most of them wanted to be brain surgeons and psychiatrists; she wanted only to be a General Practitioner like her mother's brother, who was the family doctor. After South Hampstead High School, she proceeded to one of the only three places in Britain where a woman could go to read Medicine in 1943: University College Hospital, in London, which magnanimously took eight women clinical students a year. It was during her time there that the idea of women medical students became more accepted. 'You had to put up with some teasing from the consultants and we were fair game for their jests.

'Women, to them, were nurses; all medical students were men; so we had to behave like pseudo-men. It was a peculiarly sexless relationship, which had enormous repercussions. For instance, the fact that one had been a medical student automatically called into question one's femininity. I think a lot of us had more children than most other people, in a sort of quest for femininity,' said Wendy Greengross.

No advice-giving agony aunt would recommend getting engaged after just one week's whirlwind romance but this is what the impetuous Miss Greengross did. She had just qualified, and had a scholarship to go to America to do obstetric work at the Chicago Lying-in Hospital. 'My passage was booked, but in the meantime I went off, just to fill in time and earn some money, to do a locum at Southend. I arrived on a Wednesday and there met Alex Kates, who was also down there on a locum. He'd just arrived himself the previous Sunday. A week later, I rang my father to say I'd got engaged. They were delighted because they thought I meant the boyfriend I'd been going out with before. Then they were delighted anyway, because this meant I was giving up the scholarship to America.' Wendy and Alex were married the following February.

Having qualified as Wendy Greengross, she retained this name professionally. By 1970, she was talking on the radio, doing her Dr Wendy problem page in the *Sun*, and acting as consultant to the TV soap 'Crossroads': might not all this publicity constitute advertising? So at this point she became Dr Kates in the medical register. 'I found it very useful,' she says, 'to have three names. I was Mrs Kates at home, Dr Kates in the surgery and Dr Greengross in the media.'

The family rather regarded her as 'poor Wendy who got married but still had to go on working'. 'In our family the women worked until marriage and then gave up to look after the home. So I think they were a bit sorry for me, having to work. Even if it was my own free choice.'

The first baby was born soon after they married. 'My husband was nine years older and he'd said he didn't want any children after the age of forty; and I said I wanted eight children; so you see there was no time to lose,' Dr Greengross explained. 'I fixed on eight because my husband was one of eight and I, who had only my brother Alan, felt rather deprived.'

There was, it seems, always a scheme to Wendy's family: a quick-step pattern of 'Boy, girl, boy boy girl' ('a Victor Sylvester family, I used to say'). Wendy specifically wanted a second girl because she felt having a sister was enormously important. 'My mother was one of four sisters, my father had four sisters, my husband had six sisters; but I had only my brother. So I was absolutely determined that having had one daughter I'd give her a sister. And although six years apart, the two girls have got on terribly well; perhaps better than if they'd been closer.'

They had their five children in seven years. 'And actually it is very difficult to know whether it's a bad or good thing, to have them all so quickly. I've just been to visit my eldest son in Canada, and seeing all the problems of coping with two under two, I begin to wonder how we ever managed with five under seven. But if you're in the middle of it perhaps you don't notice. It's like being in a fire: you might wonder beforehand, what would I save, the dogs or the diamond tiara? But when the fire happens, you just cope.'

Nicholas, Hilary, Trevor, Richard and Polly could not have been more meticulously and successfully planned, down to the exact month. 'My brother and I had birthdays only two weeks apart,' Wendy Greengross explains, 'and I hated that double celebration, especially as his came first. So in our family we've got birthdays in January, April, July, September and November, nicely spread throughout the year. Now that really was good planning. It all went exactly to order, the most extraordinary thing.

'Yet during my six years of medical training we were only given one half-hour's tuition on contraception. And we were lucky to have a registrar who would tell us anything at all! It was not a scheduled aspect of the syllabus.'

Dr Greengross and her husband took over a surgery in Tottenham in north London in 1950, a partnership practice. Later they pioneered the idea of the group practice – now familiar in many parts of the country, but theirs was only the second in England, and the first to be purpose-built in London. They managed to build it on a piece of open space on an old London County Council estate. But the opposition to doctors forming a group practice was enormous. Why? 'People were very much afraid that we were empire-building,' said Dr Greengross.

It was when she took a Family Planning course that Wendy Greengross began to be involved in marriage guidance. 'One week I was asked how I dealt with all the marriage problems that came up in the normal course of general practice. I was just beginning to realise that "recurring sore throats" and "tension headaches" were actually marital problems, and I hadn't a clue how to deal with those. So I looked into Marriage Guidance, and found that I was being interviewed for training as a counsellor.

'Well, I had only been married a year myself, and it turned out the training sessions were every Thursday evening, which was our one night off from the surgery, when we rather hoped to go out. So I said I wouldn't attend unless my husband could come too. They said fine, as long as he trains to be a counsellor as well. And that was how we were both selected. But at the point when I was supposed to start actual counselling I had to say, "Sorry, I'm pregnant . . ." and each subsequent time I was supposed to start, I was pregnant again, and again. So my husband did three years of marriage guidance counselling before I'd even started.

'But it gave him an enormous amount of insight into people, and I'm sure he was a much better surgeon because of it. He was a very kind man anyway; but he always talked to his patients. Some surgeons never do.'

For each new baby Wendy Greengross took a few weeks off work, but after the third child reduced her commitment to three surgeries a week, and housecalls. So how did she manage? She tried an au pair for a while, but then discovered a better solution – a sister-in-law who lived near the practice with her own two children. 'I'd cart the babies over to her and they'd stay and play with hers while I did the surgery.

'It was down to her more than anyone else that I could go on working. She was a very placid person who never behaved as if she was doing me a favour – and she even took messages as well. It was easy and comfortable and the kids were happy and they loved her. If it hadn't been for her, life would really have been difficult.

'But I did look after my kids, the rest of the time. It made me uncomfortable when people shook their heads admiringly and said,

"Look, five children and a medical practice!" I think I was afraid that it made people dislike me more. I was sure there were a lot of married women who would have liked to do what I was doing, but were trapped by husbands who said, "What do you want to work for, you've got a nice home and children!"

'I had a marvellous husband, a super husband. He always encouraged me to do things. If I was asked to do something, on TV perhaps or radio, or that sort of thing, I would speak to him about it first and he was always terribly pleased for me and for himself. I don't think I ever would have done what I have done without him.

'My marriage was the most important thing in my life. What makes for a successful marriage is commitment: that is the main thing. You know you are going to spend the rest of your life with someone; it is not a matter of asking, "Am I fulfilled, am I happy?" and if you had no differences or arguments at all it would be awful. The commitment overrules all: you have to make that effort. When I speak to youngsters now, so many seem to talk in advance about the possibility of divorce "if things don't work out". But you only get married if you have no doubt at all that that is the only possible course. Then you are committed. Then you work hard at it. Marriage is the best context in which to find out about yourself.'

Several times during our conversation Wendy Greengross emphasised that if it had not been for her husband she would never have discovered she could become one of these women who manage everything, but might have blushed unseen; it was her husband who brought her out into the limelight. 'The problem for most women is having to do battle with your husband over doing a job. That must be so energy consuming. I've been extraordinarily lucky. In my era you were supposed to be either a career woman *or* a wife and mother. I wanted to be a doctor, and it was only my husband who said: You *can* be both.'

Wendy Greengross is one of those who denies that she is a feminist even though she believes *of course* in the equality of the sexes. The missing ingredient for her is the battleground which she regards as part of what being a feminist involves. 'I had an indulgent father and husband, and I haven't had to fight, it all fell into my lap. In further education for instance, my brother and I were equal.' (Her brother Alan is former Greater London Council Councillor, now Sir Alan Greengross.)

'I regarded myself as a wife and mother first, who happened to work as well. I got so much out of my marriage. It gave me my self-confidence. It was because I felt totally secure in my marriage that I felt I could meet other challenges.'

A card on the table beside me in her study read: 'Dull women have immaculate homes.' Dr Greengross's house was not far off immaculate, but I found this card cheering. Her husband, she said, had not been a bit domesticated. 'A man with six sisters to wait on him,' she said, 'is not domesticated. And I got married with the view that the role of a nice Jewish girl is to be her husband's wife, washing up after every meal. I set myself fairly high standards. For two years I did everything. Then imperceptibly as the children got older they did a lot more in the home. They *always* had to help clear the table for instance. When there are so many of you, you have to share that; and we had shifts for other chores.'

She was fortunate in her experiences of childbirth, having been inspired by Will Nixon, the professor at University College Hospital whose houseman she became. 'He was a person who said, "Having a baby is a job for a woman, and we must listen to what the woman says". He brought in the ideas of Grantly Dick-Read the pioneer natural the childbirth expert. He insisted that when giving a mother a cup of tea, the mother should have a teapot and milk jug on a tray; she must be served tea in the proper fashion, and treated with courtesy.'

All their five babies arrived at such speed that Wendy's husband never made it to the delivery room in time to be present, until the arrival of Polly, the last one. At her birth the room contained at least four doctors including Wendy and her husband; but it was the midwife who delivered the baby. Much more important, she says, was the fact that all the babies were all right, for which she is grateful. At the time we met, Dr Greengross was anxious that Enoch Powell's Unborn Children Protection Act was going to get through Parliament, stopping experiments on embryos ('It's not that I'm on the side of the researchers particularly, but I *am* on the side of the welfare of people who have to bring up the congenitally deformed') – but the bill did not get its second reading.

One of the precepts Wendy Greengross has always lived by, she said, was *A mother's place is in the wrong*. It is oddly consoling to be told by her that whatever one thinks one does for the best is bound to turn out to be wrong.

Her girls went to South Hampstead High School, her boys to University College School, both independent London day schools. 'I'm sure I was regarded as a terrible parent by their teachers. One of the worst things was trying to get them to do their homework: one expends an enormous amount of energy on that. And then the piano lessons, and getting them all to practise. You can sit with one child for half an hour but can you sit with five? Our piano tutor used to get so upset. I think I was the despair of their teachers at school who found me lackadaisical.

'One thing that made life easier for my generation was that one could put babies in prams outside in the garden for the whole morning; of course nobody does that now. And mothers are now afraid to let their children cry at all. We didn't even think about cot deaths. I used to traipse around in public places with enormous numbers of kids, my own and others, and say, "If you get lost, wait for me at the park gates": you certainly don't do that any more either. One actually did not have to worry so much then, about their safety.

'Later, the teenage years are a survival course, and you've got to survive it. When you get through at the other end, things do improve: you begin to get a closeness and an adult-to-adult relationship. I gave hoards of advice out, even while I was going through the problems of adolescent children myself, during years of the radio programme and years as Wendy of the *Sun* (I was their answer to Marje Proops). But I never found a better summary than "A mother's place is in the wrong." Will you be angry with them when they finally come in at night, or will you be accepting? If you say, "Please bring your boyfriend home," she'll say, "Of course I'm not bringing him here," and if you don't offer she'll say, "Why didn't you invite him here?" If you know in advance that you're always wrong, you don't feel so guilty. Guilt is such a self-indulgent, diminishing emotion.'

At this moment the middle son, Trevor, came in. As a state school teacher, he was on strike that day. Joining in our conversation he gave his mother this testimonial: 'Nice kids don't just happen. Nice kids are made. My positive qualities come directly from your teaching.' 'That's very nice of you to say so,' said Wendy Greengross politely.

I reflected later that of all the women I had talked to, the one who stood out in her constant reference to their husband's importance in her life was Wendy Greengross.

Life had been, she said, very difficult for a couple of years after his death. She had been desperately ill two years ago, was quite helpless and nearly died herself. 'The children have been absolutely wonderful,' she said, 'but the other important factor in my life is that I've got a lot of interesting things I'm able to do. And if it hadn't been for my husband encouraging me, perhaps I wouldn't have these things now. It really is *only* because of him.'

Drusilla Beyfus

journalist

m. 1956
MILTON SHULMAN
journalist and theatre critic

2 daughters, 1 son
ALEXANDRA NICOLA JASON

Drusilla Beyfus

Drusilla Beyfus, a *Vogue* editor, was one of the five women I could name, before I started on this book, who combined a busy working life with a long marriage and three children (she was scathing when I dared to celebrate a mere ten years of marriage). Drusilla could always be relied upon to advise with a crisp word, and her advice was worth more than a dozen consciousness-raising feminist books because, as I was well aware, she had done what I was trying to do, and the writers of the books in question had not. Her journalistic responsibilities (as, in turn, women's editor of the *Sunday Express*, associate editor of *Queen*, home editor of the *Observer*, associate editor of the *Daily Telegraph* magazine, and editor of *Brides* magazine and at *Vogue*) have been continuous, never thrown off course by any complication in life. Her daughter Nicky, when an Oxford undergraduate and fashion model, told me once: 'My mother is a saint. And you know how provocative my father is.' Father is Milton Shulman, the theatre critic and author: a person of decided opinions, excellent stories, and one who is at his best relating these stories and opinions in the company of women. In 1953 he published a newspaper series, 'Shulman's Beauties of 1953'; his future wife, 'easily the most beautiful women's editor in Fleet Street', noted for her cynical, witty and feminine writing style, was number eight.

Drusilla Beyfus remains a considerable beauty – she was the only woman in this book who refused, with the utmost charm, to reveal the year of her birth – and she invariably has something original and pertinent to say. It was on her advice that I confined my inquiry to those who have been married for at least twenty-five years. In 1968 Drusilla was the author of an enthralling book called *The English Marriage*, consisting of interviews with thirty couples, some maddeningly anonymous, some not. By the time the book appeared, several of the named couples were married no more (Andrew and Marianne Sinclair, Joan and Michael Bakewell among others.) It is true that marriages do end after twenty-five or even thirty years, but on the whole these marriages are a safer bet. When we met for the conversation here, Drusilla and Milton were about to reach the thirty-year mark. Characteristically, Drusilla did not regard herself as a suitable interviewee – for the reasons she explains – but we met to talk, anyway, in the Palm Court of the Ritz, and later at her flat in Eaton Square.

ॐ

'Women in journalism may be admired for being able to combine work with motherhood and marriage but we are cheats,' said Drusilla Beyfus, 'because we've always had work that can to some extent be manipulated. Our work is flexible. It is inflexibility that is death to anyone with a family. For instance, my sister has to be at her desk, when not rushing to an airport on business, by 8.30 am, and has done so for twenty years. Now that is really tough. And it does *not* combine with small children being breakfasted and amused or delivered to school.

'Also, I don't really count anyone with a husband working at home. Or a husband who likes domesticity. And I don't count anyone who has got a mother who likes playing the grandmother. Nor do I count anyone who does inflated part-time work, which can be taken up at any time.

'The professions which do count are the relentless ones – the city, the law, politics, an editorship or top management. To combine those with family life, a price has got to be paid and who is going to pay that price?' Thus did Drusilla briskly narrow down the field of my study and undermine its foundations.

Drusilla regards her family background as peculiarly unusual. Her father, a novelist and poet, was blind; her mother was separated from her father. Drusilla was out in the world by the age of seventeen, earning her living shortly afterwards. 'I have always felt constrained by precedent,' she said. 'I have felt imperilled and alone, and determined to make a go of things – of marriage, for instance.'

She was always going to be a journalist, having read about the exciting life of Pat, Girl Reporter, in a schoolgirls' novel. After her finishing school, she joined a weekly paper, the *Reading Mercury* – 'Which was foolish; I should have gone to Oxford and had a lovely three years in which to reflect.' But by the age of twenty-one she was one of Fleet Street's bright young things. Here she met another writer from the Beaverbrook empire, Milton Shulman from Canada. She was much sought after, but he was most persistent. As a gesture of independence she kept on her Mayfair flat for two years after they married in 1956.

'One was much less introspective then, but there was a certain spirit of independence. I remember labelling certain objects as "mine".' They married at Caxton Hall, with Michael and Jill Foot as witnesses, and found an organ-grinder complete with monkey to play outside. The thing Drusilla remembered best about it was that they had a heavenly honeymoon, near St Tropez.

Marriage did not change her life, she says, but children did, gradually. 'I am very typical of my generation. One assumed one would obviously get pregnant, and I felt very perky about it. Healthy and happy and pleased to be pregnant. I belong to the generation that were determined not to let it affect us at all: the new career woman/mother.'

Naturally she wrote articles about the impact of pregnancy and birth, and about her husband's reactions: 'The only time he fainted was when he saw the bill' (*Sunday Dispatch*, December 1957).

'When I had the first, Alexandra, I was working on newspapers and then I went to *Queen* magazine where I was rapturously happy. After Nicola, the second, I was back to full-time work again within two or three weeks as a matter of course. It was the last baby, my son Jason, I gave in to and took the state of pregnancy seriously. I knitted socks and did exercises. I had a prophetic sense that it would be a boy which I wanted very much.

'My general recollection is that I was always working right up to the delivery room. I was certainly finishing an article as I went off to Queen Charlotte's Hospital to have Alexandra and I drank a bottle of brandy thinking I could disguise the pain. In the taxi Milton said, "These days, there's no more to this than having a tooth out," and he deposited me with Mr Humphrey Arthure, my gynaecologist, in whom I had the greatest trust. Mr Humphrey Arthure never left me for the whole of the labour. We all adored him; he stroked our backs and held our hands.

'When you were pregnant, men colleagues treated you as if you were on fire; they always seemed afraid that you might have the baby in the office, so the relief on their faces when you finally left for hospital was considerable. Afterwards, they paid not much notice: "I thought maternity had claimed you," they said and lost interest.'

Drusilla's views on help at home are decided. 'Someone has got to spend time with your children: if it isn't you, who is it going to be? Whatever your answer, you have to take a course of action that leaves you feeling that you can somehow face yourself. I feel it is probably easier to delegate when they are younger; it is later on, when they become individuals, that it is probably more important to be around.' This is the reverse of the accepted assumptions of most women, who expect to be freed once the children are at school, and tied to the home only by infants. What Drusilla says makes sense, with one caveat which she herself adds: 'If you are largely abstracted with your own concerns while they are very young, and you don't get accustomed to them, you never really understand your child and the child assuredly never understands you.'

What Drusilla did was to appoint first a twenty-five-year-old living-in nanny named Janet, who wore a uniform and a badge and stayed until Alexandra was five. There was a daily cook who made lunch, and at one stage also a nanny's-day-off nanny, which gave her total back-up. 'And everyone was perfectly happy,' she says on reflection, 'except me. Because when I was with the children on my own I realised how strong my feelings were about wanting to bring them up.' She always had trained nannies, mainly because it meant they immediately fitted in with the nanny network. 'I spent endless time,' she says, 'worrying about the nanny's health and happiness.'

When I first had a nanny myself, Drusilla told me I was doing the worst possible thing by having a Monday-to-Friday nanny while I worked, but nobody at weekends: I would be working seven days a week, she said, and she was right. I still have the same arrangement and the same nanny. But then, times have changed. In the late 1950s at the Shulmans' in Eaton Square, the nanny would have only one day off a week and one complete weekend a month. Those were good days to be a working mother, but not such good days to be a nanny.

'I once had a deadline to meet on nanny's day off. To occupy Alexandra for a while I devised a game whereby we sailed across the floor on an upside down chair, pretending we were on a pirate ship looking for Treasure Island. "Look," I said, "I can see a notice on that island over there. What does it say?" Alexandra, determined to thwart the game, looked keenly at this imaginary notice and said firmly: "It says: NO BURIED TREASURE."'

After Jason arrived, the Shulmans had an elderly Scottish nanny to live with them, who doted on the baby. Nanny would dine with them on the evenings they were at home, 'which was a bit inhibiting if you felt like a fight,' Drusilla says. 'But Milton is very tolerant and to my knowledge never complained.' Most men, it must be said, prefer not to have the nanny around during the evening meal at least. 'But I knew that if Nanny was happy, the children would be happy, and Nanny took precedence over one's convenience. And one was always much better off than friends who had a new nanny every month.

'I honestly never felt guilty about employing help. I was so very aware of the contribution they made, and because I wanted to work I was super-conscious of the necessity of having a surrogate parent for certain hours. It is having to go to an office that makes you accept this.'

There were, she confessed, years of rush and panic. 'I do remember saying, "I don't have time to water a pot plant." The children's schools were all at different times and I delivered them, setting off at about 8.10 am until they were about fourteen and could travel alone. I did an enormous amount of chauffeuring to swimming, dancing, riding, gym and parties. I remember I once went away for six weeks when I had a trusty nanny, and I left *twelve* closely typed pages of instructions such as "No butter on the potatoes for Jason."

'I had always intended the children to go away to boarding school as I had done, and that would have left me wonderfully free. But then I realised that it is actually much more difficult to find the extra time for them in the holidays, if you are not used to having them around. And anyway, my daughters said please don't send us to boarding school; or rather, they said: "We are *not* going to boarding school" and that was that. My son did board from the age of twelve, and came back to live at home when he was at college in London.

'Was it all necessary, I ask myself, the rush and panic that went on for years and years? And what does one advise one's daughters in particular? They want the same things, but they are going about it quite differently of course. Such a structured life will be out for them. I should be surprised if they were not much more relaxed about the organisation of their lives professionally and domestically. They are much less confined by the need for perfection. I always wanted everything to run perfectly smoothly, and for it to be seen to do so, at work and at home.'

Could she imagine what her life might have been without children? 'I could quite easily have borne not to have had them,' she replied. 'I'm sure that I would have gone in the same direction anyway. But on the whole I think I am a mother who worked, rather than a career woman who happened to have children. There was certainly a long period when I was very much a mother who worked. Now I am someone who works and has had her children, which is different again, and is a surprisingly nice phase. The children were a fulcrum for a very long time, during the years between the nanny stage and A-Levels.

'To me the crucial years are the ages eight to sixteen. They are all at school and people say, how lovely, they're off your hands, but whose hands are they on? You have to think about that, and possibly increase the time you are there. Unfortunately these are precisely the years which, if you are having a successful career, coincide with all the main chances.'

Did she feel she had given up things because of the children? She turned down body and soul jobs because there wasn't the time, and books which in her case she dismisses as a trivial sacrifice. 'In fact any field that one tried, one really could have done better at without the children, except as a writer. Having children does deepen your under-standing of human nature and of your own character.

'There were long years when any additional major commitment beyond my basic one of editing a magazine filled me with terror. I look at women who get to the very top, particularly in creative spheres, and are untrammelled by family and I think, how wonderful to be able to give absolute priority to your work. If you are the mother of a family and do not have a house-husband or equivalent, you do have to go easy on your ambition for a spell.

'I do think that women who work and have children tend to be super-conscientious and make extra efforts. I kept saying to myself, was all the effort worth it? What about modifying one's aims? I'm not sure. But then what would the alternatives have been? I would always have worked, and I would always have been a journalist, because if you have a talent you should exercise such ability as you have. Having children as well enables you to have a taste of a wider range of experiences; never having children would be a closed door. You would simply not compre-hend the extraordinary intimacy of bringing up your children, and their trust in you.'

In the end it is a question of conscience. 'I feel combining work and motherhood requires you to plunge into your own conscience to decide how to arrange your priorities so you can live with yourself. But I do know that a lot of people don't feel like that at all. They may feel they have a great creative talent and are prepared to sacrifice the family for it. There is no question in their minds but to pursue their art. I only know it is an endless quest to find a balance between all these dismally conflicting and competing needs, and your own needs.'

Feminism was not *Brides* magazine's great concern but I suspected that its former editor was one of nature's feminists and she agreed. 'Feminism seemed to me a restatement of the obvious. When the early Simone de Beauvoir, and the books that followed, came out, none of it seemed a revelation to me. I always felt a rather natural feminist. I looked after myself from the age of seventeen. I am all for my sex. I do take a feminist position in life. But there are unanswered aspects. I think the post-feminists are making a more realistic appraisal of what is going to happen to the family. And what if we don't have the family?

'All the attempts to dispense with the family in my generation – in China, in Russia, in Israel, – as a cradle of the next generation, have failed. And whatever women feel about men as partners we know we are *not* going to give up maternity.'

Milton Shulman is one of those men who is totally at ease with small children; his approach is not to stem his flow of racontage, but to incorporate stories children will appreciate. He once stopped in the middle of crowded Fleet Street in a large trilby hat with a green riband, and declaimed, for my children, a story about his goldfish. It seems the goldfish's mate had died, and Milton had fashioned a new goldfish from a carrot, to keep the bereaved fish company. This story went down very well.

'Obviously it does help,' Drusilla said, 'if you have got a sympathetic and supportive husband. Milton, often working at home during the day, has always played an important part. Most husbands like children well enough in their proper place, which is not under *their* feet. But most intelligent men enjoy being with their children. People overstress men's lack of interest in their offspring, I think.'

(At this time Milton Shulman was usually doing two or three jobs; he was a TV executive during the day, and a theatre critic at night; and when he left the TV company he took on a weekly newspaper column as well.)

'At night Milton was wonderful with babies, and would rock the cot for hours. I hardly ever got up at night myself. I used to get up quite early in the morning, and I worked all day, and frequently cooked dinner at 10.30 pm after the theatre, so I thought 7 am to midnight was really quite enough.'

For many years the Shulmans spent high days and holidays at a Herefordshire manor house that was lent to them. When the children were between about seven and eighteen, Drusilla would take them away for the summer and could edit *Brides* magazine, commuting by train to her office when necessary, or going up to London to record television programmes like 'Call My Bluff'. It all took a great deal of organising. 'But I loved the days spent at our retreat,' says Drusilla, 'and one can always find the energy to do the things one really enjoys.'

She and Milton have always spent a remarkable amount of time together and she approves Cyril Connolly's view of marriage as a continuing duologue. 'Our conversation was never primarily concerned with the children,' she says. 'Although he writes about the theatre he is a political animal. He bombards me with his views and ideas about moral issues and the state of the nation.'

Did she consider herself his equal? *Heavens* yes. 'But we have different qualities. He has a great deal of moral conviction about everything. He is fundamentally more rational and optimistic than I am. He is basically in good heart, which is very reassuring. So when I feel desperate and filled with self-doubt, he is encouraging.

'But he is not really interested in the minutiae of my work. He likes me to be financially independent, and fulfilled, but he would be just as happy if I gardened, or made fudge, I believe. He is extremely sound in the face of failure. Success he is not so good at, as he tends to be sceptical: but he is tremendous when people feel checked, or low, and that is a great asset.

'And it is always nice to be with someone who likes your company. I have never got the feeling that he longed to be elsewhere. He is cheering and entertaining and he genuinely enjoys the company of women; best of all he loves a female audience and in the absence of an audience he seems happy to make do with me. I don't wish to paint it as an ideal or idyllic partnership, however; you ought to ask him what he feels about it.' I did, and after a rare silent pause he said: 'Our lack of boredom has been mutual.'

In her preface to her book *The English Marriage*, Drusilla thanks her husband for his 'most uncharacteristic display of patience' while she was writing the book.

When it came to writing her conclusions for that book, she decided she could not come to any. 'There are no rounded generalisations that wrap up the state of modern marriage. It seems to me that in marriage people speak for themselves alone. I find it encouraging that the marital tie remains the most personal, volatile and unclassifiable of human bonds . . . Marriage, I am convinced, is going to be the last subject to be effectively computerized.'

I put to her the notion which the journalist Maureen Cleave, a colleague and keen observer of people, had mentioned to me – that *brains* might be the essential ingredient in managing this way of life. 'Intelligence could be the answer,' Drusilla said, 'but then there are a lot of brainy women who make a classic mess of these things. The quality needed above all is the will to do it.' As for energy, she felt energy might even be a drawback rather than an asset. 'I think a lot of intelligent people without energy plan their lives *more* intelligently. People with energy attempt to cover up mistakes, and may take on too many things.'

Perhaps it is her positive manner, but Drusilla has always seemed in command of her life. 'I don't know how it appeared to others,' she said, 'but the edifice was always on the verge of collapse. The whole undertaking felt threatened, night and day. I thought I was going to blow into a million fragments, I was never going to be able to do this thing, my own work, and have a family life. Everyone in their innermost souls knows when they are getting near the point where the strings may break: then you must draw back.

'I think living near your work is an underrated convenience. It means if there's an emergency you can always get back. I always had that convenience. I'm sure, if you asked the children what they remembered of their schooldays, they would say that I had been very much there.'

On an earlier occasion I had asked Drusilla what it had been like bringing up children in the dotty 1960s. 'To me the 1960s were a mixture of hearing the Stones' records and reading Cecily Parsley's Nursery Rhymes to my children. There was such a feeling of family life being beleaguered, that I was all the more determined to keep the home fires burning. The interesting point to me now is the survival of traditional values. I'm sure the young feel that this emphasis on change, on everything being different, has been rather overdone. Young women, it seems to me, are much the same as we were. They still want to find someone who is going to bring them happiness, who will understand and be supportive and to whom they can talk.'

If it was any consolation to anyone, Drusilla added, she had formed the opinion that there really is no perfect answer to the work-and-motherhood conundrum. 'And I must say it really was rather a relief,' she said, 'to know there was no single answer.

'Should anything go wrong with a child, you feel this is your fault, for the very good reason that it often is. Had your mind not been elsewhere, you might have been able to recognise a future problem in time.

'That's why I think it's important to get to know them as young children because later in adolescence, when they lead such secret, independent lives, you need to rely on your understanding of them acquired during the early years. You will have quite a good idea of how they are feeling by merely looking at them.'

Not having gone to university herself, she was determined that her daughters and son would, and they did. They also tend to work in her field of glossy magazines, so they see each other frequently.

'I think they know I get enormous pleasure out of them, they know I love their company. Although they irritate me intensely at times,' said Drusilla, 'and I don't think I could live with them. I like the *idea* of them. What I really love is thinking about seeing them.'

Evelyn Anthony

novelist

b. 1928

m. 1955

MICHAEL WARD-THOMAS

company director

4 sons, 2 daughters

SUSAN ANTHONY EWAN KITTY

CHRISTIAN LUKE (BARLEY)

Evelyn Anthony

If you had to picture the quintessential English country manor house it would look like Horham Hall in Essex, one of the finest Elizabethan private houses in the land. Its mistress is Evelyn Anthony, the author, whose novels emerge every couple of years; her devotees order the latest at once from their libraries, so that in any year's list of the 100 most borrowed books, she has six titles, far outstripping more noisy best-sellers like Jeffrey Archer and Len Deighton.

Yet Evelyn Anthony, a successful writer for thirty years and the mother of six children, does not feature in lifestyle articles in *Vogue*, nor appear on quiz games, nor talk at literary luncheons, nor turn up at bookish parties. 'I doubt if she is even acquainted with a single other author,' her husband, Michael Ward-Thomas, told me as he drove me from the station to the house one hot July day. The centre of her life, her passion and her reward, is that splendid house, where she is content to stay quietly put. She stepped out, when we arrived onto the gravel drive, surrounded by dogs, tall and blonde and carrying a tray with sparkling wine because it was her fifty-seventh birthday.

We talked on the terrace under a shady medlar tree, overlooking the lake with water lilies, a fountain, swimming pool, shaven lawns leading to distant woods, fields as far as the horizon, husband toiling away with his lawn-edging shears . . .

'Being mistress of this house,' Evelyn Anthony told me, 'is *the* great joy of my life.' Later she told me how the house was lost to them, and how they got it back; a story which emphasises the place her moated grange holds in her heart. It seemed entirely in character that she should have won it back. She has that spirit and tenacity, as well as the mocking green eyes of a Becky Sharp.

She is the author of 27 novels – 11 historical, 16 thrillers. Her latest, entitled *No Enemy But Time* (the quotation comes from Yeats), is set in

Ireland and was, she said, more personally and emotionally involving than anything she had ever written before.

୬◑

Evelyn Anthony, born Evelyn Stephens, whose grandfather founded the Stephens ink company and whose father invented the Dôme trainer for anti-aircraft gunners, was not expected to become a working girl at all. She was expected to marry in her debutante year, by nineteen at the latest, a beautiful girl like her. 'But I tended to drive men off by badgering them and talking about religion and politics. Also, I was a Catholic and that was a disadvantage in those days, unless you found another Roman Catholic to marry. It really was "Do come down, but I'm afraid my father wouldn't have one in the house."'

The only child of Christian Stephens, a fond father, she was educated by the nuns of the Sacred Heart Convent, Roehampton, and before that by a governess named Miss Ethel Bossey. Every afternoon she and Miss Bossey would go for a two-hour walk and had to speak either French or Spanish. Her father was the one who encouraged her to read history and literature. 'But I was not encouraged to be independent; I suppose I was lacking in confidence but I've made up for it since. My mother was a complete Edwardian, well into her forties when I was born. I felt, even as a child, "If only I had been born a son . . ." If I had been a son my father would have come into a great deal of money. I was never reproached with it, of course, but I did pick up an inkling of it and part of me strove to be bold and brave and athletic in order to be *like* a son. I adored my father. He was my companion, intellectual and clever.

'You may not believe this now but I was extremely pretty. The deb season wasn't as lovely as we all used to make out, though. I was always slightly contentious and silly; I wasn't really a huge social success. But I was proposed to, yes. One of the proposers is godfather to one of the children.

'It was suggested that I might have got into Oxford to read History, but I suddenly got fed up and passionately wanted to do something in the war. We were in a naval port where my father was stationed, I was fifteen and it was the school holidays, when the terrible raid on Southampton made me furious. I wanted to do something positive at once so I joined the firewatchers. I only did one night's duty before they found out my age and sent me promptly home. Then when I left the convent at seventeen at the end of the year I squeaked into the Red Cross, first as a filing clerk with the RAF Wounded and Missing section in Belgrave Square, then in the personnel department, which I loved, and where I made many lifelong friends. The war was the most important thing that happened in my young life. I can't see my life without seeing it in terms of that. One longs to tell the children, sometimes. We did take some of them to visit Dachau when we were in Germany a while ago, and I think it made its impact.'

She met her future husband at a ball, at the Dorchester she thinks, when she was twenty-two. He was in naval uniform and it was love at first sight. 'But we didn't get married, because Michael didn't have any money or a job and I was very immature and neither family was very keen on the idea of the match.' So he went off to Northern Rhodesia for four years, and would send her flowers each year on the anniversary of the night they met, December 10th.

'Then my father died and Michael wrote to me and I was very touched, so we had another go. Again, because of family pressures it broke up, and he went back to Rhodesia. Within a year, his father died. We said: "Right, we're not going to tell any of them;" so I lied to my mother and he lied to his, and we had a six months' engagement. I kept chickening out, the run-up to the wedding was most dreadful. We started our married life in the face of family resentment.'

It wasn't that Michael's family was particularly anti-Catholic, she explains, but there was prejudice on both sides ('With hindsight I was an intolerable little papist prig,' she says). 'My family were alarmed by Michael's reputation as a very "fast" young man. Add to this that we were both only children with – to put it mildly – possessive parents, and you have the framework for a miserable engagement. Marriage was taken far more seriously then than it is now, when live-in girl and boy friends are welcomed into the family without a second thought. Divorce would have been a family tragedy. Perhaps these old-fashioned attitudes had some bearing on the fact that thirty-two years later we can say we proved them all wrong.'

Within eight years there were six children: Susan, Anthony, Ewan, Kitty, Christian and Barley. Barley was christened Luke but known as Charley-Barley, and Barley stuck. 'I had all these children,' Evelyn Anthony says, 'because I truly believed that was my religious vocation in life: to give life. It was to do with my true belief and my Catholicism, although I'm not as adamant or as bigoted as I used to be on the subject. I still believe, though, that if you marry, the best thing you can do is bring human life into the world. When we married and I didn't get pregnant immediately, I thought I wasn't going to have any, and it was a terrible worry. But the great thing was, my dear husband who was not a Catholic and who perhaps didn't realise what bunny rabbits we would be, said, "I don't care, I didn't marry you for children, I married you for you, and we'll adopt".'

She felt very well when she was pregnant and worked like mad. When Michael, who was a socialist in those days, accused her of being a drone during their courtship she had started writing short stories for the men's magazines of the day, using a man's name, Anthony Evelyn (she chose Anthony after her saint). One story about bull-fighting was published. Then at twenty-three she wrote her first historical romance ('Very cringe-making to read it now but I was terribly young') and soon afterwards, two US Literary Guild awards came her way, worth £10,500 each, the best possible boost to confidence: for *Anne Boleyn* in 1956 and *Victoria*, 1957. 'It put me on the map and gave my career just the lift it needed.'

'I think I would have always wanted to work. I know I was pleased to have something of my own, and when you are a young woman you chiefly want to be published and if money comes too you are delighted. Money starts to work into the equation: it gives you freedom and it is a tangible sign that you are accepted and recognised for what you do.'

In those days before the women's movement Evelyn Anthony would be interviewed about how she managed to have six children and to have written ten books. There was never a nanny. She did the day-school runs. 'But that was a bit of a cheat because I always had domestic help, a lot of help. There were foreign girls who were always very nice, and you could meet someone for lunch and the children would be better off than with some old dragon of a nanny. I wasn't a bit martyred by motherhood. Also, the eldest boys went off to prep boarding school at seven or eight.'

One interview which captured her in 1966 (alongside another career-woman mother Margaret Thatcher, then Opposition spokesman on Treasury affairs) cites two male servants as Evelyn Anthony's domestics: a cook named Nice from Nigeria, and Salifu from Upper Volta. Michael had been travelling in Africa for many years and Evelyn joined him for six months in Ghana where Michael was director of a mining company producing industrial diamonds. All the children (five of them at the time) came too. 'Nice and Salifu were cook and chief steward respectively to the General Manager, and worked for us on the mine at Akwatia. We offered them the chance to come to England and see how they liked it, and they stayed with us for seven years. They were the days when there was still an optimistic feeling about the freedom of Africa.'

She feels they got better as parents as they went along. 'We may have fussed over Susan too much as she was born with a hole in the heart,' she says. It is Evelyn Anthony's belief that Susan was a Lourdes cure; someone brought back a little bottle of water, which she gave to the child, and at Great Ormond Street, she says, they could find nothing wrong with Susan after that.

All six children are now variously dispatched into the world. One son is in the furniture removal business, one a student in France, one an army officer with the Blues and Royals, the second mounted regiment of the Household Division, escorting the Queen on ceremonial occasions. Horses, and three-day eventing, have been a feature of their lives. 'Our children brought themselves up really, they were such a tribe,' Evelyn Anthony says. 'Very clannish and self-contained. They would chase friends away if any came. "Let's get rid of them and go down to Noggin's Wood," you'd hear them say.'

In 1967 Evelyn decided to give up her successful historical romances, with titles like *Valentina* and *Anne of Austria*, and concentrate on thrillers, with titles like *The Rendezvous*, *The Legend* and *The Assassin*, often with a wartime or espionage background. They proved to be even better sellers than her romances. *The Tamarind Seed*, which she thought of during a short holiday in Barbados, when she saw the tamarind seed, shaped like a slave's head, in the museum at Bridgetown, became a film with Omar Sharif and Julie Andrews. Her productivity has been regular and dependable. Did the women's movement impinge on her life at all? 'As a woman who worked and earned,' she says, 'I always had independence, and I wanted to be considered intelligent enough to manage my own affairs. What I resisted in women's liberation was the apparent regarding of the uterus as a deformity we carry within us, and the antagonism towards men which I find sad. My attitude is that within a marriage you have to keep your end up. Particularly with a strong man, which he is. Nobody thanks you for being a doormat. It is a question, I think, of taking what you need from the women's movement and leaving what you don't. Those who went overboard for it tended to throw away everything.' She is, by age and upbringing, one of those women who claims to feel twitchy if she sees her husband carrying a tray. 'I see myself as the boss who keeps the establishment going while the other boss is away.'

'It's a tightrope, if you run a big family, because you want to be positive and decisive, without being so overpowering that the others feel they can't decide anything for themselves. I'm very conscious of it.' The clue to staying together happily for more than thirty years in her view is laughing at the same jokes, and noticing the other person is there. 'We're friends, that's the real secret. We're very companionable and never bored.' Despite her years of success Evelyn Anthony is still a worrier. 'Things worry me for much longer and far more deeply now than when I was younger and weaker. And if I don't have anything to worry about I make something up.' Laughter. 'I'm still shy of literary parties. I'm a popular writer, but I'd need a stiff Scotch to face them. We tend to see all the old friends we've known for twenty-five years or more, and cling to them.'

Her hobby, in *Who's Who*, is 'buying things at Christie's'. 'There is no point in having money unless you enjoy spending it,' she says. 'We live at an extravagant rate and I spend like water. But I love buying things for the house. Anything that makes it look nice. I buy it presents. When you earn your own money it gives you the right to be irresponsible. That's when a nice royalty cheque has just arrived. Then I start a new book, and work harder to justify having been to Christie's.'

The story of Evelyn, Michael and their house is comforting. They first saw Horham Hall by paying 2s 6d at the gate with other visitors. Ten years ago, the cost of maintaining its crumbling fabric, and of bringing up their large family, combined with the soaring inflation of 1973–6, forced them to sell the house and go into tax exile in Ireland. Ireland was fine, and the children rode, but Evelyn always longed to come home. 'And suddenly one day we heard that the chaps who had bought it were selling again – at a ridiculous price.' Alexander Shand and John Phillips, men of taste and means, had done laudable things like adding central heating, efficient plumbing and finest quality curtains in the oak-panelled dining room. 'But we said no and no and no, at their price. Interestingly, nobody else came to see it (there was the threat of Stansted airport again) and then, ten days later, our bid was accepted. I think it was meant. On 15th October 1982 we were back home, bringing with us the dogs who had been here before, a wolfhound, a spaniel and a Jack Russell, and they all went shouting through the front door as if they'd never been away.

'Everything seemed to be perfect. Then there was a rainstorm and water came pouring down the stairs: we were home. I never want to live anywhere else ever again. I can tell you so many people who wouldn't have it as a gift. But it's our home and all that that entails. It's where the children grew up. If ever I'm depressed or worried, I've only got to see it and my spirits lift.'

She says she can sit down anywhere in this house to write. She always could. She could always shut off the household even when it was crowded with six children under ten and two African servants in the flat in Cadogan Square, twenty years ago. That was the point at which she made her switch from historical romances to more challenging thrillers. She is not a sentimental writer; her prose has muscle. 'And research is all a con,' she says. '*The Grain of Truth* was set in a country I'd never even visited. You don't have to go anywhere.

'I think I would say that I have been much more a mother who happens to write, than a writer who happens to have children. My whole upbringing stressed the importance of bringing up a family before any other consideration, and I was mentally and emotionally geared to put them first and my writing second. I didn't find it difficult, because doing it the other way would have made me both guilty and unhappy. I was lucky to have that "shut-off" capacity; I could switch roles almost instantly. This isn't common, because I know women writers who have actually had to take a room outside the house in order to concentrate. Had I attempted this, I'd have worried like mad about what was happening at home.

'What writing means to me is, first, a need to express myself in telling stories: in communicating to others the things that excite and interest me. I'm by nature a tense and anxious person, and writing is a tremendous safety valve. It gives me a sense of freedom, because I can spend my own money with a clear conscience and above all, I feel that at the end of the day I've justified my existence by working for some of the good things in life. That is very important to me. But I find it impossible to talk about really, because I have a horror of being an egocentric bore.'

Dr Jill Parker

General Practioner

b. 1925

m. 1951

PETER PARKER

Sir Peter Parker industrialist, businessman,
ex-chairman British Rail

1 daughter, 3 sons

LUCY ALAN OLIVER NATHANIEL

Dr Jill Parker

The first striking characteristic of Jill Parker is her humour: she seems, in a languid way, to be gently mocking, refusing to take things particularly seriously. Jill Parker is the wife of one of the nation's busiest public figures – Sir Peter Parker, former chairman of British Rail, now chairman of the Rockware Group, former Labour candidate. She has always worked as a doctor in general practice within the National Health Service, and they have four children.

In 1973 they bought Minster Lovell, a historic medieval farmhouse with some interesting old barns and a couple of meadows along the River Windrush in Oxfordshire. The house stands beside the picturesque ruins of the Minster of which the farmhouse was once part; it had previously been owned by an Oxford college and had been lived in by a tenant farmer. Two years later Jill Parker began to create a garden which has now become a source of personal pride ('the focus of my life') and of general acclaim. There is a circular garden of old roses which looks as if it has been there for ever. (She has published a beautiful book called *The Purest of Pleasures: The Making of a Romantic Garden*, which tells its story.) On one of the occasions we met, the garden was open to the public under the National Gardens Scheme. Lady Parker was showing people round, quite unperturbed (in white shirt, billowing skirt, hair drawn back in ballet dancer's bun) by the hundreds of visitors. The actual interview took place in the Parkers' flat in a mansion block in Kensington, near Jill Parker's medical practice which, whatever her husband has been occupied with, has continued on its even keel. It was when I interviewed Jill Parker that I first formed the conclusion that there is a sort of officer class among women whose unassailable assumption is that they will get on with the job in hand, do what needs to be done, reap the rewards and not – *ever* – grumble about the effort it all requires.

Jill Parker opened the conversation with a sort of declaration: 'I think of mine as an extremely privileged position. There are very few men who can say that they work at what they like doing best and get paid for it, while somebody else pays the rent. You don't actually have to call yourself a feminist unless conscious of some sort of frustration, I think.'

Gillian Rowe-Dutton, as she was born, was the youngest of three daughters of Sir Ernest Rowe-Dutton, a Treasury manager and financial adviser to the embassies at Berlin and Paris. 'We all adored him and he gave us a tremendous work ethic. We were a very close family. My eldest sister has died, but I am still close to the second. What my father instilled into us was that you worked; you worked jolly hard, and if you earned money that was a rather disreputable thing to do. I think there were probably two dirty words in his view – one was money, a very dirty word; the other was getting your name in the paper, which was an extremely dirty word.

'A lot of our life was formed by the war. I was fourteen when it broke out, and at St Paul's Girls' School in London; before that we'd lived in Paris and Berlin when my father was there, so we were fairly snooty, self-sufficient kids. We didn't have many friends. But we were in London all through the war, and through the Blitz. And somehow the idea of not working afterwards did not arise.

'It was taken for granted that I would read Medicine. That may have begun when I read a biography of Marie Curie, at the age of nine or ten. My mother was absolutely not academic, a vicar's daughter, very maternal, intellectually very simple. I don't think she cared about not having a son, but I'm sure my father must have wanted one. As the youngest I was the favourite, the scatty one. It gave me some closeness with my dad, since I was still running around in shorts when the others were growing up. There was a lot of reading going on in our house. My father had been at Trinity College, Dublin, and at Oxford, and was a rather classical fellow. Chemistry and botany I was quite hot at. I went up to St Anne's College, Oxford, and I *adored* it. The year I went up, '43, no men were going up except a few tubercular red-heads. They took a dozen women to read medicine and they told me, you can come and be number thirteen but you must behave yourself. I was so afraid of being sent down I avoided every collegiate thing, I thought I'd better keep a low profile. And since I was having a cheery life, I thought I'd better keep an *even lower* profile.

'Then in 1945 the university was flooded with middle-aged heroes aged twenty-two. Including Peter. I was doing clinical work and house jobs at the Radcliffe Infirmary in Oxford. Peter was reading History and he did everything: politics, sport, acting, ran the Labour Club. Was I immediately enraptured? Yes, but he was still with Shirley Williams and I was with Ken Tynan. Ken Tynan was brilliant. He was a one-off, there was no one else like him. Alas, we parted the worst of friends. The fact remains, he was a startling fellow.

'We had quite a jolly hectic time at Oxford, you might as well say it was a marvellous generation. But Peter went down six months before I qualified and went off to the States for a year. He thought he'd got away, and was just shaking the dust from his feet when after six months I thought that's enough of this, and got an extremely minor fellowship in obstetrics at a little hospital in Brooklyn. Peter was at Cornell and Harvard in upstate New York; my parents were then in Washington as my dad was the first British director of the World Bank. So off I went to the States and if I felt in need of family I could whizz off to Washington.

'I didn't know much about obstetrics, I didn't even know words like calibrate, but I did have my Oxford-England voice and I could try to impress people with that. I had a very good year and we plighted our troth during our last week in America. We came home, and before long Peter fought a Labour seat, Bedford, his home town, which he jolly nearly won. It was an 1800 majority for Christopher Soames, the only marginal seat whose Conservative majority was reduced in '51.

'It was taken for granted that I would go on working after we married. There's a funny thing about being a doctor. Once you're a doctor you've got to be a doctor. You can't stop being one – that's what's so claustrophobic about it. I wish sometimes I *didn't* know how the liver worked. I'm only a GP, "the lowest form of medical life", but it's the matrix of my professional mind. It seems to me amazing that people can look at their hands and not know what's going on inside, how the joints work.

'In my first job I was earning £700 a year and Peter was earning £500, so I made the most of it. We were both very keen to have children. He came from a very close family too and the whole point, with both of us, was the family. We had a marvellous year on our own first in our one-room flat off the Fulham Road and then, after eighteen months, we had Lucy. I was pre-pill; we had caps, and the children came just as and when we wanted them, but there was a late miscarriage in the middle, so the family falls in two groups of two: Lucy and Alan, then Nat and

Oliver. The fourth one was born when I was thirty-nine and I felt then that another pregnancy would seem to last a few *years*.

'The first job I did was deeply boring and nine-to-five: junior medical officer at Unilever. What did I do? Bugger-all. That is to say, it wasn't my idea of doctoring. Very little contact with patients and a lot of bureaucratic administration. Then I got pregnant for the second time and they gave me the sack, which they could in those days. I stayed at home for about six months with the second baby and wasn't sure what to do.

'We had an endless stream of au pair girls, which I think was confusing for my generation of working mothers. I would absolutely play it differently now. I was always so apologetic about the children. People used to say, it's not worth training a woman for anything, she'll just have babies and give it up. One did want to show them. And one felt too, "My dad paid for all this." And anyway I *wanted* to work. But there was a definite feeling that you were very much in a man's world and you had to bend over backwards to be reliable so that nobody would say, "Oh God, she's got *children*." But one was only ever as reliable as one's hopeless Spanish au pair. That was a real tightrope, trying to look as if you didn't have children.

'Today I'd be bolder. I'd say: "You're jolly lucky to have me! *And* I've got these wonderful children." I admire the way young parents now are far more self-confident about that, they even let their kids ring them up at work . . .

'I started being a GP when Alan, the second, was a baby. There was a practice in Brunswick Gardens and the first I knew of it was there was a huge white rabbit in the garden and a red face appeared and said, could I have my rabbit back? He was a GP who lived over the wall, and when we introduced ourselves it turned out he was looking for a locum.

'I had already done the occasional locum job, but I was petrified of real patients. I used to think, Oh God they're going to die and it'll be all my fault. But I stuck with the practice from that day to this, retreating into part-time when Peter went to British Rail. The joy of general practice, and of staying in the same practice, is the continuity. And the surgery is just five minutes from here' (the Parkers' flat in Kensington).

I asked what had been Sir Peter's role in the domestic scene and she answered, 'Zilch. He never did a thing. But if I was a doormat, it was voluntarily. It never occurred to me or to him that he should be domesticated. His mother and mine – though totally different – did the same. My dad didn't know where the cooker was and I don't think Peter does now. But then, you don't want to say, "My husband's brilliant at cleaning the lavatory" do you?

'In our family all the children are totally undomesticated apart from Nat. Lucy has just bought a little flat and is very keen on it but she's not a natural housekeeper. Nat is the one who will clear up and say "Mum, we're out of cornflakes," quite naturally.'

Jill Parker had her first two babies in Queen Charlotte's Hospital, the second two at home: four in nine years. They went to a local primary school round the corner.

'Life at home during the school years was pretty disorganised. I'm not one for clearing up the night before and setting the breakfast things ready. It was a hell of a scramble in the morning and I was jolly tired much of the time. Now, I'm appalled at the amount of time we spent on just seeing that the socks were white.

'I was very fond of my mother-in-law, a very powerful woman. Peter's two brothers had been killed in the war which made it very important to stay close to her, so we'd go down to Bedford at weekends and take the kids, so there was a great deal of ironing little pleats. Peter was a marvellous son, and it was good for the kids to know their grandparents, but it was a tiny house and the kids had to behave, so it wasn't restful. We went back to Ireland for holidays; Ireland has always meant a great deal to me.

'In our family marriage was regarded as almost the most important, crucial work. It was drummed into you. Marry or not but, my God, make it work. I'm certainly not the divorcing sort. I would have had to go through hell to do it, I would think of it as the worst possible thing. For your marriage to smash would be the worst smash you could have, worse than bankruptcy or an accident. I've always taken that as read.'

Of all the women to whom I addressed a question about what was the reason for a lasting marriage, Jill Parker's reply was the most straight-forward. She said: 'We're potty about each other.

'Increasingly so,' she added. 'Thirty-three years more potty than we were thirty-three years ago. It does sound rather wet, I'm afraid. But we've never been able to have rows. I'm very uncomplicated. I think Peter's much more complicated than I am. I was brought up to think that scenes were the most awful thing that could happen. Some people do have scenes, I believe, and that's the way they work. It's just not part of how I can function. I probably suppress my anger. I don't *feel* anger. But if I did, I would probably suppress it.

'I can't imagine the children coming between us. I think it's quite funny that after a certain stage one tends to have secrets with the children as opposed to with your husband. "Whisht, children, your father's going to sign his name": which means, for Christ's sake don't ask him for money till the day after tomorrow.

'When they were young our weekends were filled with children's activities, trudging about doing Londony things. We always did things together, that was the point. If you wanted to write letters in solitude you'd have to set the alarm and get the letters written before the day began.'

Jill Parker claims she is totally unambitious in the vertical sense. 'I don't want to climb the Harley Street ladder. Medicine is for me a one-to-one relationship, doctor-patient, and that is all. Peter Parker has plenty of ambition so I would never put my ambition first. If Peter said, "Let's go to Peru," he would have already taken into account the fact that I would stop being a doctor. I think the sort of life we lead, the fast, middle-class, top management life (the kids, the mortgage, all the commitments) makes you feel trapped. There is a terrific momentum, you can't afford to earn less or do less. But you have to leave a corner of your mind free so that if you say, "Look, I do think we should go and dig this well," you can say, "OK, we leave Tuesday." You have to know that you could scrap everything at any time. If you feel a bit free of it, it's easier to sustain. I make it sound like a tightrope, which of course it is if suddenly something goes wrong. You do have to keep running.

'Long ago we decided not to base our decisions on whether a thing costs money or not. Of course you need money, but it's totally relative. To some people we're incredibly rich, but to oneself one's never rich. A lot of people would be staggered if they knew we don't have background money at all. There has never been unearned money in our lives: we've had to make it all.

'We had no idea that Minster Lovell would ever come into our lives but that is our home now, and the children's sometimes. It is the focus of my life, the garden, the weekends at Minster. It means Olly and Nat can have our London pad to have orgies in all weekend. They're actors, it's ideal.

'Peter's diary is fixed months ahead, so I get a list from Peter's secretary saying what's happening every night in October, and I can tell the practice I cannot be on call on October 17 so I'll do it another Wednesday instead. There are only four of us in the practice and I can still keep up the same amount of work every week, whatever happens in Peter's life.

'I do think that the person who has done the worst disservice to women is Superwoman. It means that whereas I had to be apologetic, now women have to be *super*. This is the difference. I have never tried to do everything. I do not sew on buttons.

'I don't see how one could be anti-feminist: I look on feminism as improving the quality of women's lives. The Cause could not have got under way without Germaine Greer. But my eldest sister was the wife of a clergyman in Nottingham in a four-room council flat. And two nights a week she would – apart from the clergyman's wife stuff – turn over her living room to about twenty really poor women to do a sort of Keep Fit and have a cup of coffee. *That's* improving the quality of people's lives.'

What about the satisfaction of having everything, the husband, the family, the career? 'There isn't any; it makes one depressed. One feels, it can't last, it makes me anxious. I feel infinitely lucky of course. I think it's amazing that one gets to be sixty, for a start. We're both immensely healthy. One looks in the mirror and thinks, Crumbs! I say, what luck, I'm terribly healthy today; think about all the good things.'

She went out into the kitchen to make coffee and whistled the entire time.

She said, when she came back, that there was still something she would like to do and that is to write, perhaps a medical thriller. 'When I stop – and I'd have to put an arbitrary date on my stopping, about sixty-five, – I'll start on it. Peter won't stop, he'll go on indefinitely till he fades. The Railways were a 24-hour-a-day job. Now he's got a bit of time to play tennis with the boys, and for his Blake. William Blake is his passion. And he is more active than I am in the SDP. We were always Labour before. I've found it tragic not to be able to point to a really idealistic Left wing any more, to tell the children that's what politics should be all about. Or an idealistic Right, come to that.

'I could have earned a lot more by working in private medicine, but only at huge cost to the children. Anyway I could never have been happy in the private sector. I have always worked within the National Health Service, and think of it as the best context in which the doctor-patient relationship can flourish. I believe the faults and weaknesses of the NHS are largely imposed from outside pressures. I was a full-time partner in the practice until Peter went to the Railways, but I never worked at weekends: that was axiomatic. If they wanted someone who worked at weekends they'd have to get someone else. I found that the children didn't mind me working as long as they knew that when I said I'd be home I'd be home.

'In retrospect I think I worked too hard when they were very little, really tiny. I left them more than I would now. I think they missed out.

'I've come to believe this through my daughter-in-law, who has never worked at a job *and* is totally undomesticated as well, and doesn't want to be, ever. The children come absolutely first with her, and I think that's brilliant. She's the other end of the spectrum. She doesn't feel unliberated. She is not pre-feminist, she doesn't feel obliged to do the housework, she doesn't feel tied down or imprisoned in her home, she's got the freedom to live her life as she pleases. She says: "The place is a tip and I don't care, it's the kids that matter, and I'm jolly well going to play with them." Her husband is the son who got sacked from Bryanston for supporting Black Power and every kind of sheer rebellion at fourteen, and is now working in the City. He was such a wild boy, and now he's the one with the mortgage and wife and kids. It's so funny.'

Alice Thomas Ellis

Anna Haycraft
writer and painter

b. 1932

m. 1957
COLIN HAYCRAFT
publisher

5 sons, 2 daughters
WILLIAM JOSHUA (*d.* 1978) THOMAS
OLIVER ARTHUR ROSALIND (*d.* 1971)
· SARAH ·

Alice Thomas Ellis

Alice Thomas Ellis is the author of five novels and the mother of five surviving children (there were seven). Though not a kitchen table novelist (she writes in her bedroom) it is in her kitchen that she is presented to the world: sometimes in a long white apron at the Aga, like a woman in an old Welsh cottage cooking for a crowd; sometimes at the table while the family come and go, talking, smoking, having a glass of wine. Her house has few mod cons. It has still a scullery with ancient sink. Unlike its neighbours in the Regency crescent in London it has no white paint. The playwright Alan Bennett, next door, allows a homeless old lady to camp in his driveway in a van which adds to the general air of eccentricity that hangs about the Haycraft household; Anna Haycraft is Alice Thomas Ellis's real name. The house is full of dim nooks and thousands of ancient books. People come in and out the whole time; there are few quiet moments in this interview.

There were years of her life, before she became a fiction editor and then a fiction writer, when she was exclusively a mother, and didn't even pain: though she had been a painter. But she is in this book because she is one of the most original voices to be heard on the subject of the family, marriage and domesticity (she has found a congenial niche writing a weekly column in *The Spectator* called 'Home Life') and because her novels are extraordinarily good. 'I wrote the first,' she has said, 'because I was fed up with feminist whining and whingeing. I'm afraid there's no other word for it. I felt women did themselves no service by adopting such a Poor Me posture. It seemed to me a travesty of womanhood. I wanted to show a woman who is very powerful, like so many of the women I know.'

'I was an only child,' says Alice Thomas Ellis, 'so perhaps having seven of my own was a compensation. My children always say they're never going to have any children, ever.'

She was born Anna Margaret Lindholm, in Liverpool, but when her father was away at the war she and her mother went to live in Wales at Penmaenmawr in a cottage under a hill. 'It was where we went for holidays when I was tiny, and it was heaven.' She would walk a mile to the station for the train to Bangor, and another mile from Bangor Station to school. 'The sort of grammar school where you get your certificates and that sort of thing and wear a uniform and get *naicely* brought up. Bangor had been an Edwardian watering place with a Grand Hotel and it had the air of a large village.'

Art was Anna's strong suit. 'The head mistress and the art mistress used to argue English-at-university vs. art college. But university seemed to me a bit of a dowdy idea; there was still that awful image of bluestockings in cardies and cocoa, while art schools were black stockings and much more *me*. I still visit my old art mistress, Miss Smart. Only now I call her Daisy.

'Father came out of the war as an invalid. He died at the age of fifty-four but my eldest son William remembers him; he was five when he died, and absolutely adored him. He used to embroider nightdresses for the children.'

At seventeen she went to Liverpool Art School and this was when she first met Beryl Bainbridge, one of her three closest friends, who was in those days an actress at the Playhouse. 'It wasn't until years later that we met again in London at the gates of Hampstead Comprehensive where we both had children. We fell on each other. That's what started me on the whole fiction thing. She gave me her unpublished novel, *Harriet Said*, and I found I had a gift for editing. I knew what she meant even when she didn't, if you see what I mean.'

But what happened directly after art college was that she went into the Convent of Notre Dame de Namur in Liverpool, a Belgian order, as a postulant. Her parents had belonged to the dotty Church of Humanity, based on the teachings of Auguste Comte, but Anna had converted to the Catholic Church at nineteen. 'But I was invalided out of the convent with a slipped disc and I went to work for Leonard Cheshire's charity, general dogsbodying.

'Working for Leonard Cheshire was extremely interesting and I was going to go back to the convent but I was carried on by the course of events. Leonard Cheshire introduced me to a man, and I went to London and lived in Chelsea.' This brisk narrative is the extent to which Anna wishes to linger over that period, but the Catholic Church and what has happened to it are subjects that obsess her still.

'I went and shared a flat with some girls, thirty bob a week in Bramerton Street in those days, wonderful what one could do, eh. I went to work for the Comtesse de Hautecloque, Françoise Tollemache, in a delicatessen in the King's Road, behind Markham Square on Chelsea Green. We sold little pies and things and roast chickens. It was rather bliss, before Chelsea turned. Pubs and clubs, that's what we did. Every night, the White Hart to the Marquis of Anglesey to the Pheasantry. That's what we did every evening and everybody seemed to know each other.

'Then one day Colin came into the deli to buy a pie. I was wearing a pinny. He was working on the *Daily Mirror*. I think he proposed the next day on the steps of Bramerton Street. I think I said yes at once.'

They were married in Penmaenmawr a few months later.

The post arrives at this moment bearing the news that Alice Thomas Ellis is in line for a PEN award and if she wins, she will have to make a gracious speech. She says she would rather die than speak. After appearing on TV when her novel *The 27th Kingdom* was a Booker Prize nomination she said, 'I'd rather have eighteen visits to the dentist than one TV interview.'

When they married, Colin encouraged her to carry on with her painting, but the babies got in the way. They settled together in Markham Square, Chelsea, and came to this house in Camden in 1961. It cost £4500, which was modest even then. They already had three sons, William, Joshua and Thomas. Oliver was born a year later. 'Four under five; rather hair-raising. I was tired beyond belief. But I did love being pregnant. And I did think: "This is me. This is what I came for." I did a bit of painting, but mostly I fussed about food and made them little nighties.'

Her son Arthur, aged seventeen, had materialised in the kitchen at this point and was listening. 'Why did you choose to have *seven*?' he asked his mother. 'Odd,' she said serenely: 'A child reaches this age and has never asked this question before, nor have you ever explained it.' Then, addressing Arthur: 'You do not practise birth control if you are a Catholic.'

To me she said: 'I'm not good with little children; grown children are more interesting. But there was always this curiosity, what on earth was the next one going to be like? Then they arrive, this odd mixture. You think they'll all come out alike, like Smarties, or snakes, but they don't, they're totally different. One of my dreams of heaven is to be a sow with all the children latched on to nipples for ever, so you know where they are.'

Colin didn't seem to mind having so many babies, she said. 'Except when the nappies were draped everywhere, cloth in those days, and no washing machine. He used to get blisters on his thumbs from wringing out nappies. I don't really like babies much in general but I did adore them, and I loved breast feeding. I could just sit there and sink down into a novel. I got through the whole of Dickens while breastfeeding. I fed them all until nine months, and Arthur until he was two, and Sarah till she was three. I just went on longer and longer when I realised the end was nigh. I was forty when Sarah was born, so I decided it would be the end.' (Seventeen years between first and last.)

There was now a violent rattle from the washing machine. 'Janet will fix it,' said Anna placidly. 'Janet used to be Sarah's nanny,' she explained, 'and now she's mine.'

'We were poor as churchmice of course. Good nourishing vegetable soups, squished up for the babies; baked potatoes; brown bread and butter was a treat, jam very rare.' Colin left journalism and went into publishing. After working for George Weidenfeld, in 1968 he took a partnership in the old firm of Gerald Duckworth, which he now owns, and installed it in an old piano factory just down the road from where they live. In this tiny company (twelve on the staff) one son works the computer, and Anna runs the fiction side.

One reason Anna's books are appreciated by women, and indeed are more about women than about men (as Jane Austen's are), is that she likes the company of women. 'Women laugh a lot,' she once said, 'which is odd when you come to think of it. Why should anyone laugh when there is death?' The memory and experience of death is present in Alice Thomas Ellis's work even when she is being witty and hilarious. Being bereaved of two children is not an experience that leaves a writer unmarked.

When Arthur was two, her sixth baby was born: the first daughter after five sons. Her name was Rosalind, and she died at two days old. 'The priest buried her and I went up the next day with a little wreath, one of those dreadful municipal cemeteries. We're now all going to be buried in Wales. My friend Caroline and I both worry about where our daughters are buried, but I don't suppose it matters all that much.'

Caroline is Lady Caroline Blackwood, Robert Lowell's widow. Caroline, Beryl Bainbridge, and Zélide Cowan are the trio of friends closest to Anna and vital to her. 'One would have died,' she said, 'without one's female friends.'

The telephone rang and it was of course Beryl. 'Beryl,' said Anna. 'Did you get that bit about Lucretius? Colin has all these things at his fingertips. Oh *dworling*.' A pause. Beryl (I later discover) is commiserating about yesterday's review of Anna's new novel. The reviewer seems to have failed to grasp the essential Anna. She says to Beryl: 'Me and Janet have decided to invite him to tea and poison him. But I'm told he's very nice really.' The cleaning lady, fag in corner of mouth, appears in the kitchen to ask have we got anything for cleaning the windows?

'It must have been three years after Rosalind that I had Sarah.' Sarah is now fourteen and, having dyed her hair the colour of ginger biscuits, has gone off to boarding school. Her birth coincided with Anna's getting down to write her first novel, *The Sin Eater*. 'I wrote it in a terrible temper. I thought the rest of the world had gone mad. Women were whining all over the place about how they hadn't got any power, so I invented Rose. I wanted to show a woman who *is* powerful, like so many of the women I know.' She thought that by inventing the name 'Alice Thomas Ellis' she could protect herself against the glare of exposure. 'I didn't want to do interviews and all that stuff. My life is boring, there's nothing to say about it. Everybody else has had fourteen husbands and travelled all over the world. I'd never been anywhere until Diana Melly took me to Marrakesh a couple of years ago.'

Writing her own books developed from editing the novels of others. 'Everybody I knew was writing books, so I wrote one. It was literally true that I wrote the first on the backs of envelopes. That's why I write this size' (she shows me a page of manuscript, in tiny writing like the Brontë sisters' thumb-sized infant notebooks) 'and then I give the sheets to Janet to type.

'Working and having children is a terrible problem, there's no getting away from it. Painting you can't do with children around. I was still painting when I started writing. Marina Vaizey told me the time had come to have an exhibition, but I just couldn't take it seriously enough.

'The problem with writing is different – writing you can do in bed. But it's the getting on with it. You sit down at the tripewriter, you peel a banana, you get up and wash the floor, you say, good God it's time the cat had a walk. Writing is the last thing you want to do. A weekly deadline is a good discipline I find, so having to do a piece for *The Spectator*'s jolly good for me.'

It is now seven years since the second son Joshua died at the age of nineteen, after months in a coma following a fall, a dreadful time. 'It wasn't a good idea, losing Josh, was it?' (she addressed those of the family who were nearby – Janet, and another son who had just come in, Thomas).

I asked was it true what Elizabeth Longford said, that in marriage troubles are halved by being shared? Could it be true of grief? 'No, because when it's something like a death, there's nothing to say. It's not a pain halved at all, because you feel the other person's pain as well. It's worse, it's doubled. It is the most severely testing thing for a couple. I've known people break up after the death of a child, it's so hard to cope with. You never do get over it. But you go on. And when you lose a child you find that almost everyone you know has lost a child at some time.'

She still cannot bear to go into Joshua's room.

She has written, sometimes, about Joshua in her column, and about death in general. 'I went to the grave of our second son on his birthday. He is buried in the churchyard which lies across two fields and a stream from the house. In the summer I met one of the women from the village there, and I said no one had ever told me, and I hadn't known, that one would go on missing them so much for so long, and she said her daughter had died in infancy over forty years ago and she still mourned her. There are those who have seen it as their duty to convince me, for my own good, that the dead are well and truly dead and we will never see them again but I can't take that seriously. I always feel remarkably cheerful in the churchyard and don't want to leave. One of these days I won't have to, since we have acquired the land from the grave to the wall, and there is plenty of room for the rest of us . . . It is comforting to know where one is going to end up. Lends a sense of security.'

Women and children to the hills, the Raj refrain, is applied still by the Haycrafts every holiday, so that her 'Home Life' column, and indeed her actual life, is punctuated by these periods in Wales. 'At first we rented a forestry cottage up in the mountains with no electricity and running water only when the pipes hadn't broken. What we have now is a palace compared to the one before. Colin gets an awful lot of work done when

I'm in Wales. I think he misses me quite a lot but I don't have time to miss him.

'I've never had as much as a week of solitude myself. I've had two days, and it's bliss and wonderful and the house stays so tidy. I can enjoy two days of it but I wouldn't know what I'd feel after a week alone because I've never had it.'

If you look for the rock at the centre of Anna Haycraft's life you conclude that she is herself the rock. 'An awful lot of people lean on me. There is no time in my life for despair. One can say, "I think I'll have a nervous breakdown" but one couldn't by choice.

'I sometimes feel musclebound, I seem to be so incredibly tough. That year that Joshua died, and Caroline's husband and daughter, and one of my dearest friends, and both Janet's parents, every time the telephone rang it was dreadful news. That's when you need women, you see. They know what you're feeling because they're the same, and men are not. I really do feel that: despite having sons whom I get on with like a house on fire, I feel very strange about them. *They are totally different.* Men and women are like cats and dogs as my friend Deirdre says.

'There's no reciprocity. Men love women, women love children, children love hamsters.'

The character called Charles Bohannon in Anna's novel *The Other Side of the Fire* perfectly expresses this incomprehension between the sexes. 'He found women unfathomable. You gave them everything – love, loyalty, security, children and either they ran off with a dago or they flopped around in hysterics, crying for the moon.'

What makes her marriage to Colin last while others do not?

'Roman Catholicism is one thing,' Anna said. But Colin is not a Roman Catholic – he says he is an 'indifferentist' in matters of religion.

Being monogamous is very important to her, she says, and what she wants to know is what can anybody possibly gain from changing partners? 'If you leap from bed to bed how can you learn anything about another person? People expect so much from sex, but the person you deeply love may be being deeply unpleasant for a bit, and change. Life is very short, as I am increasingly aware.'

('Well I think adultery is a filthy habit,' says Rose in *The Sin Eater*. 'Like using someone else's toothbrush.')

She does acknowledge the factor of lasting affection in marriage. 'As he comes through the door my heart lifts a bit,' she said. 'And if I see him unexpectedly in Camden Town I think, Ah, I know him. He's also my brain. He knows everything.' (Colin Haycraft took a double first at Oxford) 'and anything I want to know I ask him. It saves me a hell of a lot of time in the library.'

At this point Maureen the cleaner came along and said through smoke that something had got lodged in the hoover. We all had a blow at it but it was no use. 'Janet will fix it,' said Anna. 'She even mended the telephone the other day. Took the front off and fiddled with the wires!

'Without Janet I could do nothing. Life wouldn't be anything without her.' (Janet was even at this moment mending the hoover.) 'Where did I find her? Her father used to be Dick For Value in the market, so I've known her since she was a little girl. She lived at home with her mum and dad and they got on marvellously and she was taken to museums and got her A-Levels and could have gone to university but she came here when she was eighteen or nineteen to be nanny to Sarah. She reads, she travels, she drives, she cooks, she does bird-watching, calligraphy, she types, she arranges my life, she delivers, she mends things, she *runs me*.' In Janet Perry, as capable a young woman as you would wish to meet (moments later she was whizzing off to deliver Anna's copy to the *Observer* and *The Spectator*), Alice Thomas Ellis has found what some older male writers would expect in a wife.

'My life may look like chaos,' she said, 'but it's controlled. What's important is remembering the essentials. You've got to know where the children are, and you can forget the cocktail party, but *people have to eat*.'

'The boys have split and gone off and lived with people but they've all come back home. William, Thomas and Arthur live here and I like it. It's the economics of it, they can't afford their own place; when I was young you could cope on five pounds a week from Françoise at the deli. Mind you if we hadn't been pretty we'd have been dead as they say. But I've told the boys if they come here and live with their wives and their children I'm moving out.'

I asked if her children were Catholics too. 'It takes my kids a long time for these things to cross their minds,' she said. 'William is twenty-eight and just beginning to think about spiritual matters and has become a profound thinker while he works his computer.'

Anna at nineteen joined the Catholic church for its beauty and comfort and although she still goes to Mass she does mourn the full formality and ritual of the old Church.

'But I've got this mate who used to be a monk who's very careful of my spiritual welfare. What I'd like to do is go back to the monastery sometime. There's an awful lot about religion that needs to be taken up again. I could start now, getting down to it again, reading, going on retreat, much more going to church. But there's plenty of time, if we live.'

Professor Elizabeth Anscombe

Professor of Philosophy, University of Cambridge

b. 1919

m. 1941

PETER GEACH

Professor of Logic, University of Leeds

4 daughters, 3 sons

BARBARA JOHN MARY CHARLES
JENNIFER MORE TAMSIN

Professor Elizabeth Anscombe

Professor Elizabeth Anscombe, referred to in textbooks and on her office door in Cambridge as G. E. M. Anscombe, stands apart from movements and fashions of thinking. Until October 1986 she was professor of Philosophy at the University of Cambridge, the legatee of Ludwig Wittgenstein, whose pupil she was. For years she wore his gown, even more ragged since someone tore out the precious L. WITTGENSTEIN nametape. We met some time before her recent retirement.

She is a Roman Catholic, married to a fellow professor of Logic, Peter Geach, and they have seven children. This is intriguing enough. A Cambridge philosophy graduate, Terri Apter, said in her study *Why Women Don't Have Wives*, that Professor Anscombe is in a different league from the fictional image of the Catholic woman whose life is crippled by repeated pregnancies. 'Prof Anscombe is an upholder of the Pope's encyclical on birth control, and is therefore quite unmodern in her no-nonsense association of sexual intercourse with the production of the children . . .'

Several people were quite surprised to hear that Elizabeth Anscombe had agreed to let me come and talk to her about combining motherhood with professional life. The impression I gained was that she was regarded as much too lofty a thinker to dwell on such humdrum questions, and was intellectually scathing about philosophical lightweights. However, I was also told that when confronted by someone, as it were, *innocent* of philosophy, Professor Anscombe could be perfectly agreeable. As indeed I found she was.

She has a nice big square face and wears her dark hair in a bun. She wore what could be called an unstructured jacket and serviceable trousers, and sat in her office in Cambridge at a desk scattered with learned journals, bills, statements, wine labels, books. Later she drove me from the Sidgwick lecture site in Cambridge to her college, New Hall, in a battered and rickety van, the sort you can sleep in. She and her husband had driven to Poland in such a car, she said. She also told me cheerfully that they had decided en route that the whole of northern Europe is bathed in the smell of pigshit.

Elizabeth Anscombe was the third, late-born child of a South London schoolmaster and his wife. 'My mother was a parson's daughter who had started at Aberystwyth University but had to leave and go into teacher training when her father died, leaving debts. She became a village schoolmistress and married rather late in life, at thirty-eight. She had twin boys a year later, and I was born when she was forty-four. I never heard her grumble about giving up her job, though she had been interested in it, and she did teach her own children.

'When I was seven she started teaching me Latin. My father was a carpenter by hobby, and had a big workshop in the garden. On school holidays I would have to go to him every day and recite the four conjugations of regular Latin verbs, *amo* to *audio*. And if I made a mistake he would say, "You don't know it; go and learn it again," and I had to come back and recite it right. I owe it to him that I learned them so well. It seemed perfectly OK to me that he should expect this. But I remember weeping, when I was about eight, and I translated "that" in "he said that . . ." as *illud*. I hadn't learnt indirect speech and I didn't understand why *illud* was not "that" in this instance. My mother found it difficult to explain. My chief debt is to her, though.

'My father taught Physics at Dulwich College, the school my brothers went to. He was also head of engineering and he noted that the boys who came over after a year or two in Classics were much better than those who had never done that. So he formed the opinion that learning the classics was of great value, even to scientists.'

When Elizabeth was fourteen her mother went to see the headmistress of the local Girls' Public Day School Trust school, Sydenham High, to ask if Elizabeth could take Greek, which she had started at home. There was a timetable problem but the headmistress asked, 'Would you be considering sending her to university?' Mrs Anscombe said, 'Oh, yes, of course,' not unnaturally, says Professor Anscombe, since both she and her husband were graduates. 'Oh well,' said the headmistress, 'if *that*'s what you're thinking of, certainly.'

'I became interested in philosophy at about sixteen when I began thinking about certain questions – and after a while I discovered that this stuff was called philosophy. Young people are frightfully ill-informed and naive: I could have gone to Girton to do Classics but I thought, if I went there it would go on being Classics, whereas at Oxford, Classics turned into Philosophy. I didn't realise, then, that you could change courses, and I could have read Moral Sciences at Cambridge. However, my father was very generous and didn't insist on my taking the Girton scholarship, which was double the St Hugh's one, and he let me keep my scholarship money for my own pocket.'

We talked about the continuing single-sex status of her old Oxford college, and the catastrophic effect on the numbers of women Fellows in the colleges which have gone co-ed. 'I expect, when I'm a hundred,' said Professor Anscombe, 'I'll be saying, "I remember when there were 250 women Fellows, and now there are only thirty-three."'

'It was perfectly clear from the start that if all colleges went co-ed, the former men's colleges would get a lot of the best women, but the women's colleges would *not* get the best men. The standard of women's colleges used to be well above that of the ordinary men's colleges. I remember, when I first taught men from Oriel, thinking, "Well, *he'd* never get into Somerville." They weren't hopeless, they were just not nearly as bright.'

Elizabeth Anscombe met her husband at Oxford: she was at the end of her first year and he was three years older, in his final year at Balliol. They married on Boxing Day, 1941, and Miss Anscombe went on being 'Miss Anscombe' and living in Oxford while he was away elsewhere. When she first became pregnant she was still a Research student living in Newnham College.

'I think I did once ask my husband how many children he wanted and he said, "Perhaps five, to begin with." And I said, "In that case, we'd better wait till you've got a proper job!" There were nineteen years between the firstborn and the last. I suppose my eldest daughter hardly knows her youngest sister.'

Terri Apter's description (in *Why Women Don't Have Wives*) of Professor Anscombe's attitude to her family is illuminating. The cares which arise from having 'too many' children – all those visits to the dentist or doctor, all those shoes to tie in the morning and clothes to wash in the evening – are commonplace, says Apter. To concentrate on these denies the fact of children as a 'given' and not something one always chooses to have, or not. 'She does not burden herself with responsibility for the children's well-being in a neat and middle-class notion of "well-being" ... She did not know precisely what a child would need, but she was confident that she would find this out when a child, and children, arrived. The strength of her position comes from her knowledge that there was no way she could possibly have given up her philosophical work ... She does not feel herself, her work, to be threatened. The children that are born to her are not "unwanted". They are given to her. They are a natural outcome of the sexual aspect of married life. They are gifts for whom she must care, but ... it is unimportant whether they are organised in a conventional fashion.

'She solved problems as they arose, and worked alongside her children, encouraged her children to care for one another, and found the energy to give her children the attention they needed and still need, because she remains attached to them, and continues to see them in her care even though they have become adults. She displays a high-mindedness and purity and innocence that few of us could emulate, and her household is not one that many of us would want to imitate' (a reference to that kind of scatty but high-thinking household which I call 'gumboots-academic') 'but she can serve to remind us to reconsider what we assume is so important – a falsely controlled household, with a mother trying to enter the child's world in a Sesame Street fashion.'

Professor Anscombe read this description of her attitude and said she regarded it as flattering. 'Two of my children, at five and eight, were expelled from their convent school in Abingdon for fighting on the bus. But also there was a letter saying that sometimes they didn't have enough buttons on their blouses, and their shoes weren't done up. I was not as attentive to these matters as the nuns thought I should be. I remember my husband wrote a letter back to the nuns saying he was sometimes in that state himself, and *he* was not threatened with dismissal.'

Elizabeth Anscombe declares that she was very relieved when the Pope's encyclical *Humanae Vitae* came out (to the surprise of many Catholics, as even the pontifical commission had reported in favour of contraception in certain circumstances) in August 1968. 'I already had seven children by then, and because of the teaching of the Church I never practised contraception. But I had begun to think that the Church was going to let it go slip, just by saying nothing about it, as they did with usury. In about 1820 the law was very strict against usury, and then nothing more was ever published about it; and I thought perhaps it was going to be the same with contraception. It would be much more serious because not so many people practise usury, whereas the teaching on contraception affects everyone who is capable of having children.'

Was she ever dismayed at the prospect of another child? 'I can remember being a bit worried about the third one, and thinking, oh dear, I'm going to behave badly about this, I mean grumble about it.' Did you like babies? I asked. She narrows her eyes in thought, as she does in careful response to all questions which others might answer without a moment's hesitation. 'Yes, I did. I can remember the first one: I'd never handled a baby before and I looked at her with *astonishment*. Once they were there, I didn't behave badly in fact. It may be of some use to say one's prayers about it: "I know I'm going to behave badly about this unless I'm helped" and I suppose I was helped.

'After that they seemed to be fairly matter of course. And anyway, they weren't endangering what I wanted to do in the way of academic work.'

It was when I saw Professor Anscombe that I realised that the academic life is the ideal option for anyone planning to raise a family and work simultaneously. Unlike creative writing, it brings a regular salary and a commitment to deadlines for lectures and papers, with all the discipline that entails. Nor is teaching regarded as a cop-out. The mistress of the house is expected to have higher things on her mind, and is excused the lower things.

But it was not enough merely to know that Elizabeth Anscombe had scant regard for neat middle-class homes and an unconventional respect for children's lives. I still needed to ask how she managed to get her work done with seven children to bring up.

'The answer,' she said, 'is that I had very good servants. That is to say, I had an absolutely marvellous charwoman who came from nine until lunchtime, and cooked lunch and things for the weekend and made superlative pastry. Mrs Colter had one baby herself, and I think her husband didn't want another, so when I had another she would say, "It feels as if it was mine." The children were very fond of her; I heard her say, "I brung 'em all up." She was very quiet, very thorough, very busy, whisking round the place, putting things right, stopping the children quarrelling.

'She was with us for twenty-one years and she was super. I'm positive if I was still in Oxford she'd still be with me. She was a member of the Salvation Army, and I believe one of the things they believe is that you have to have a cross to bear. Possibly Mrs Colter regarded us as her cross. But she was very fond of us all, and when she came to my second daughter's wedding last year she got on with my present help like a house on fire.

'It is essential, I believe, to get on with one's help. It is very simple if you follow this simple rule: they must quite like you. It's very quick to see whether they are good. If they are good, don't get on their backs about anything. If they are good, let them do things their way.

'After the third baby I decided it was a bore having babies in hospital and there was a very good domiciliary midwife service in Oxford. The nurse came every day to bath the new baby until the last one, when times had changed and they said: "We now get the mother to bath the baby." Then Mrs Colter would say, "Can I bath the baby?" And she took that over.

'I had altogether three people expressly to help with the children. The first two didn't last very long. Then Jessica Scott appeared, a woman I knew who had spent her life teaching backward children privately. When my second daughter was expelled from her convent school we were stuck, so I asked Jessica Scott if she would tutor Mary, which she did for a year until the child went to Oxford High School. Mary would go every day to her. Several years later Mary mentioned that Jessica had made her learn "Intimations of Immortality" or "Ode to a Nightingale" and I said "At eight? Did you understand it?" and she said, "Of course not; but I *had* it."'

'Jessica was on whatever they give you if you have no pension, so she was fairly hard-up although she did have her home. She came to see me and said, couldn't she come and do the children at bedtime, and give them their supper? That's what the people I employed did, gave them supper and saw them into bed. But she mustn't earn more than 30 shillings. I thought she meant she would just come sometimes; but she came every single day, including Sunday. Oh yes, I was *very* pleased. She was a teacher by bent, and she read to them every day and went to work on Barbara's handwriting and formed her into someone with decent handwriting. I wouldn't have been nearly so good at all that. I remember trying to teach two of them Latin, and they dropped their grammar books down a drain.'

The children were named Barbara, John, Mary, Charles, Jennifer, More (for Sir Thomas More) and Tamsin. For much of their childhood their father was lecturing in Birmingham (1951–66) and later became Professor of Logic at Leeds. 'No doubt if I hadn't had a job,' says

Professor Anscombe, 'I would have moved to where Peter was. But he liked Oxford and it seemed to be a natural consequence for us to be based there. He very much doted on the babies. He did know how to feed a baby and how to change a napkin. In fact all the children have memories of having been made to feed the newest baby, and change nappies. But it united them: if any outsider turned on any of them they lined up together in defiance.

'I have heard,' she added, 'that my husband used to fly into great rages which at least the eldest boy found terrifying. He only said this later. At the time he never appeared to show much terror.'

Holding the fort at home, Professor Anscombe had a rule that the children might not burst into her study when she was giving a tutorial. But the fact of giving tutorials at home is another of those singular reasons why academic women can weave together a family and a career. 'It seemed to me,' says Professor Anscombe, 'that 10 hours a week was the upper limit for tutorials and not feeling overdone. When Michael Dummett went to Ghana and I took on his St Edmund Hall students, I was doing fifteen hours a week and I found that dreadfully heavy. I did all my teaching at home apart from lecturing twice a week.

'I suppose I must have worked at night; I don't remember very distinctly. I used to do the lecturing and tutorials in the morning when Mrs Colter was there, and I had to be in the house with care of the children from two o'clock or so in the afternoon until five, when Jessica came. In academic life it's easy to arrange that you work when there is somebody else there. I was so incredibly lucky with the marvellous Mrs Colter and the lovely Jessica Scott. I think I must have been rather neglectful about some things, as you can see from the buttons story, and there were things I did not bother about much, things that other people do bother about. It seemed to me for instance that it was no use having good silver for one's table, because it would get lost. I said I would have just the teaspoons after my mother died and sure enough, they did get lost.'

Another striking factor about these women's lives of an earlier generation was how much less fetching and ferrying they did for their children. The streets were safer for children to go alone; the activities fewer; and anyway, Elizabeth Anscombe did not have a car. 'We never did anything very extravagant and it was years before I learned to drive a car. We used to go to a place in the country each summer, and we would go by train and hire a car when we got there. But mostly one didn't do much getting around. Or we went around on foot. When they went to the convent in Abingdon there was a bus; otherwise they walked.'

Still, aren't seven children something of a trial? 'There was a time when I found one child a bit too much and he'd better board for a term. There was another baby on the way then. We boarded children in Oxford twice. No, three times; we were going abroad for a year and Jenny didn't want to go.'

'I think I'm lazy,' said Elizabeth Anscombe. 'I don't have high standards about dress or the household, and I don't do nearly enough work. I find it easy to relapse into laziness, and have a vaguely guilty feeling and wish I'd got on with the stuff I should have been getting on with. I've never felt guilt about the children, but that's one of the advantages of an academic job, you're available even if you're only saying, "Oh shut up, I'm doing some work." It's such an elastic-sided life.

'I'm rather vaguely a feminist. I don't like women's colleges throwing up the sponge. There was such a lot of hard work put into developing them, and running them on a shoestring.'

Professor Anscombe is one of those rare women whose job is exactly comparable with her husband's and whose status is equal, or superior. 'There are ways in which my husband is my superior,' she says. 'He knows a lot of logic: I am a mere spectator of logic. He has an incredibly good memory and a vast store of knowledge, far greater than mine. But I would guess that I am a lot more disposed than he is to think that you should try to see what other people mean.'

Their eldest daughter did not want to go to university and took up nursing, training at University College Hospital in London. But she then went to America, where she took her Master's degree at Yale Psychiatric Institute and proceeded to a doctorate; she is now a professor at the City University of New York and is married, 'But alas,' says Elizabeth Anscombe, 'no children.'

The second daughter, Mary, read Philosophy. 'But she's been pretty eccentric about getting a job or publishing any stuff. She stuck around at home and took nine years over her PhD and won't publish her dissertation. She's married now and we miss her at home; she was such a marvellous cook.

'John is a luthier who restores harpsichords and makes viols in Shropshire. I ought to have recognised his musical talent straight away. Neither my husband nor I were musical, but one day I was playing a record of the Archduke in my study and the door was open into John's bedroom and he shouted, "Very good music, Mummy!" at the age of about six. I should have woken up then and given him a musical education. He learned to play his instruments later, and became so enthusiastic about gramophone records and concerts that he forced almost all his brothers and sisters, with the exception of Mary and Tamsin, to learn to play. John and More and Charles and Jenny play all the time when they're at home together; that's what they come to Cambridge for, although it's hard to drag More from the arms of his computers.'

Charles read History at Oxford and is working in Minnesota; Jenny read Greats at Oxford and teaches Classics at Malvern College. 'Jenny taught Tamsin Greek and then shipped her into the school and on to read Greats too. She is a frivolous and lazy girl, so Jenny must be a good teacher.'

Professor Anscombe's eyes narrowed for a long while when she pondered the elements required for a good marriage. 'Doing a certain amount of noticing what the other person's likes and dislikes are,' she said. 'And having a lot of conversation.'

Elizabeth and her husband have travelled around in recent years, spending five months in Germany in 1984 when each won an Alexander Von Humboldt prize.

'The danger with us is that we go on just chatting instead of getting on with our work. Of the children, some of them stayed around a lot and liked our company, and others did not. My husband likes reading to people. One holiday he read *A Tale of Two Cities* to us all, which was very enjoyable; the children were so excited by it they clamoured for two chapters at a time instead of one. I still get read to at night. No, not philosophy. More often stories of crime, mystery and horror.'

Alison Smithson

architect

b. 1928

m. 1949

PETER SMITHSON

architect

2 daughters, 1 son

SIMON SAMANTHA SORAYA

Alison Smithson

Alison Smithson, as half of the Smithsons, has spent her entire adult life in partnership, personal and professional, with her husband Peter. In *Who's Who* it is Peter who gets an entry; but their buildings and their published papers are all acknowledged 'A. and P. Smithson'. The couple are two of the British architects whose name is known to the lay public, and they have made their mark on post-war architecture with their New Brutalism.

Living and working together within the same walls for more than thirty years, they have shared not just their family life and three children, but a vision. They are a self-conscious pair in this respect; commitment to their work is central to their lives. A room in their house in Kensington is set aside for the Smithson Archive.

On the telephone, Alison Smithson's voice (which I had expected to be brisk and busy) was listlessly quiet and slow. She has large, dark, woebegone eyes and a look of dreamy remoteness. When we met I discovered that she and I shared a home town. We both spent our childhood in South Shields, on the north-east coast of England, a place which etches itself very particularly on its inhabitants. In a town where almost everyone used to go to sea, our fathers were both involved instead in something apart: her father was head of the local art college, my father left the sea to become a cartoonist. But our perceptions of our childhoods there are quite different. I, having left the place at fourteen, have a residual affection for South Shields; she has not.

In 1971, another working husband and wife team, the social scientists Rhona and Robert Rapoport, produced their study *Dual Career Families Re-Examined*. One of the five closely-observed couples in that study were the Smithsons, disguised as 'the Bensons, Architects.' The term 'Dual-Career Family' meant what it suggests, father and mother pursuing active careers and family lives; but 'Career' had to indicate some work with a high degree of commitment. This study by the Rapoports was scientific and intensely investigative. The prolonged inquiries affected Alison Smithson deeply; she found them harrowing and disruptive. Anything that gets in the way of architecture, she told me, is 'unbelievably upsetting. I used to get the absolute shakes at all their questions.'

Fifteen years later, Robert Rapoport pointed out to me that working wives have now become such a commonplace, that to question whether married women should work at all has become almost an irrelevance. Nevertheless, the chapter about 'the Bensons' is still fascinating because of the whole-hearted rigour of the Smithsons' partnership. As Alison says, she has spent virtually twenty-four hours a day with Peter for thirty-six years.

୫ଚ

Alison Smithson was an only child, as was her husband Peter. 'My mother and Peter's both came from the generation of mothers who had been trained to do something. My husband's mother had worked as a teacher; my mother met my father at art college and they discussed things very much together. At home there was a natural assumption that I would be professionally trained as well: my father felt education was the great liberator. A lot of my generation were mystified by Women's Lib when it came along because we didn't feel caged at all. We literally did what we wanted.'

Alison went to four different schools: Miss Lee's private school in South Shields; Sunderland Church High School for Girls; George Watson's College in Edinburgh (when evacuated during the war); and back to South Shields High School for School Certificate. She went on to King's College, Newcastle – now part of Durham University – to study architecture. There she met Peter Smithson from Stockton-on-Tees. He went on to the Royal Academy School in London, and they married in 1949. At first they both worked for the old London County Council.

While working at the LCC they won the competition for Hunstanton School, Norfolk, their first commission. Their theoretical writing began almost at once, when they published their ideas and intentions for the school. 'After the school,' she says, 'we had already made a myth of ourselves.' They moved from furnished rooms in Bloomsbury into a house in Chelsea, where their joint career began in earnest. Their most noted work, the Economist Building in St James's, 1959–64, and Robin Hood Gardens Estate, Tower Hamlets, 1963–72, started then.

'We just used to work all the time. When Simon and Samantha were born I think the most difficult business was going out. I never went out unless to take part in some meeting or a lecture to do with architecture. Work came first. We never entertained very much, we never had the energy.

'I always maintained the same amount of work I would have done if I hadn't had children. We had to be equal, equal, equal. Peter might have changed the odd nappy, but we did everything else together; the studio was part of the house and meals were made by the two of us. Cooking together is the last relic of that 50–50 equality and to a certain extent it has always been symbolic. We ran a very tight ship, sometimes rushed off our feet for eleven months and then nothing to do for four or five. Architecture is all-consuming. It is not only our work but the thrust of all our emotions.

'We took up rigid ethical positions: on state education, for example, because my husband was against our having any expenses that would oblige us to take on jobs we didn't want to, like hospitals. So the children went to local primary, then comprehensive schools.

'And we had to be equal in all things. If the two of us could have typed the manuscripts or done the accounts, we would have done. But I taught myself to type and did all that. We would each edit the typescripts. On each project we talked through everything, and we knew exactly who would do what. But we did each develop an individual style. My husband thought of Coventry Cathedral' (a design that was not adopted) 'as a great square, and turning the square on the diagonal, this whole diagonal language of his. The curvilinear language of the House of the Future was mine. Things like our first chair designs were done very much together.'

They sit at drawing boards facing each other to work. Such details of their daily working life do not spill readily from Alison Smithson: she says she has always resisted any form of looking back. 'I never revisit a building,' she said emphatically, 'and neither of us has even taken potential clients walking round our buildings, as other architects endlessly do. We're much more like Le Corbusier or Mies van der Rohe, who are somehow in the head.'

One of their consuming interests in the 1960s was Team X, the international 'family' of innovative architects who met to discuss ideas.

'At small meetings Simon would sit at a bench with model scraps. Just as, in the office, before school age, Soraya would work feverishly cutting things out. They were like carpenters' children really.'

Alison stressed that she would have been distraught not to have had children. 'It is not possible to contemplate not being married; not being married would have been not being. And not having children would have been no success at all. I would have died if I had not had children. It made me feel more feminine; if you are working at something I think it makes you anxious to prove that there is another side to you.'

Peter, on the other hand, had been hesitant about marrying for all the conventional reasons like being tied down. 'But in fact some part of you,' he told the Rapoports, 'accepts very ruthlessly that you're not going to marry someone who's dumb, because you can see a lifetime of boredom ahead of you. So you steer miles away from that sort of person.' Peter Smithson was more attuned to the views of Le Corbusier, who believed that having children interfered with the creative life. 'We found that drawing, provided you were prepared to work hard, is very much like writing a novel,' he told the Rapoports. 'You can fit things round each other.' The Smithsons deferred the birth of their second child specifically to fit in with an international meeting of Team X. Peter Smithson's view was that a very large family would have been 'brain-shattering'.

The dual career family study reported that when the Rapoports began their interviews, Alison Smithson 'spoke rarely and in a slow, soft voice. The interviewers felt that she was somewhat depressed. She character-ised herself as "tense" . . . By the end of the interview series she was ebullient, and indicated that the early impression was partly a phase phenomenon, in that she does have marked ups and downs, and partly a reaction to specific difficulties both with domestic help and in their working situation.'

Peter Smithson, by contrast, had participated more enthusiastically in the Dual-Career interviews, they said. 'He has a somewhat sardonic manner but at the same time communicates warmth.' But the most striking aspects of the couple were that they had persisted in their creative independence along a thorny path ('four out of five of all the things we do turn out wrong') regardless of public disapproval. Their dedication was almost ascetic despite an aesthetically beautiful house, a comfortable car and foreign travel every year. They likened their way of mixing work and family to the scene 'in a craftsman's workshop before the industrial revolution, with everyone in the family lending a hand'.

Alison Smithson added for me a gloss on this reference to 'foreign travel every year'. 'At one point Samantha was very upset that all the children in her class at school were going on package holidays. I said, for goodness' sake, one doesn't do that.' (At the time they had a 'solar pavilion' in the country where they would go for weekends.) Then the Smithsons were appointed to design the new British Embassy in Brasilia, a commission which later fell through. 'We took them to Brasilia with us when the embassy seemed a goer, and they looked so happy on the beach we thought, perhaps Samantha is right. So for the next seven years we went on package holidays to Djerba in Tunisia.'

It was a curious life. Alison Smithson kept a detailed diary, at the Rapoports' request, for several days in May 1967. I fell upon this with some relief. I read it on a day when I was feeling myself battered by innumerable mundane intrusions to my work. On a Bank Holiday Saturday, when my husband was working all day at his office until 10 pm, my day was circumscribed by children's meals and activities while I longed to be at my desk. Then I opened Mrs Smithson's diary, and found a detailed résumé of the minutiae of her family/working life: '12.00: Change to warmer clothes and put wool socks and cardigan on youngest daughter; bring washing out of rain. 1.45: Read to youngest daughter; both get ready to go to exhibition; put toys away; make two telephone calls (1) to engineers (2) this evening's arrangements; edited book; coloured party invitations . . .'

Mornings were punctuated by getting children off to school on time ('son's watch left in Wiltshire'), evenings are piecemeal: 'Son switched TV off to do revision; chicken in; scrape potatoes, put on; son in bath; typing manuscript; jigsaw with son; eldest daughter and husband return; supper; typing manuscript; cut eldest daughter's hair.' Getting the shopping done, in Portobello Market or the West End or nearer home, features alongside visiting project sites. Telephone calls to colleagues, and studying plans, are interrupted to tidy children's rooms. Endlessly, Alison is found typing manuscripts for 10 or 20 minutes at a time, as in: 'Breakfast; type manuscript; air clothes upstairs; iron dolls' clothes made for daughter's birthday; cut out nightie; telephone call re book contract; shop at Boots; call eldest daughter's school to see if all OK; project papers; chair designer friend arrived late; son doing tests . . .'

Although even diaries do not necessarily tell the full story, I was for once able to imagine what their life was like. Husband and wife's patterns of activity were quite similar: there was no sex-stereotyping in the division of labour. Like many very busy families, the Smithsons imposed additional activities on themselves, like keeping turtles which forever needed their tanks cleaning out. And even a short foray to the local shops ('laundry, chemist, thread, plant, fish, buns, felt-tips, polish') took ages 'since baby trails and observes other people'.

The living-in students who stayed at the Smithsons' house in exchange for babysitting were an essential adjunct to the household. 'The student tended only to appear minutes before we went out and would be in bed when we came back. They used the office kitchen and only ate with or cooked for the children when babysitting (always spaghetti with tomato sauce).'

There was a secretary who might help with shopping, and the elder children were trained to treat housework, and meal preparation as something to be shared by all when necessary. A housekeeper ('wonderful Mrs Blake') also came in for a few hours five days a week. Mealtimes were strictly regulated: lunch was at 1 pm without fail. In the two gardens Alison did planting and pruning: she calls this 'women's gardening'; 'men's gardening' was mowing and killing weeds.

Although she is able to drive, Alison never did. Other professional women she knew would ask how she managed to get around and get everything done. Well, she never did school runs or chauffeuring to ballet classes and Brownies, though her children were involved in all these activities; and the schools and shops were nearby. Also, she emphasised to me, walking and using public transport were her 'observing society' sessions.

In their rhythmic daily routine, which meant Saturdays and Sundays were only slightly different from weekdays, they felt it was essential to manage their energy in a rational way to be conserved for important things. When work pressures were severe they had to make special provision for family life; this is clear from the diaries, in which putting Letraset on a model boat is given an equal mention with studying plans for the redevelopment of Stockholm.

The conclusion the Rapoports reached was that the Smithsons had developed their sense of Couple Identity to a very high degree. 'Their work pervades their lives and they both feel it would be a bore to be married to someone who did not share this central preoccupation.'

The reason I have quoted from this study to such an extent is that when we talked, Alison Smithson continually referred me to the report

ALISON SMITHSON

as an accurate reflection of how the family had lived in those years. Of all
the couples in their study, the authors declared, the Smithsons had the
greatest overlap of personal, family and work worlds.

One conspicuous difference in their lives today, apart from the children having gone their various ways, is that Alison Smithson, who did
not lecture before, in 1978 began accepting the invitations she used to
turn down. They both had a reputation for saying no, in the days when
telegrams came, inviting them to some Third World destination, all
expenses paid. However, students still come to question Alison on the
role of the female architect, or on the Smithsons' history.

She feels in retrospect that her two elder children were affected by
having such well-known parents and being taken about with them. 'I
think the children got a lot of aggro from people because of us, people
questioning them and chipping at them. We once found that someone
was doing a case study on Soraya when she was in primary school, to see
what had penetrated from home: real police state stuff. But she has
survived, and she was furious in 1985 not to be mentioned when she was
with us at an occasion reported in the *Architectural Journal*.

'People were unbelievably mean to Simon when he went to
Cambridge; he would get hammered into the ground by some architect;
years of spleen would come out. One lecturer came in saying, "I hear this
is Smithson's year . . ." It was monstrous. Perhaps that was one of the
reasons he was keen to get away to Harvard.

'But the children always attracted a lot of attention. We would go and
look at Greek or Roman sites and give the children flower-presses and
tell them to go off and find sherds, and if you're very busy it's easy to lose
sight of tiny children. I was a real Tabitha Twitchett . . . always losing
her children.'

Their life was a continuing workscape even when they weren't
engaged on enormous projects – Alison says the buildings she feels most
attached to are the ones she would have enjoyed seeing built – and it
carries on today. Alison, having stuck to state education for her children,
and hearing her daughter now talk of private schools for her children,
has published her ideas about education. These involve reducing the
school leaving age again to fourteen, with the perpetual possibility of
re-entry at any time later, so that people learn when they want to, and
don't prevent others from learning. 'My idea is a parallel "opting out"
from eight or so onwards, using old church halls and baths and so on,
staffed by retired people with interests in train-spotting, ping-pong,

stamps, darts. Any skill is better than none, and a threshold to other things.' She also has ideas on housing: all council rents, she suggests, could be regarded as a national mortgage which could be transferred from place to place. 'This handing over of responsibility would change attitudes overnight.' She is concerned at the way cities have changed, with the disappearance of casual corners, street life, and other aspects of urban living which once made a city childhood absorbing, and now make it dangerous or isolated.

Her mind bristles with ideas as much as ever. In the 1960s the Smithsons represented an intense duet of criticism of mainstream modern architecture. The lean years without much work case-hardened their steely commitment to their own ideas. 'They conceive and bear buildings like children,' one commentator said.

'In an architecture-centred house,' Alison Smithson says, 'the children were our three best buildings. I still think that. They are very good-looking, and very much admired.'

Now that the children have gone – Samantha with oil-man husband and children to Borneo, Simon to work in America, and Soraya to art school – the upper family part of their gabled and turreted house is chiefly for storage, sewing and ironing rooms. The Smithson studio is on the ground floor and basement; its meeting room reverts to family use at Christmas. The Smithson Archive is in the back study.

It is, Alison Smithson confirms, something of a strain to be together all day – 'It's a wonder one still has a different point of view at all' – and when Peter goes away, say to a summer school in Italy for two weeks each year, it is a holiday for her, suddenly giving her an immense amount of time and space.

Much of their discussion of work used to take place in their comfortable Citroën, 'a glass box in the sun' as they drove down to Wiltshire at weekends. Their essays would be put together on these journeys; Alison says the children didn't enjoy the journeys much.

Over the years there have been 'his' and 'hers' buildings though both their names go on each one. 'In the beginning there was an element of competition; now, one doesn't feel nearly the same pressure to come up first with an idea. Whenever my husband said, "Stupid woman," I would remind him that I was his best pupil. But I am a hard taskmaster too, I have a Tyneside aggressiveness and if I get excited my voice shouts. He minds his own business more than I do; I let my thoughts and worries spill over into other things. We take things very seriously, but we have a northern sense of humour permanently linked to disaster. Sometimes it's touch and go whether I go up like a rocket or collapse in laughter.'

Her dislike of looking back made it an emotional punishment to edit a diary of their country place, which she has published lately. 'A double agony because of remembering the cat we used to take with us, who died. He became quite a different cat in the country.'

The work goes on. 'We are both very conscious of wasted time. I hate crowds, and we never get into situations you can't get through quickly; for instance we'd never shop in a supermarket on a Saturday. We were always easily bored and very easily frustrated; my husband, who has a fantastic verbal memory, gets furious if someone tells him the same story twice.

'We have to keep working,' she says, 'just to keep eating bread. We're just like artists who have to keep painting. And if we succumb to arthritis we'll just have to start cutting up paper, like Matisse.'

Sheila Kitzinger

childbirth educator

b. 1929

m. 1952

UWE KITZINGER

President, Templeton College, Oxford,
the Centre for Management Studies;
former diplomat

5 daughters

CELIA NELL TESS POLLY JENNY

Sheila Kitzinger

❦

No symposium on the subject of childbirth is complete without Sheila Kitzinger. Her name is now synonymous in Britain with the natural childbirth movement. I first met her at an exhibition of photographs of breastfeeding; I was newly pregnant for the first time and as luck would have it, she was about to start a course of classes at the National Childbirth Trust, which she urged me to join. On the memorable night when my waters broke – a month before the due date – I rang Sheila for advice. The hospital had said, if your waters break, ring us *at once*, but having been to her classes, in Sheila I trusted. Her response was characteristic. 'Don't tell the hospital yet – just have a soothing brandy and a lovely night's sleep.' Too excited to sleep, we went out on Hampstead Heath at midnight in the rain, then sat up talking till dawn. The baby was born the next day, and among other things for which I was grateful to Sheila Kitzinger, I was always thankful not to have spent that last night of pre-motherhood in a hospital ward. I never did follow the Kitzinger preference for home births, but I think a hospital ward is the place to be after the event, rather than before.

Sheila is a large, peaches-and-cream woman with a blonde top-knot and what can only be described as a maternal radiance. She started out as an anthropologist, became an ante-natal teacher and developed, from the pioneering work of Dr Grantly Dick-Read, her own approach to the psychoprophylactic technique of preparation for birth, and the psychological adjustment involved in childbirth. She is the author of a dozen books on the subject, and the mother of five daughters who have grown up into highly individual young women.

Sheila's husband is Uwe Kitzinger, whose former career as a diplomat and academic has meant long periods of separation for the Kitzingers. But now he is president of an Oxford college they both live in their Tudor manor house in a village near Oxford, which is where I went to see Sheila for this interview. We sat in the drawing room before an open fire and beneath one of Sheila's vivid paintings – of Uwe, lying naked except for his eye-patch.

✦

Sheila Kitzinger's mother, Clare Webster, was the inspiration in her life. Her father retired early after a stroke, and it was her mother's passions and concerns which animated the family.

When her mother died, Sheila discovered a memoir Clare had written in 1952. It is an illuminating document because it shows how she came to be a mother of the inspiring kind. In it, Clare remembers her girlhood and the men going off to fight in World War I. Her pacifist instincts tussle with patriotic sentiments; she becomes a Quaker, and nurses the wounded. Then comes the year 1918, a few days before Christmas. Her mother (Sheila's grandmother) is busy in the kitchen, happily looking forward to all the family being reunited, when suddenly a telegram arrives: her eldest son has been killed in France.

After his death, Sheila's mother's conviction grew that war and enmity must not prevail. In the next war, she took in evacuees; after the war she organised celebrations with PoWs, encouraged her children to travel abroad, and continued to work for international friendship and world government.

She wrote this memoir in the year of her silver wedding and also the year of Sheila's marriage. 'Our adorable children, how confident they look!' she wrote of the farewells after the silver wedding party.

'Can their generation save the human race? With a protective arm on mine and the knowledge that he holds my heart, my husband and I walk off the station platform together, a twinge of loneliness at the parting but a feeling of thankfulness for the useful citizens our children are becoming. And so back to our home to begin our work for a larger family – the Save the Children Fund.'

Clare Webster's high-minded precepts about good citizenship and interest in other countries – rather like those of Dickens's Mrs Jellyby – clearly influenced her daughter. Sheila remembers the house being always full of people from different backgrounds, and in her own studies of childbirth such as *Women as Mothers*, she has always been interested in women's lives across the world. She went from Bishop Fox's School, at Taunton in Somerset, to Ruskin College, Oxford, to do a diploma in Social Anthropology, then to St Hugh's College to do an M. Litt.

degree. She met Uwe Kitzinger, the son of German Jewish refugees and one of the most brilliant undergraduates of his generation, on a flight across the Atlantic.

'We both had student research fellowships during the long vac. We'd never met before but I'd noticed him in the American Embassy, waiting for his visa. I thought he looked funny but he had a nice smile. And there we were sitting next to each other in one of the old Flying Tigers, chasing the sun. I was in rhapsodic mood, writing it all down in a glowing letter to send to my mother, and Uwe was being sick into little bags. But in the intervals between being sick, he started being intrigued. Once we landed, I went to Chicago and he to Washington and Illinois, and we didn't run into each other again until the next term.' Uwe achieved a Double First and was President of the Oxford Union.

They married when she was twenty-four: a Quaker wedding. 'I did not promise to obey,' Sheila says. Uwe went to work for the Council of Europe in Strasbourg and she was teaching at the University of Edinburgh, but this commuting arrangement in marriage was precisely what they had agreed. 'We've never really settled down in one place together; we always worked in different countries. We wanted to fly wing to wing – as birds do, on the same current of air. It is very complicated indeed, because the fantasy is that when you get together it's so exciting you can't wait to rush into each other's arms, but there are so many practical things to discuss, like the stopped-up lavatory or the leaking roof or something about the children.'

Sheila gave up her job in Edinburgh and went to join her husband in Strasbourg intending to write a sociological study of the diplomatic corps, but soon realised that she would never be able to publish any such thing. Uwe liked the diplomatic society, but Sheila emphatically did not. 'All those wives having their nails done and their hair done and their massages, and having coffee and exchanging recipes, and the line-ups at dinner parties. There was even a club for Oxford and Cambridge *men*, but women had to keep out of the way, until I insisted on being there when the meeting was held in our small flat.

'I was always a misfit there. My work had fallen through, and I didn't know what to do. I started off by having honeymoon cystitis for a year, and then a late miscarriage. I felt I must be in very poor taste. Not only did I not fit the expectations of the diplomats and their soignée wives, I must have seemed very gauche and grubby, I didn't know how to behave. I did silly things. We did some lively and fun entertaining but *not* with little gilt chairs and pâté de foie gras. I was a vegetarian from the age of nine and a half, so I gave them wheatgerm and kelp.'

Six weeks before they left Strasbourg, their first daughter Celia was born at home. Sheila was twenty-five. 'I'd read Dick-Read at Oxford and I was already interested in the subject of birth from the point of view of anthropology. There *was* no anthropology of birth. There was the great Margaret Mead and that was all. There were whole anthropological books in which the subject of giving birth was never even *mentioned*.

'My first labour was two and a half hours from start to finish. We'd been at a marvellous reception the night before with wonderful food. The Council of Europe was still in session when the baby was being born, and I needed some stitches so I had to go to the clinic and we popped into the office on the way. There at the office was George Brown, and he said, "What a good dinner that was last night," and I said: "We've had the baby! I'm just going to hospital to be stitched." His mouth dropped open.

'I suppose a faint feminist consciousness was raised that day, when I heard the obstetrician say to my husband afterwards: "I've stitched her up nice and tight." I was furious and deliberately walked the stitches loose the next day.'

Having come back to a home base, a cottage in the Oxfordshire village of Freedland, the Kitzingers proceeded to have four more daughters in the next six years. 'I wasn't besotted with babies, but once I was having them I thought I'd have quite a lot. Better go at it hook line and sinker, rather than spin it out.' Celia was not yet two when the twins, Nell and Tess, were born.

The National Childbirth Trust was just being formed in those days and Sheila, a founder member, started running classes at home in her cottage. She was already wholly in favour of home births; all hers were. 'I was always surprised that a woman should want to go into hospital to have babies. I don't think I comprehended the fear they felt, because I didn't feel it myself.'

She was fully occupied with motherhood, childbirth and ante-natal teaching at home for several years until the fourth daughter, Polly, was born. Within a few days of Polly's birth, she started writing *The Experience of Childbirth*, which remains her standard work on the great subject.

The Experience of Childbirth had an enormous impact in 1962. The photographs alone were a breakthrough; they show Sheila giving birth to Polly, smiling down at the baby emerging from between her thighs. Understandably in those days Victor Gollancz, her publisher, found them rather shocking.

I reminded Sheila that when she was working on the revised version of that book in 1976, and wrote to me inviting suggestions (it was three months after my first baby) I had two principal ones: (1) to improve the section on sex during pregnancy, which she had written about excellently elsewhere, and (2) to excise the suggestion that expectant mothers should leave food ready cooked for their helpless husbands when they went into hospital. I felt this must surely be as anachronistic as the advice not to bother about cleaning the grates when you came home with the new baby. How did she come to put such things in, I asked her.

She said: 'Well, I was like that when I was newly married. Maybe in a way, I erected a situation where Uwe didn't do anything at all at home. He was teaching at the University of Saarbrucken half the week, in Oxford the other half, and he would dine in college at night. He would come in at 11.30 and tell me all about it. I was at home with the children a great deal, and it was I who did all the putting to bed.'

At this point daughter number four, Polly, who had joined us, interrupted to say: 'We put each other to bed.' She added. 'Sheila didn't have fixed ideas about bedtime. It was my eldest sister who taught me to brush my teeth.'

'You must remember,' said Sheila, 'my mother was a great admirer of A. S. Neill, and I'd had Montessori teaching so I was a great believer in a free environment for children, and unlimited opportunity to express themselves and be creative. It was very important for me and Uwe. Uwe regarded family life as an Outward Bound course; everybody had to join in, in the garden or sailing in the cold wet Solent. With water, his philosophy was drop the baby in and if it swims it's a good experience. I remember Jenny fell in the River Windrush at the age of three. Uwe looked, and Peter Huntingford (the gynaecologist, who was staying with us) looked, and I was in pale blue trousers and pale blue top but I jumped in, of *course* I jumped in, and came up covered in duckweed. I always remember the way the two men just stood there, watching.

'I knew from the beginning of our marriage that if I wanted children they would be my responsibility. Uwe did want children too, but if I'd gone to live with him in the usual way we'd have had a nanny and a governess and a conventional family life, in diplomatic terms, out there.

But there was work I wanted to do that was not ancillary to his. I was not prepared to get involved in his work even as the wife of the president of a college, which he is now. He knew I wouldn't.

'Uwe would happily play chess with the children but it was only a year or so ago that he learned how to peel an onion. I knew perfectly well that he was like that when I met him but you always marry rather hoping to change the other person, don't you? On the other hand, I couldn't stand a man who plumped up the cushions,' said Sheila.

In her book, *Women as Mothers*, Sheila makes the dedication: 'With dedicated thanks to our daughters – Celia, Nell, Tess, Polly and Jenny – who increase my knowledge and understanding, and whose growing up is an education for their mother.' The definite impression from Sheila is that her daughters raised her feminist consciousness, which started off low and is now as high as could be found in a wife and mother.

'But Uwe did do something very important for me. I decided I wanted to go to Jamaica to do a field study. I needed an anthropological field where the role of mother and child was central to peasant life, so he took a job as professor of government, which he wasn't that keen to do, at the University of the West Indies. We were nine months there, when Jenny was two. We took a Scottish girl out with us. I used to go out on my fieldwork from 6 am till 3 pm, so that I could see the girls in the late afternoon.'

I asked about mother's helps. 'It was really like having another child in the house most of the time,' said Sheila. 'One ran off with a lot of my clothes, two had babies. They tended to need more help than I could give. In Oxford there was a Moral Welfare Officer who sent along a catastrophic series of girls, one on drugs, one who arrived with her teddy bear. But there was a very nice Czech girl and one marvellous one with a sports car, which the children loved. But it was all a bit chaotic, and the villagers got quite used to seeing our children climbing out naked onto the roof.'

Polly added some graphic details about what it was like being one of the five blonde Kitzinger girls. 'Sheila used to lead us through Oxford all holding onto a rope and all dressed the same. She would choose a length of cloth and have it made up into five little capes, so we were quite a sight. All the schools we went to got used to a succession of Kitzingers, famous throughout the schools and identified with each other. We never had the right school uniform. We were renowned for being different from everybody else.'

What happened to their mother-centred domesticity when Sheila's developing importance as a childbirth educator took her away from home, is vividly remembered by Polly. Sheila went on a lecture tour to America, leaving the girls to be looked after at home by an old friend who had two children of her own. 'It seemed ideal, but it was dreadful, wasn't it?' said Sheila.

Polly said: 'We were used to being in control of our own tea-making, and she came along and said things like, "Now all wash your hands." She didn't like us running around naked; she locked us in the bedroom on Bonfire Night because she said it was *dangerous* – we always used to go to the bonfire – so we jumped out of the window.'

Sheila got a telegram at Boston saying, '*Come home immediately your children need you.*' It was from Celia's headmistress. 'I did feel guilty,' said Sheila, 'but I didn't go back. I didn't really question what I was doing because I knew I should show the girls that a woman's life doesn't have to be restricted to motherhood and domesticity; there are battles to be fought and won.'

Wasn't Uwe at home at the time? I asked. 'No,' said Sheila, 'Uwe's attitude has always been, "Well if you're away I might as well be away."'

Polly's childhood memories are of a sisterhood that was a closed circle. When her father was political adviser to Christopher Soames in Brussels, she says, Uwe's homecomings meant the atmosphere at home changed completely. 'He would ask: "What have we all achieved this week?"'

But it was fun to be one of five sisters. 'I was proud to be a Kitzinger. We children were a unit. As regards housework, we had to do quite a lot. We had a work rota from when Jenny was two, when we came back from Jamaica: one would make breakfast, one would hoover. There were dreadful arguments about it of course.'

Sheila Kitzinger has almost always worked from home and usually in the midst of the family. 'I could never have excluded the children from the room where I worked. Although I do remember that at the playpen stage, it was I who would get into the playpen sometimes, and give them the run of the house.'

She has always been a dawn riser since the breastfeeding years, and she writes in bed, these days using a dictaphone. Polly has no recollection of ever being told to keep out of her mother's way. 'I do have the capacity to continue working while all hell is breaking out around me,' Sheila says. 'I can switch off and intervene when necessary. A mother of a family who writes gets accustomed to this. Now I know Uwe could not do that. Uwe has his study across the courtyard, quite separate from the house. If I'm working in bed in the early morning he'll traipse downstairs to the study, where he has his waterbed.'

Every summer they would go *en famille* to their house in Languedoc. Polly interjected: 'Sheila and Uwe stayed at three-star hotels on the way and they'd drop us by the roadside in a tent.' True, said Sheila: 'We'd spend four or five days getting down there. All the leatherette on our big Toyota car was nibbled and chewed by frustrated children who wanted to bite each other. When Uwe and I stopped for meals in restaurants we'd suddenly see five little faces pressed against the window.' 'Sometimes,' said Polly, 'the waiters took pity on us and brought us out a plate of peaches and melons and ice-creams and things.'

Once there, the girls were free to go off, Swallows and Amazons-style, sailing in their own boat on the big salt-water lagoon. One day Polly and Jenny were arrested by the *gendarmerie* when they were found alone in their boat on a canal. 'They thought we'd run away.' 'I had to explain to the *gendarmerie*,' says Sheila crisply, 'that in England we encouraged initiative in little children.'

On another occasion they remembered, at home in England a children's officer called to ask why the children had been left alone in the house one evening. 'It was ridiculous,' says Sheila. 'Celia was nearly sixteen. Someone in the village had obviously rung up.

'I remember also a paediatrician saying, "I admire you for your happy neglect of your children. You talk to them as if they were adults."'

How like their mother are the daughters? Celia, a psychologist, who read Politics, Philosophy and Psychology at St Hilda's College, Oxford, is doing a post-doctorate on justice in schools. She wrote the lesbian chapter in her mother's book, *A Woman's Experience of Sex*, and Sheila and Celia are now writing a book on the conflict between the values of the home and the values of the outside world. Sheila beamed confidently that they were going to have such fun talking about it. Tess is a computer engineer in Connecticut, married to an American; Nell is a gardener; Jenny is a research anthropologist at Cambridge, and a radical feminist; Polly at twenty-five said she emphatically does not want to get married and does not want a nine-to-five office job. 'She ran away to sea,' her mother says fondly. Polly had been reading Philosophy at the University of Sussex but abandoned it to deliver a boat to Yugoslavia, whereupon she decided to take a navigation course. 'I want adventure,' she said. 'I'm not interested in money or security, I want freedom and choice and travel.' At present she is with the Oxford Women's Health Information Service as their publicity worker. Sheila chipped in to say that she had once worked in an office herself – while she was running an Open University course – but formed the opinion that the whole system of working in offices is so much wasted time.

The Kitzingers gave their girls all possible varieties of education: High Anglican primary school with long assemblies, comprehensive school for the twins, Bedales (the progressive mixed public school) for Polly after O-Levels because Sheila and Uwe were living in France at the time and gave her the choice of local *lycée* in France or boarding at home; Jenny chose the French *lycée* and later went to Westminster, the boys' public school, in the sixth form as a day girl. It is said that Dr John Rae, who was then headmaster, declared that the school would not forget Jenny Kitzinger. Celia also went to a boys' school, Bryanston, but discovered that the girls were expected to be an improving influence on the boys. 'When the boys did something wrong they had to go on a run,' Sheila says, 'and when the girls misbehaved they had to darn the boys' socks. Ridiculous! So by mutual consent Celia was removed.'

It is in Sheila Kitzinger's preparation-for-birth classes that her obsession with maternity is best observed. She sits cross-legged and comfortable and expansive, in her kaftan and top-knot, before an open fire in the white-walled Tudor hall of Standlake Manor, her pupil mothers lying on squashy cushions before her. She is tirelessly interested in each expectant mother's feelings. With evangelical zeal she urges every mother present to be in tune with her body and to understand precisely the progress of the growing baby inside her. To this end she produces a succession of fruits and vegetables: a fig (the uterus before pregnancy), a small avocado (six weeks), a large avocado (twelve to twenty-four weeks) and a plump marrow (six months). A husband who has come along for his obligatory preparation is asked to put on a butcher's apron filled with twenty or thirty pounds of sand, so that he can feel what his wife will feel, carrying her bump around shortly before labour.

All this is explained by Sheila with tireless relish and a beaming smile. No student ever forgets the sight of a football emerging from the neck of a jumper (Sheila's graphic visual aid to show the birth process) nor Sheila's sensual insistence that birth is akin to orgasm, if one could only tune in to waves of pleasure instead of oceans of pain. Her enthusiasm is a legend in the childbirth industry. Something about her makes women want to tell her about their births and the intimate details of their marriages. I certainly told her all mine in the confidence that she would not be bored.

Since every husband is expected to play a full and active role in both the birth classes and the accouchement itself, it was interesting for us, during one of our classes with Sheila, to have a tape-recording played of the birth of Sheila's last daughter (there were no videos in those days, so it was sound only). Across the dawn chorus of birds outside the bedroom window, could be heard the voice of Uwe Kitzinger, welcoming the new baby: 'Oh, you little darling . . .' But although dutifully present and emotionally involved with the births, Uwe seemed in other respects, did he not, an old-fashioned, unreconstructed male chauvinist? Rather like many other absent-minded professor types – immensely chivalrous, but rather distanced from the nitty-gritty of real family life.

Sheila tells me this was quite true of Uwe for a long time. But she added: 'Now he's trying very hard not to be. After thirty-four years of marriage we have recently made some important changes in our lives which – though it's exciting – has been quite hard to do. For the first time he has started learning how to cook, and is beginning to enjoy doing things with me in the kitchen. He tells me that he always used to think of "the family" as everyone gathered round the fire playing chess. But now he realises that the real thing, the family togetherness, was going on in the kitchen as we prepared the meal, and that he missed out on it for years.'

When I asked Sheila about future plans and unachieved ambitions she said she had *lots*. 'So much to do!' she cried. 'The whole revolution in women's health care, the need to find a better environment for birth, the books I want to write! The next one will be *The Crying Baby*. It's about the whole assault on a woman's self-image, and on her health, and on family relationships, when a baby cries. A fundamental and common-place factor, but so important. I've just done a book for children on *Being Born*. And I want to paint much more . . .' Her mother would approve.

Before I left Standlake Manor I had to see the oak-beamed bedroom with its stark white walls and Turkish rugs, a room Sheila describes as 'womb-like'. Its centrepiece is the four-poster bed designed by Uwe, seven feet square, draped in brilliant ethnic spreads in flame, crimson and yellow Batik and patchwork designs showing birth-symbols, lit by halogen lamps. Here the Kitzinger children were conceived and born, and here they would all pile on weekend mornings, the hub of a rather extraordinary family life.

Postscript 1987

Postscript

❧

I had to write this book, because it was one I wanted to read. I hoped to learn something. In my house there were at least four shelves entirely given over to books about women and not one of them answered my questions about marriage, family and work. There was plenty of advice about playing constructive games with one's toddler: there was plenty of polemic about how women must remain independent persons; but scant evidence of anyone combining everything over a lifetime. The basic difficulty of feminism, as Margaret Forster said in *Significant Sisters*, is still the one recognised a hundred years ago by Elizabeth Cady Stanton, mother of six: 'The woman is greater than the wife and mother, and in consenting to take upon herself these relationships she should never sacrifice one iota of her individuality.' But how? 'Women may wish to agree,' as Margaret wrote, 'but come the testing time and the woman is rapidly submerged by the wife and mother, sometimes never to reappear.'

The twenty women I talked to seemed not to have been submerged. There are legions more out there: some who have managed the compleat life, with varying degrees of satisfaction; many more who are, like me, in the very thick of it – wondering if luck will hold for another decade or two, and if it does what the children will do when it's their turn to run their lives; and thousands more who have just set out on this rocky path: married, or expecting to be; contemplating a first or second child, hoping to keep up with work and wondering how to manage without the whole edifice collapsing about their ears.

I know there is no such creature as Superwoman, and no resemblance between these women and the red-fingernailed Shirley Conran heroine. Nor can I claim that the compleat life is one that every woman would contemplate as a desirable goal. Of the hundreds of women I've interviewed over the last twenty years – writers and actors, politicians and women of ideas – the vast majority lived their lives quite differently:

287

quietly solitary, or chronically disrupted with serial marriages, grand affairs, love-children and complicated step-families. Their lives were all the more interesting for these vicissitudes. I can think of many an indomitable old lady to whom nothing would appeal less than domesticity with one man for life, and a brood of children to consume her energy – and look at all the achievements and globe-trotting adventures she managed without such hindrances. Think, for instance, of three prototypes of the distinct courses women's lives may take: Elizabeth I, Elizabeth II, and Elizabeth Taylor. To marry not at all, to marry seven times, or to marry once and be mother of four: the latter course may appear to be the least thrilling, but in her quiet way HM the Queen is a twentieth-century role model, having combined work with marriage and maternity for nearly forty years. This is, after all, what women now tacitly assume they will be able to do.

It is always dangerous, of course, to write about real people's lives. There is always someone who will tell you, 'Of course she's quite mad,' or, 'But her husband's famous for his affairs,' or, 'I know someone who lived next door to them and the children ran wild.' I know. The pitfall of presenting people's own view of themselves is that even when you appear to strip a layer and reveal an undercoat, there may still be several tatty old coats hidden beneath. Even the most seemingly honest and straightforward of interviewees may retain her secrets. The only way round this would have been to write about pseudonymous or anonymous people. But I would never be interested in either reading or writing a book full of pseudonyms. And I like and admire these women too well to insist on probing further.

The reason for liking and admiring was simple: I am linked to them by common experience even though I am as different from any one of them as they are different from each other. The common experience is the husband, the babies, the professional commitment. It's taken centuries to make the combination available to women, yet now that it is achievable, with no profession barred to women and almost complete control over family size, one can't be sure that future generations of women will wish to take up the triple challenge at all. In fact it looks to me as if these women I talked to, of the post-suffragist, pre-1970s women's movement generations, might prove to be both the first and last of their kind. There is no indication that their daughters will produce children at anything like the rate their mothers did. The 90 children of the interviewees are never going to produce 360 children in geometric progression; they will not even replace themselves. The middle-class breeding breed is fading fast.

We are more wary than ever of the concept of Happy Families. Even in the best regulated families the assembled characters may resent, criticise and mock each other. It would be a very odd family which pronounced itself perfectly happy all round; also a dull one. Nor did anyone convince me (not that anyone tried) that motherhood today is any easier than it ever was, women's movement or no women's movement. But at least the Compleat Woman has given motherhood a whirl; and they were all pleased to have done so. All motherhood ends in separation at some stage, at which point a woman must be thankful that she has forged another role in life. It is good for her self-esteem.

It seems easier to be thankful, twenty-five years on, in that quiescent stage when the most testing trials of motherhood are over. A woman of fifty or sixty whose husband is still beside her, whose children have grown, and who has a comfortable domestic base (the house itself was vitally important to most of these women) and work she can carry on doing as long as she likes, has reached a very pleasant plateau. But it can be a long hard road to get there.

To keep right on to the end of that road, these women had to be remarkably resilient, competent and energetic. Even if they denied the energy factor, my impression was that they bristled with it. There was something dauntless about all of them – rather like their Victorian forebears who travelled into unmapped jungle and desert and thrived on adversity.

Of all the women I spoke to, only one – not included in the selected twenty – positively disliked the prospect of the future because she dreaded retirement. What would she do without a school to run? People told her she could get on with her hobbies, she said, 'But you can't do your hobby all day long.' The higher a woman flies, the more galling the prospect of coming down to earth. And the husband who flies less high than his wife is another consideration: the demands made on a truly equal partnership can be additionally complicated. Hence my curiosity about how these marriages managed to thrive. I don't think I found more than a few really useful clues. There are, as I have said, far too many imponderables, and absolutely no fixed rules. The one conclusion I drew was that in most cases, the wife's determination to carry on pleasing herself *and* her husband was an underlying strength. She would never give up either on work or marriage, and so the marriage adapted itself to her life. The men seemed to see that a busy, dedicated wife is preferable to an under-occupied restless one. These men, by and large, shared a respect and admiration for their wives which is far removed from the more commonplace incomprehension and veiled contempt for women one senses in men who still cannot imagine an equal partnership.

I met about a quarter of the ninety children of these equal marriages. If any generalisations can be made about such a diverse group of people, I'd say that they were remarkably competent types, and there was never a suspicion that any of them resented their mother enjoying a role outside the family. On the contrary, they were positively proud of their mothers. One mother might say, referring to her eldest daughter, 'X's whole life is a revolt against our standards', but if you met X, you would find a spirited young woman who is getting along splendidly (unless you rigorously compared her with her mother at the same age, and found her less of an achiever). In any case there are vast differences between siblings: I met a sober-suited undergraduate one day, and another day his younger brother whose hair stood up in green spikes. What the two boys strikingly did share was their warm concern for their mother, who beamed upon both of them. 'I love having teenagers around. Despite all the anxieties, they're more interesting than infants,' several mothers declared.

Belonging to a generation which is not too modest to talk about sex and fidelity, I found the general reticence on these subjects surprising in these women. I ended up knowing far less than I had hoped about what part sex played in their relationships and whether fidelity had been important. Don't those with long experience of monogamy wish to declare its advantages in contributing to a simpler and happier life? After all, the nation is (as I write) bombarded with warnings that promiscuity can be fatal, and there is a current fashion for articles on the loss of interest in sex among the young (eg 'The New Sexual Apathy', *Harper's & Queen*, January 1987.) In this context it ought to be appropriate to speak up for the pleasures of nuptial sex, and the excitingly danger-free benefits of monogamy. Perhaps their reticence is to do with not wishing to sound self-congratulatory? As one interviewee said to me at the outset: 'I really do not want to be *envied*.'

Readers who found themselves saying 'Ah, but . . .' as they read these interviews ('Ah, but she had money / luck / help / no nine-to-five job / long gaps between children . . .') echoed my own doubts and reservations. When I embarked on this project I had four children under seven, three of them under four; I had to go to the office four or five days a week, and collected children from school every day; I often worked well into the night. I would wallow in self-inflicted self-pity until I met another interviewee whose life, I would discover, was even more crowded with commitments even after her brood of young had flown. None of them, none of us, is Superwoman. We are by turns industrious woman, harried woman, organised woman and sometimes cunning woman, because we all agree that one can always find time, in the most hard-pressed life, to do what one really wants to do, whether it is dancing the tango, playing the harp or writing a book (during the year since this book was first published, no fewer than eight of the inter-viewees published books of their own). The thing I really wanted to do was to ask a certain kind of woman how she managed to live a certain kind of life. I burned with curiosity about it. I knew their answers would fascinate me, however peculiar and various they were. And they did.

Acknowledgements

𝒫

Among the many books I have turned back to repeatedly in the course of writing, certain ones stand out as being particularly informative, and I acknowledge with gratitude:

Significant Sisters by Margaret Forster (Secker & Warburg, 1984)
Why Women Don't Have Wives by Terri Apter (Macmillan Press, 1985)
The Sceptical Feminist by Janet Radcliffe Richards (Routledge & Kegan Paul, 1980)
Dual Career Families Re-Examined by Rhona and Robert Rapoport (Harper Colophon/Martin Robertson & Co, 1976)
Inventing Motherhood by Ann Dally (Burnett Books, 1982)
The English Marriage by Drusilla Beyfus (Weidenfeld & Nicolson, 1968)
Woman on Woman, edited by Margaret Laing (Sidgwick & Jackson, 1971)
Ever Since Eve by Nancy Caldwell Sorel (Michael Joseph, 1984)
The Macmillan Dictionary of Women's Biography, edited by Jennifer S. Uglow (Macmillan 1982)

The author and publisher would like to thank the following for copyright illustrations:

The cartoon, 'The Parliamentary Female' (1853), from *Punch Almanack*, by permission of *Punch* magazine; a detail from a cartoon by Posy Simmonds from *Mrs Weber's Diary*: the artist, Jonathan Cape Ltd and A. D. Peters & Co. Ltd; the cartoon, 'A Suffragette's Home': the Fawcett Society Library and the Mary Evans Picture Library; the photograph of Alice Thomas Ellis and family: Nic Tucker and *Harpers and Queen*; the photograph of Elizabeth Longford and family: Patrick Lichfield.

The author and publishers also gratefully acknowledge permission to reprint quotations from copyright material as follows:
Why Women Don't Have Wives by Terri Apter: Macmillan Press; *Enid Bagnold* by Anne Sebba: Weidenfeld (Publishers) Ltd; *The English Marriage* by Drusilla Beyfus: Weidenfeld; *The Unquiet Grave* by Cyril Connolly: Hamish Hamilton Ltd; *Enemies of Promise* by Cyril Connolly: Routledge & Kegan Paul; *Inventing Motherhood* by Ann Dally: Burnett Books; an essay by Eva Figes in *Woman on Woman*, edited by Margaret Laing: Sidgwick & Jackson Ltd; *The Dialectic of Sex* by Shulamith Firestone: Women's Press; *Men* by Anna Ford: Weidenfeld; *Significant Sisters* by

ACKNOWLEDGEMENTS

Margaret Forster: Secker & Warburg Ltd; *The Female Eunuch* by Germaine Greer: Aitken & Stone Ltd for MacGibbon Ltd; *The Powers of Love* by Celia Haddon: Michael Joseph Ltd; *Women as Mothers* by Sheila Kitzinger: Collins Publishers; *Malespeak* by Irma Kurtz: Jonathan Cape Ltd; *The War Between the Tates* by Alison Lurie: William Heinemann Ltd; *Memoir of a Thinking Radish* by Sir Peter Medawar: Oxford University Press and A. P. Watt Ltd; *Dual Career Families Re-Examined*: by Rhona and Robert Rapoport: Harper & Row Publishers, Inc, New York; *The Sceptical Feminist* by Janet Radcliffe Richards: Routledge & Kegan Paul; 'The Black Art' in *All My Pretty Ones* by Anne Sexton: Houghton Mifflin Co, Boston, Massachusetts; *Outrageous Acts and Everyday Rebellions* by Gloria Steinem: Jonathan Cape Ltd; Mrs Mary Stott for quotations from her book: *Forgetting's No Excuse* (published by Virago/Quartet); *Letters to Alice* by Fay Weldon: Michael Joseph and the Rainbird Publishing Group Ltd.